HOME FROM THE DARK SIDE OF UTOPIA

A Journey through American Revolutions

CLIFTON ROSS

Foreword by Staughton Lynd

AK
PRESS

Home from the Dark Side of Utopia:
A Journey through American Revolutions

© 2016 Clifton Ross
This edition © 2016 AK Press (Chico, Oakland, Edinburgh, Baltimore)

ISBN: 978-1-84935-250-5
E-ISBN: 978-1-84935-251-2
Library of Congress Control Number: 2015959319

AK Press	AK Press
370 Ryan Ave. #100	PO Box 12766
Chico, CA 95973	Edinburgh EH8 9YE
USA	Scotland
www.akpress.org	www.akuk.com
akpress@akpress.org	ak@akedin.demon.co.uk

The above addresses would be delighted to provide you with the latest AK Press distribution catalog, which features books, pamphlets, zines, and stylish apparel published and/or distributed by AK Press. Alternatively, visit our websites for the complete catalog, latest news, and secure ordering.

Credits:
"An Old Clown to his Son" first appeared in *The Americas Review*, vol. 24, nos. 1–2, Spring–Summer 1997.
"Proud Sinner's Prayer" was first published in *Translations from Silence: Selected Poems by Clifton Ross*, Freedom Voices, 2009.

Cover design by Josh MacPhee | antumbradesign.org
Interior design by Margaret Killjoy | birdsbeforethestorm.net
Printed in the USA

CONTENTS

FOREWORD
by Staughton Lynd

I

In *Home from the Dark Side of Utopia*, Clifton Ross offers an account of his personal pilgrimage through several varieties of religious extremism, counter-cultural life in Berkeley, and Latin American radicalism.

Ross's journey began with a childhood on military bases. It appears to have left him with an image of a hermetically-sealed world of close-cropped lawns and unrepealable dictates from above. Ross discerns a kinship between what he experienced growing up and a vision entertained by both the Right and Left that is Utopian and apocalyptic. Accordingly, his version of the Emerald City is, first, a world in which decision making is decentralized and communal, but also, and just as important, a world in which the desired social transformation comes about in a spirit of experimentation, with an understanding in advance that what happens will be a patchwork of failures as well as successes.

These are problematic objectives in the United States. To begin with, America is home to three hundred million people who are notoriously non-communal: a "lonely crowd" (David Riesman) of individuals who increasingly "bowl alone" (Robert Putnam).

Moreover, too many Americans believe that the good life will be achieved suddenly, almost magically, as a "world turned upside down" or in a miraculous moment of "rapture." Even the most inspiring of our home-grown prophets on the Left tend to imagine the coming of the Good Society as a rush of events that will produce a qualitatively different state of affairs in a very short period of time. James Baldwin and Malcolm X seem to have anticipated some version of a fire that would sweep through established institutions. The Wobblies' theme song, "Solidarity Forever," imagines a new world coming into being, after such a fire, from "the ashes of the old." I think that fire is a form of violence, a hoped-for shortcut to social change that doesn't work. My own daydreams are of little green things that poke up after a fire through the blackened forest floor.

What can be distressingly rapid, in my experience, is the collapse of Left organizations. Having lived through the disintegration of Students for a Democratic Society, the Student Nonviolent Coordinating Committee, and the Black Panthers, I am left with a sad but stubborn belief that it is just as important to try to understand our defeats as to clarify the character of the new world to which we aspire.

Through a number of initial chapters Ross struggles with the conflict between the hope for a Kingdom of God that would materialize all at once ("when the stars begin to fall") and the common-sense delays of ordinary life. For example, a visit to Berkeley by Daniel Berrigan gave rise to an epiphany. Berrigan cut through clouds of "cosmic millenarian reverie" to call for confrontation with the nuclear arms race and with a demonic, cold, rational utopia, as well as for empathy with the needs of the poor. Yet Berrigan in his own way fixed his gaze on "the end" and "embodied the prophetic voice of the apocalyptic vision."

A by-product of this state of mind for many young radicals is a quest for a particular society in which the promise of the future is, at least for the moment, displayed. Lest I seem to be exempting myself from this generalization, let me be clear. In high school and the first years of college I supported the Soviet Union. This ended when a friend quoted Trotsky's ultimatum to the Kronstadt rebels ("surrender or I will shoot you down like pheasants") and Bukharin's abject response when accused in the purge trials of the 1930s of being a "running dog" of imperialists who wished to destroy the USSR ("Citizen Prosecutor Vishinsky, you have found the words"). After reading Martin Buber's *Paths in Utopia* I held out the incipient State of Israel as a model of decentralized socialism until another friend told me, "Staughton, they stole the land."

My wife and I used our two- or three-week summer vacations to make five short trips to Sandinista Nicaragua in the 1980s. I was resolved not to deceive myself again this time. But I did. Not until I read Margaret Randall did I fully grasp what it signified that the highest official in the Sandinista women's organization, AMNLAE, was not elected by the membership but was appointed by the predominantly male Sandinista directorate.

I still view Zapatismo through a reddish haze but I fear I may have much to learn. I may discover that young people in the Zapatista villages still leave for the coast or for *el Norte*. Alcoholism and male chauvinism may remain stronger than one is led to believe. Above all, the Leftists who shepherded the emergence of Zapatismo in those wet mountains may have had, and may continue to have, a good deal more influence than they let on, just as in Sandinista Nicaragua.

II

This brings us to the question of Venezuela, which takes up the second half of *Home from the Dark Side of Utopia*.

I have never been to Venezuela. I do not speak or read Spanish well enough to learn very much at a distance. I am unable to offer a reliable assessment.

Nevertheless, I think the compendium of facts about contemporary Venezuela that Clifton Ross has assembled demand attention. In *The Dark Side* he tells us how he acquired them, year by year, visit by visit, friend by friend. They are most conveniently available in another of his recent books, *The Map or the Territory: Notes on Imperialism, Solidarity, and Latin America in the New Millenium* (New Earth Publications, 2014).

Leaving aside currency manipulation, which I do not pretend to be able to summarize intelligibly, the following are facts offered by Ross (in one or the other of these two books) about the Chavista years:

1. Agricultural production has declined significantly. Articles such as coffee, rice, and white corn are now imported. Food is increasingly scarce and its cost has increased.
2. Industrial production in the nationalized industries has declined across the board, including the production of cement, aluminum, steel, and oil. Oil and gas are imported in significant quantities.
3. The government has created new trade unions parallel to existing unions. Arrangements that the government

calls "co-management" and "workers' control" have been resisted by the elected officials of existing unions. Union demands for collective bargaining contracts governing the wages, benefits, and working conditions of employees have been disregarded.

4. Many co-operatives have been created but only 10 or 15% of these are "active."

5. Many announced projects were never built or were abandoned when halfway complete. An example is the national paper company, Pulpa y Papel, CA, for which more than half a billion dollars was appropriated but that remains "an empty field with a fence and a cleared space and nothing else."

6. Between 1998 when Chávez became head of the government and 2014 the percentage of those living in poverty rose from 45 to 48%, and the number of those found to be living in "extreme poverty" rose from 18.7% to 23.6%. A 2015 study by the same agency, after the drop in the price of oil began, reported 73% of Venezuelan households living in poverty (see pages 320–321 of the present work).

7. Health care in hospitals has suffered. Of 6,700 neighborhood clinics that were founded in 2003 to bring health care closer to the people, 2000 or almost 30% had been abandoned by 2009.

8. Street violence in Venezuela is now second only to Honduras in Latin America.

9. I have left to last the propositions that are most difficult to prove because they are non-quantitative but are also obviously the most important. They include claims that many government subsidies go only to those who support government directives; that the essential rights of free speech and free association

are severely restricted; and that elections may be efficiently conducted but that election results are manipulated, as when the polls are kept open at times and places when the government is losing to allow party members to be brought in to vote.

From my perspective as an historian forced out of the university and turned lawyer, these allegations call for what lawyers call "shifting the burden of proof." That is, one or more among those who believe that Clif Ross distorts reality should bring forward the evidence that they consider rebuts or explains numbers like those set forth above.

III

More important than the critique of anything existing is careful discernment as to where we should be going.

Clifton Ross and his wife Marcy Rein have edited still another book, made up of oral histories by participants in the new social movements of Latin America, entitled *Until the Rulers Obey: Voices from Latin American Social Movements* (PM Press, 2014). In it they argue that too much uncritical attention has been lavished on leaders like Subcomandante Marcos (Chiapas), "Lula" (Brazil), Evo Morales (Bolivia), and Hugo Chávez (Venezuela). In one country after the next, Ross and Rein found persons with names unknown to readers in the United States who, in the manner of indigenous decision making through the ages, sit in a circle when they meet, seek consensus, and are prepared to act as well as talk.

In *The Map or the Territory* there are some paragraphs near the end that express, as well as I know how, the spirit in which those of us disappointed by the various versions of "real existing socialism" should proceed.

Clifton Ross says that we must build resistance to power by means that are "autonomous, critical, often oppositional." The solidarity sought must be of two kinds.

One is localist, focusing on our own communities. The other is international: organizing low-wage workers in the United States and reaching out to workers in the countries from which so many come; the climate justice movement; the Boycott Divestment and Sanctions effort. I would add: encouraging soldiers of all nations engaged in meaningless, aggressive wars to lay down their arms and join hands.

PREFACE

"...living in a world without any possible
escape... there was nothing for it but to
fight for an impossible escape."
—Victor Serge, *Memoirs of a Revolutionary*

This is the story of a "heroic quest" to find a hidden door
that opens into a better world. In that sense, there are two
major elements to the story: the hero, and the door. In this
narrative, each time the door opens a different place is revealed, and each time the hero passes through door he is
transformed. The final doorway opens into the book you hold
in your hands. Now it's your turn to pass through the door.

Readers familiar with the archetypal heroic narrative structure will know that it is circular: the hero (who we'll now call
"the protagonist," to avoid the unwanted connotations of the
word "hero") leaves home on a search into the unknown for
a treasure. The protagonist faces, and wins, challenges, and
then, after a series of adventures, returns home. And then, in
a dream, the location of the treasure is revealed to be, of all
places, buried beneath his bed.

The context from which the protagonist sets out is offered in the first chapter, but something should be said here about the more exotic waypoints to make the journey more comprehensible. I spent some thirty-five years (at the time of this writing) writing about, and doing solidarity with, revolutionary movements in Latin America. This memoir lays out the story of how I came to that work, and how my understanding of an anti-imperialist struggle has evolved over the years.

My first contact with Latin America happened when I landed in Nicaragua in 1982 as a rather naïve (I should say, *very* naïve) Christian solidarity activist. The Sandinista Revolution had been in process for nearly three years at that point, and it was responsible, in ways I didn't even understand at the time, for revolutionary upheaval that seized the entire region in those years. My story also took me through work with the Zapatista struggle, primarily translating, co-editing and publishing what was the first book of their material to appear in English.

However, the bulk of this book concerns my work with the Bolivarian process of Venezuela, and this is the point that my understanding of the work of an anti-imperialist solidarity activist began to change. The section on Venezuela encompasses roughly half of the book, and it was the epiphany and denouement of a very long journey.

I am approaching, again, the beginning of my journey where I discover that the world isn't at all what it appears to be. It is the responsibility of all of us who understand that to look beneath the surface for the truth concealed there. That is the treasure, the location of which only our dreams will reveal.

Clifton Ross
Berkeley, CA
February 2016

ACKNOWLEDGMENTS

Thanks to my anonymous home group: you know who you are. Thanks also to many of the people mentioned in this book who read or skimmed it and offered helpful suggestions, in particular, Garry Lambrev, Ben Jesse Clarke, and Michael Duffy. Special thanks to Kevin Rath, who helped me wrestle some of the ideas down and bend them to the will of the manuscript. Our many Saturday discussions were not in vain. Finally, eternal gratitude to my partner-in-life and all that goes with it, including good-natured arguments, disagreements, refutations, and blissful evening peace agreements. Truly, without Marcy Rein this book would not have been possible.

ON BASE WITH G.I. JESUS

This story would make very little sense to the reader without some context, which in my case was apocalyptic, utopian, millenarian, and military. Those were the constellating forces of my consciousness, almost like a blueprint for the way my thinking would be ordered for my whole life. Since they play such a pivotal role in my thinking, and hence my intellectual development, it seems appropriate to start there, with what those elements signify. If you think you've got it, and you already know what I mean by those gangling terms, you can skip to chapter one where the story starts. What follows for the next few pages is what you might call the cultural, intellectual background to my story.

I was born and raised in the Air Force, growing up, in that sense, everywhere and nowhere at the same time. The bases were all designed according to the same ordered logic, and regimented down to the detail, even if the details changed from base to base.

The bases were conceived as a uniformly ubiquitous utopia (u+topia: "no where") circumscribing the planet Earth. Even the lawns and shrubs had military haircuts, the traffic flowed at a precise pace, and the men all wore the same blue uniforms, with only slight differences to indicate rank.

Life on the base was directed and regulated with sirens, bells and a strict discipline from which no deviation was permitted. It was a Manichaean[1] world that distinguished itself from the civilian world, demarcating its utopian territory with the fenced base perimeter. The fences, always topped by barbed wire and defended by regular patrols, also reflected a state of mind: within, the allies, those submitted entirely to the military code in utter and total obedience to the Nation and its Mission.

Outside, beyond the base, was, if not the enemy, at least the "other," either the occupied, or the defended, civilian world: undisciplined, lazy, disordered, and aimless. It was always there, offering evidence of a "locale" outside the gates of the base: a medieval church tower, quaint village houses or possibly a long shopping strip, or series of bars, often with a few derelict women hoping to snag some hapless GI to buy them a drink. It all depended on the location of the base how the civilian world surrounding it took form, but it was always "the civilian world" or "the Economy," populated by "civilians," and it had none of the regularity and uniformity of the military base. The Economy was a strange and mostly foreign world but I adapted, as "brats" do, and grew up bicultural, able to adeptly move between the Base and the Economy with relative ease.

Central to the military was a sense of family, community, team, in short, the aim to be a single united force. The military was, as Lewis Mumford so aptly pointed out, the "first machine," a human machine. And central to that unity was the idea of "The Mission," which entailed an absolute faith in, and total obedience to, superior authority, especially those with superior rank. Although you might never truly understand what the Mission was, it was, nevertheless, everything. It defined your life. The military was, in short, a form of civil religion. Combined with Christian millennialism, it was a powerful, intoxicating, and apocalyptic faith.

Even though the military distinguished itself from the civilian world, it defined itself against The Enemy. The enemy might change (for most of my life it was "Communism" and more recently it has become "Terrorism") but the roles remained eternal: the military was Good, and what opposed it, the enemy, was Evil.

This was the Manichean basis for another element of this secular apocalyptic faith that had great symbolic significance: the nuclear mushroom cloud symbolized God's wrath toward all unbelievers, be they Germans, Japanese, or the Godless communists, and HE (for this was also a Patriarchal faith, and God was male, presumably with all associated attributes) had given this weapon to *us*, the United States. As possessors of the atom bomb the US government, through its military, was proven to be the *de facto* agent of God's justice, and [North] Americans, His Chosen People.

The US military accommodated this apocalyptic worldview without *explicitly* propagating it, quite possibly because of the Constitutional separation of Church and State. Nevertheless, the warrior and the priest have traditionally been seen as a single caste and, as such, often accompanied one another in war making and the construction of empires.

And so the military reinforced a civil-religious worldview based on the skeletal backbone of Judeo-Christian religion, stripped of all identifying symbols and doctrines, and it also heavily relied on the apocalyptic anxiety, terror, and enthusiasm to bind and unite its cadre in a dogmatic faith in the Commanding Officers. Indeed, whatever I later learned in "civilian Christianity" was reinforced by the airtight system of military thinking, and vice versa. The military utopia that we lived out on base was the perfect expression of US civil religion as it had developed from Colonial times right up through the twentieth century.

If we see the apocalyptic-utopian-millenarian idea everywhere we look in the modern and post-modern world, that's probably because it *is* everywhere. As the English philosopher, John Gray, puts it, "if a simple definition of western civilization could be formulated it would have to be framed in terms of the central role of millenarian thinking."[2] From this millenarian foundation come ideas of progress, revolutionary ideologies, even the idea of self-improvement so popular in the West: everything is rooted in the Judeo-Christian apocalyptic.

While apocalypse (Greek: *apocalypsis*, "revelation") and millennium (Latin: *mille* + *ennium*, "thousand years") and utopia (Greek: u+topos, "no place") all have different meanings, in a sense they emerge from a common matrix. Apocalyptic and millenarian movements are related and often indistinguishable, although believers in an apocalypse (calamity) don't always have faith that a "millennium" (or thousand-year kingdom) or utopian state will emerge from disaster. Conversely, utopias, and the rupture with present reality that they imply, aren't always conceived as necessarily being preceded by apocalyptic disaster. But all three words express the same sharp departure from reality, either by divine intervention or great human will, and the institution of a new social and political order. Through this book I will consider the three phenomena together and often refer to them collectively by the acronym "AUM" (apocalyptic utopian millenarian).

Millenarian thinking goes back to explanations for the failed first century apocalyptic prophet known as Jesus "Christ,"[3] although apocalyptic thinking in general goes back much farther, with some tracing it to Zoroaster, or "Zarathustra" who lived in what is today known as Afghanistan, around 1500 B.C.[4] Millenarianism, then, emerged out of the apocalyptic faith of Jesus and his disciples as a response to the "cognitive dissonance" of "belief disconfirmation" resulting from Jesus's execution for the political crime of treason or subversion. Both "cognitive dissonance" and "belief disconfirmation" were ideas that sociologist Leon Festinger arrived at through his study of a flying saucer cult in the mid 1950s. In his study, when the flying saucers failed to arrive (belief disconfirmation) believers had to deal with the "cognitive dissonance" or the gap between their beliefs and the reality.

Similarly, when Jesus failed to overthrow Roman imperial rule and become the new king of Israel, and the disciples had to deal with the belief disconfirmation and cognitive dissonance of his failure and death, they did so by, in a sense, rewriting the story. In the new narrative the gospel writers (and later Christians) had Jesus ascending to heaven and promising to return in the near future to set up a kingdom and rule over the entire earth. In the Revelation or Apocalypse, the final book of the Christian *Bible*,[5] there are references to a "great tribulation" and a "thousand year reign" (millennium) of Jesus that Christians understood in various ways. The early Church believers were convinced, based on Jesus's own words in the *Gospel of Mark*, Chapter 13 that he would be returning within the lifetime of his disciples. When that didn't happen Christians began to develop doctrines as a coping mechanism for the cognitive dissonance of yet another failed expectation.

The "Book of the Revelation of John" (*Revelation*) was one such response, which portrayed a second coming of Jesus as a cosmic event in which even stars fell from heaven, evil was vanquished, and the "Heavenly" Jerusalem descended to the earth, with streets of gold and walls of jewels. The Revelation was to become the basis of Christian millenarian tradition and the numerous conflicting understandings of the future reign of Jesus on the earth. The emerging church tended to downplay the importance of Revelation and leave the entire second coming of Jesus and the final judgment as vague future events. This became known as the "amillennial" view, and one that St. Augustine and much of the historical Christian Church adopted and taught. But there were other currents within the Church that were excited and inspired by the apocalyptic passages of the Bible, most notably the 13th century theologian Joachim di Fiores, whose apocalyptic and millenarian ideas continue to influence movements to this day.[6]

The millenarian tradition split between the "pre-millennialists" and the "post-millennialists," the former believing Jesus return would initiate his millennial reign on earth, and the latter believing his return would come after a peaceful millennium. The two millennialist traditions had very dramatic, and also very different, effects on Western religious and secular culture.

According to pre-millennialists, the return of Jesus would be sudden and chaotic and represent a dramatic rupture with the present order of the world, and then the thousand-year earthly reign of Jesus (the millennium) would begin. It could be argued that this view was more in keeping with the apocalyptic, messianic tradition of "Second Temple Judaism" (the "apocalyptic" era that ended with the Roman destruction of Jerusalem in 70 A.D.). This apocalyptic view inspired the revolutionary excitement of the radical medieval sects, and it also left its mark on modern revolutionary currents.

The post-millennial view emerged in the 17th century among the Protestants, particularly the restorationist Calvinists, Unitarians, and Puritans. This view held that humanity would progressively improve as a result of the first arrival of Jesus and the outpouring of the Holy Spirit, and then gradually the earth would enter into a great millennium of peace, followed by the final judgment. This was the view of many early social reformers, heavily influencing the Abolitionist movement, and even may have contributed to the theory of evolution as conceived by Charles Darwin.[7] Post-millennialism certainly was the foundation for the Western belief in "progress" since, according to the early Puritan thinkers, "the earthly paradise is to be merely the last, culminating state in the series of progressive stages which can be discerned in history."[8]

This post-millennial view was certainly a major part of the foundational structure or ordering principle of North American religious and secular thought as it emerged, but there were also strong pre-millennial elements. Either way, the American Revolution was an expression of what came to be known as "civil millennialism."[9] Millenarian prophecies, drawn primarily from the books of *Daniel* and *Revelation* in the *Bible*, were "basic to the formation of American revolutionary ideology in the late eighteenth century" and among the primary incitements to the American Revolutionary War.[10] And the focus of all human history, according to this perspective, was the beautiful, magical "New World" that, among other things, inspired Thomas More's Utopia, and awakened other millennial dreams, especially among English Protestants. "God, it began to be thought, is redeeming both individual souls and society in parallel course; and, in the next century, a new nation in a recently discovered part of the world seemed suddenly to be illuminated by a ray of heavenly light, to be at the western end of the rainbow that arched over the civilized world."[11]

Obviously, that land was the United States of America. "More than almost any other modern nation, the United States was a product of the Protestant Reformation, seeking an earthly paradise in which to perfect a reformation of the Church," Charles L. Sanford wrote.[12] And it's clear that the apocalyptic, millennial ideal continues to be very much alive in the US today in both its religious and secular forms[13] and even, as John Gray argues, the cornerstone of the Western world itself.[14]

Within this civil religious framework, especially as it was conceived in mid-twentieth century North America, the world was a battlefield for the war between the Children of God and the Children of Satan. And, during the years of the Cold War, if "we" were the Children of God, it was clear who the Children of Satan were. What I didn't understand at the time was that the system of "Godless communism," which our "Western Christian Civilization" was opposing, was as much an outgrowth of the apocalyptic as our own system.

If the dominant thread of apocalyptic thought in the US was post-millennial, the pre-millennial apocalyptic was dominant in the USSR. Frederick Engels saw the "chiliastic dream-visions of ancient Christianity" as "a very serviceable starting-point" for a movement that eventually "merged with the modern proletarian movement."[15] Karl Marx's first published writings included such mystical texts as "On the Union of Christ with the Faithful" and the apocalyptic vision for the impending Revolution in which he and Engels shared a faith had roots in Judeo-Christian millenarianism. Modern utopianism and other currents of socialist, communist, and much other Left wing traditions were all, to varying degrees, modern products of Jewish and Christian apocalyptic thought, or showed at least some tinge of the apocalyptic worldview. The Revolution of Marxism and Leninism that would lead eventually to "communism" follows the same mythic structure of sudden and complete transformations into an idealized world that we find in the Apocalypse of John. Both Marxism-Leninism and apocalyptic Christians assume the struggle of a noble class of people (workers, believers, respectively) against diabolical evil (capitalism, or the "World, the flesh and the Devil" respectively), which the noble class wins. After the consummation and victory of the struggle both see an utterly transformed world, some version (a secular version in one) of a "heavenly city descending to earth," the scene that ends the *Book of Revelation*.

And then there are all the other apocalyptic, utopian, and millenarian movements organized in the shadows of these two Goliath utopias of the twentieth century. Anarchism is a very diverse tradition that defies most categories, by definition. Still, the utopian and millenarian spirit clearly imbues much of this segment of the Left. Bakunin's destructive impulses, for instance, had something deeply apocalyptic about them, and a millenarian spirit was also quite evident in the Spanish anarchists he influenced.[16] In an account of one dramatic moment of the Spanish Civil War as the city of Málaga went down in flames, Gerald Brenan heard an anarchist echo the apocalyptic sayings of Jesus as he said, "And I tell you—not one stone will be left on another stone—no, not a plant nor even a cabbage will grow there, so that there may be no more wickedness in the world."[17]

On the extreme margins of the US empire the apocalyptic idea plays a major role among the Christian Identity movement, Survivalists and many other far right organizations and movements. And of course there is ISIS in the Middle East,[18] and the apocalypticism of Al Qaeda and other Islamic fringe groups, all of whom inherited their apocalyptic sensibilities from Christianity and presumably from the Prophet himself.[19]

Like everyone of my generation born mid-20th century, my worldview was formed between the millennialism of the American empire, and the apocalypticism of the Soviet. This dichotomous consciousness became the "motor force" of the 1960s and the shadowy reality that came to be known as the Cold War. Both sides of the binary were secular ideologies with deep roots in a Judeo-Christian apocalyptic ethos that would remain foundational, despite polite denials (in the "Western" countries) or even violent attempts to extirpate it (most notably in the Soviet Union). In the same way the Catholic Conquistadors built their churches on top of the indigenous temples, and often of the same stones, the modern world has been erected on the foundations of an apocalyptic faith, utterly transforming it in the process.

CHAPTER ONE

FROM MID-CENTURY TO THE SIXTIES

My father, William "Harmon" Ross, was a farm boy who grew up in Depression and Dust Bowl-era Oklahoma. As a desperate teenager he'd hitchhiked to California and gone to work in the Oakland shipyards at the beginning of the Second World War. He'd lied about his age to join the Navy during that war, and then reenlisted in the Air Force. When I knew him he was loud (due to having gone mostly deaf from working around jet engines) and he had an accent so thick he could have wiped it on his jeans. He had what one relative called "a meanness" to him, which I could have attested to even before I could speak. He terrified me until I got old enough to fight back, but even then he could make me shake in my boots.

While moonlighting as a bartender when he was stationed in Seattle, Washington Harmon met my mother, Mary Carol

Crane, an ex-Marine who'd been raised in the Hoovervilles of Seattle. She could match wits with Harmon, which she often did, but he had the louder voice and that alone commanded submission from the whole family. She'd had a wild youth, but after the marriage she'd settled down, eventually converting to Billy Graham's particular brand of millenarian dispensationalist Christianity.[1]

Besides poverty, the two sides of my family had something else in common: their diverse ancient lineages had only recently been homogenized into white Protestantism. My maternal grandmother had neglected to tell her anti-Semitic spouse that she was Jewish, and neither my mother nor the grandchildren (like me) knew that we weren't really Protestants, nor therefore, in those days, qualified as "white." On my father's side a not-too distant ancestor also took advantage of a hole in the American apartheid wall that separated WASPs out from all others to leave the Cherokee tribe and join the dominant nest. Miscegenation had already lightened her complexion, making the defection from the tribe relatively easy, and leaving her people behind probably seemed a small price for my great-great grandmother to be able to manage her own life, far from the control of the Indian agent and the Bureau of Indian Affairs. And so it was that both branches of my family became white, Anglo-Saxon, and Protestant, and generations of ancestors with their non-white and non-Christian traditions were disappeared or shunted off into the underbrush around the family tree.

Other than these similarities, the two branches of my family bore little resemblance to each other. Despite my mother's recent conversion to a rather conservative Evangelical Christianity, she was still a liberal compared to my father's side of the family: they were Pentecostal Holiness of the Assembly of God variety, with a moderate sprinkling of, what by comparison were "moderate," Southern Baptists. Most of my aunts and uncles on the Ross side, then, spoke two languages: An Oklahoma dialect of English and the "unknown tongue" of the Holy Spirit. I grew up with a personal understanding of the term "holy rollers" those summers I went to visit relatives in Oklahoma before we eventually moved there. I watched grown adults, who were the most unemotional, reserved, and opaque of people all week long, transformed on Sunday mornings. They would enter and take their seats at the pews and tap their feet to the music of the electric guitar, drums, and choir as it sang the old favorites like, "I'll Fly Away," and "I'll see you in the Rapture." The temperature would rise until the first few would be "touched by the Spirit" and soon begin dancing out from the pews to babble, shriek, moan, wail, groan, cry, and roll in the aisles of Tyler, Oklahoma Assembly of God Church, the old one-room school house built early the previous century by none other than my great grandfather.

My father never quite readjusted to that culture when he returned to Oklahoma in his mid-forties. The military and service overseas had changed him, so while his family "danced in the Spirit" and spoke in unknown tongues, he sat quietly with my mother in the pew, both of them with their heads bowed.

Because my father had made the US Air Force a career, my first memories of religious instruction took place in a more regimented and rationalized context than the rollicking holiness world he'd grown up in. My earliest memories of church took place in the US military chapel. Here God's representative, dressed in an awe-inspiring officer's uniform, led our Sunday school assembly in choruses of "Climb, climb up Sunshine Mountain" and "Onward Christian soldiers." This latter was among my favorites as I was able to march in place along with the rest of the assembly as we sang this hymn, our hearts welling up with pride as we looked forward at the Chaplain, himself marching in place at the front of the assembly flanked on one side by the Christian white flag with the blue square containing the red cross and on the other side, mirroring it, the Star Spangled Banner.

My mystical civil religious instruction was complemented and reinforced by my love of magical fairy tales and the stories of comic book superheroes. I lived in those worlds and in my own imaginary land because the outside world was full of violence, sudden dislocations, and monsters, like my father, and the other kids, many of them bullies, at the (military) base schools. I understand now that my father was just trying to toughen me up to survive in an uncertain world and life among the other children of the warriors, and for that, he thought, my sensitivity and dislike of sports, and fighting, would have to change. As he saw it, the best way to change his son was by the use of fear or force, the latter of which involved beating, verbal abuse, slapping, and an array of techniques he'd probably been subjected to when he grew up on the farm in Oklahoma or during his years in the Air Force. It was, alas, a losing strategy.

On the other hand, my mother was moved by my sensitivity, creative hunger, and curiosity, so she encouraged me to follow my passions, and she was always eager to hear and read the stories and little books I wrote. She was an eternal child, playful, with an insatiable curiosity, a passion for learning, and a rebellious nature that even more than fifty years of marriage to my father never managed to destroy.

We lived a fairly settled life on bases in Germany and then in the "Economy" on a farm near Alconbury, England. It was at this latter base where Master Sergeant Ross was prematurely delivered from his life as a jet engine mechanics instructor by a heart attack at the ripe old age of thirty-four. Certainly the fact that he was NCOIC (Non-Commissioned Officer In Charge) with a great amount of responsibility and therefore pressure, and that he was drinking and smoking too much, and eating a very poor diet, all contributed to the condition. But the heart attack itself had been precipitated on Christmas Eve by his commanding officer who had, six months before, ordered him to work out a lesson plan on his office blackboard. As Santa Claus was preparing to deliver presents to all the good little boys and girls (and, no doubt, lumps of coal to the communist children), my father's commanding officer came into the office as Master Sergeant Ross put the period on the final sentence. He looked it over silently, nodded, and then said, "Sergeant Ross, erase the board." Incredulous, my father began to reply, "but sir, this is six months…" but the officer cut him off. "Sergeant Ross, I think you know what an order is."

As my father erased the board, he felt his left arm go numb.

We arrived back in the US from England the year before England, in the form of the Beatles, arrived in the US It was the year before the US jumped, with both boots, into Vietnam with the infamous Gulf of Tonkin incident, and the year before the Civil Rights Act of 1964 was signed by President Lyndon Johnson. All those factors would come to bear on my life in some way or another, and to a greater or lesser degree.

I wasn't prepared for the racism in South Carolina. The military bases had long before been integrated, and until my first year in public schools off base all my classrooms had been integrated. School integration in South Carolina didn't take place for two more school years when, suddenly, the African-American students entered to take seats in the back of the classrooms. I remember trying to make friends with one black student named Calhoun, only to find to my disappointment he refused to speak to me or acknowledge me.

My father was a conservative and I remember him calling Martin Luther King a "communist," but my mother was anti-racist and wouldn't allow the "N" word to be spoken in our house. When African-Americans attempted to enter the white Presbyterian Church in Sumter and were blocked at the doors, the story made big news in *The Sumter Daily Item*. I asked my mother why white people wouldn't let black people into their churches, and, with a disgusted look on her face, she said, "because they're ignorant."

No such attempts were made by blacks to enter the Hickory Road Baptist Church in Cherryvale, the little community across from Shaw Air Force Base, where we lived. The church was white and strictly Evangelical, and its members were probably more racist than Sumter's Presbyterians. Cherryvale itself was white from the center to its margins. But just outside the margins were the cotton fields that ran to the edges of swampy forests and there, down winding, sandy dirt roads, were the tin-roofed, bleached-wood shacks of the black families. They would come through Cherryvale, but rarely would stop unless it was the vegetable vendor, the old man who rode around the neighborhood with his horse-drawn cart, brimming with fruits and vegetables he had for sale. But mostly I was oblivious to the racism, and eventually accepted it as given, because I was white and it didn't concern me—or so I thought in those days.

Already in the fourth grade I noticed that my teachers were more interested in the "correct" answers than they were in the true answers. I'd learned that the hard way in my final exam in history, science, and social studies when I missed only two questions. To the question "Who discovered America?" I wrote, "Leif Erikson." As to the shape of the earth, I had written "egg-shaped." Despite my arguments, my teacher insisted that my answers were "not the right answers." This was the real beginning of my education about education.

Then in sixth grade a scrawny bald kid wearing a strange double-breasted grey shirt was introduced into the classroom as the new student. His name was Michael Duffy, and we would soon become best friends.

For the first few weeks Michael kept to himself. He claimed to be in communication with Martians, and I would often find him on the playground looking off into the sky, obviously in the midst of sending them telepathic messages. He said he was requesting that they pick him up. That it was time for him to "go home." I wondered if there was something to this, and I hoped they might take me along with them when they came to pick him up, so I often stood nearby when he was "in communication."

Eventually Michael was able to let go of his identity as a Martian to become just another boy on the playground, and that was when we really became friends. For the rest of the year we spent most of our free time together writing a book about two young boys who were inseparable friends and had all sorts of adventures together. Michael and I, by contrast with the heroes of our stories, had very few big adventures, but we had lots of fun imagining them.

Eventually we decided to serialize the book and publish it in the form of comics that we duplicated with carbon paper, and eventually with a mimeograph Michael's father had in his antiques and junk store. We started selling the comics for the price of lunch, since we knew every student arrived at school with at least a quarter in his or her pocket.

Michael's memory of this incident is far sharper than mine. Years later he told me that we were called into the principal's office one day after lunch and had our money, and comics, confiscated. It was becoming clear to me that I lived in a world of total coercion: from home, to school, to life around the military base. This awareness conflicted with the world my parents told me I lived in. They had instilled other values in me, among them, perhaps the highest among them, being "freedom, democracy, and independence." But where was the freedom? And what democracy? Certainly not at home, nor, as I had discovered, at school. I began to suspect it was a total lie. It wouldn't be long before I would have that suspicion confirmed, and by none other than my father.

One older friend, my next-door neighbor, Buddy Dorsey, eventually left school after passing two years through nearly every grade, that is, advancing by "social promotion" all the way to the eighth grade. There, however, the "Peter Principle" kicked in and he hit the glass ceiling of junior high, since social promotion didn't apply beyond the eighth grade. At first he tried to make a living selling rose trellises and doing odd jobs that didn't seem to suit him, and so he joined the Marines and shipped off to Vietnam. Not long after, he was hit by a friendly mortar, which took out part of his skull and left him with a metal plate in his head and partially paralyzed. He returned home a quieter person, a good part of his life gone missing with fragments of his skull.

That was when I began to wonder why we were in Vietnam, so one evening I asked my father. My father was a conservative, but he was also an honest man. He sat down on the end of my bed and looked me in the eye. "I'll tell you why we in Vietnam," he said in his thick Okie drawl. "We in Vietnam cause we got us a war economy in this country. If we pulled out of Vietnam we'd go right into a depression." He stood up, looked at me and nodded. "That's why we in Vietnam." And he concluded, "we gotta have us a war to keep the economy goin.'" Then he turned and left the room.

I sat there shocked for a moment. Was that really it? We were selling our young men, sending them off to die, to "keep the economy going"? I felt my whole world suddenly turning upside-down. Then everything I had believed was, indeed, an enormous lie.

And so I rebelled. In seventh grade my rebellion became too much for even Michael to accompany. I joined an eighth grade group of Southern hoodlums who combed their hair back "greaser" style, wore the collars of their shirts turned up, taps on their shoes, and smoked Marlboros out behind the bathrooms. I did all that in perfect imitation, following them the next year into eighth grade where I was able to sit in the same classes with most of them who had, fittingly, failed the grade.

But already, unbeknownst to me, another path of rebellion was opening in the great world beyond my own little Cherryvale. With the magic of television, the big cultural changes of the moment were coming, even to Sumter, South Carolina. The Beatles were the major point of departure in the culture, although it would be a couple more years before we fully grasped what we had departed into. The counter-culture that had been seething in the subterranean realm of the collective unconscious of the US was preparing to explode into public view with sex, drugs, and rock and roll.

Randy Gossett was another friend who lived down the road from me. Together we'd started smoking cigarettes and drinking on the weekends. Randy's older brothers, Gary and Jeff, were beginning to listen to strange music and wear odd clothes and grow their hair over their ears. Jeff, the oldest, one night ended up in the hospital for from a strange new drug known as "LSD." It was the first known incident of such a thing in Sumter County, and Sherriff Byrd Parnell, a reputed member of the KKK and future president of the National

Sheriffs' Association (1973–1974), and his entire force decided they were going to have to watch the Gossett boys, including Randy who was, at that time, passing through his second year in the sixth grade and waiting on his "social promotion" to seventh.

I was in the eighth grade and at school I found a copy of *Life* magazine dedicated to a strange group of people in California called "hippies" who believed in free love and took LSD and other drugs. Gary Gossett, the middle brother, began wearing blue tinted glasses and playing drums in a rock band that Jeff had named "White Light." Unlike the numerous local Motown covers bands (most of them named "The Tempests" or something like that) White Light played psychedelic music. Gary drove the school bus and seemed to manage to live in both the straight and hippie worlds quite well, but Jeff was another matter.

Jeff, I knew, "knew." Jeff didn't fit, by any stretch of the imagination, in the "straight" world. He was a "head"; his hair was growing longer and longer, and he wore a leather fringe jacket, and he became my hero. That presented a real problem for my father because Jeff was not only a hippie, and a drug user, but my very perceptive father was also quite clear that Jeff was not "straight" in another way: he was a homosexual.

One day a friend a couple years older than me invited me into his garage. He had something he wanted to tell me about. We went into the garage and he looked around to make sure we were alone. Then he put on a record. It was Bob Dylan's "Rainy Day Women." I'd never heard Bob Dylan before, and I didn't much care for the song. Then he pulled out a bag and asked me if I'd ever sniffed paint. I shook my head. He pulled a can of spray paint off the shelf, sprayed into the bag, then covered his face with the bag and began breathing deeply. Soon his eyes glazed over and he handed me the bag. I took a few deep breaths and then my head began buzzing and the music changed and I remember very little else, except that I liked it. This incident led to a small group of us, Randy, his friend Chuck, and one or two others, gathering in the woods near our old fort so we could sniff glue, or glue and lighter fluid.

Fortunately, this was a "stage" most of us passed through quickly, although one of the gang stayed there a little too long and became a rather demented character that eventually had to be withdrawn from seventh grade.

Soon our little gang was raiding the parents' liquor and medicine cabinets, the latter containing a wealth of inconceivably diverse treasures as only exist in military families, since military doctors were renowned above all others for their free dispensing of prescriptions.

We were a ragtag bunch, although Michael had a definite style, perhaps due to his earlier long sojourn among Martians and his work with his father. Through his father's antique business he managed to pull together a consummate wardrobe of a top hat, a tuxedo and a cane. He would often be seen in this outfit, wearing blue or black jeans, and tennis shoes, or just going barefoot. But he was the exception. The rest of us dressed in some hippie fashion that was more down at the heels, and we thus earned the disdain and opprobrium of the culture we rejected, which in this case was the good folks of Sumter.

The young Southern gentry of Sumter called us "Shaw Trash" and we called them "Grits." They dressed in tasseled loafers, dress pants, double-stitched shirts with button down collars and London Fogs and wore their hair short, or in bangs, discreetly cut in a perfectly straight line above the eyebrows. They cruised the streets of Sumter in their Mustangs, listening to Motown, but hating blacks and always looking for someone to beat up on.

We lived up to our names, wearing long hair, patched faded and holey blue jeans and often going barefoot or, when the sand was too hot, in tennis shoes. We listened to Jimi Hendrix, the Beatles, Steppenwolf, and anything rock, and believed in peace and unity of all people. They drank beer and liquor; we smoked pot and took LSD. To them we were the reincarnation of the Yankee Army, and to us, they were redneck racists. Perhaps both sides were right.

I suspect that Project MK Ultra was responsible for the fact that so much LSD was floating around Shaw Air Base, and I took as much of it as I could, sometimes for days on end. I know for a fact that our little group was under surveillance because I saw the men in the black Galaxy 500 wearing black suits and dark sunglasses who would often show up at the Piggly Wiggly where we congregated. They would sit there, taking notes, and occasionally taking photos. Once I had a bad LSD trip and was picked up walking through the base and taken into the Air Police (AP) station for questioning. A man who identified himself as being from the Office of Strategic Intelligence came in during the interrogation and he described to me everything I'd done that day, down to conversations I'd had.

And the more drugs I took, the crazier I naturally got. Those days, my father would later tell me, he slept with a pistol under his pillow, wondering when or if he might need it to protect himself from me. At some point in the middle of these insane few years, I suspect just to be able to sleep again, my father brought home a storage shed he'd bought from Shaw Air Force Base surplus, and put it in the backyard. He told me he didn't want me living in the house, but he was willing to continue feeding me, as he was legally obligated to do, as long as I lived in the shed.

I didn't take the offer amiss: I was quite happy since now, at the age of sixteen, I would have my own space to take whatever drugs came my way and quietly travel astral planes in the safety of my military surplus shed. My friends and I named my shed "The Time Machine" and I decorated it with a black light and posters that Randy drew for the space. Randy, Michael, and I spent our evenings there, drinking or using drugs and listening to music. I remember one night in particular we listened to the title cut of Steppenwolf's new album, *Monster*, over and over. The song explained all US history and its beautiful chorus to this day brings tears to my eyes: "America, where are you now? Don't you care about your sons and daughters? Don't you know, we need you now; we can't fight alone against the Monster."

But I knew my search was coming to an end as I found myself veering closer to self-destruction than I'd ever been before. My life was disintegrating and I felt lost, confused, and out of control. My father was going through his own crisis and in 1970 he bought a farm in Oklahoma and within a few months we moved back to the community he'd grown up in. But before we moved back to Oklahoma I had an experience that changed my life.

CHAPTER TWO

SAVED!

Jackie Adair was a friend of the family and she knew I was in deep trouble. She'd recently been "born again" and she invited me to go with her to Rock Hill to meet some "Jesus freaks." I accepted her invitation and we drove up and met a young Christian hippie couple and after a long conversation, I prayed with them and became a Christian. The conversion was immediately dramatic, perhaps intensified by the amount of LSD and marijuana still in my system. Over the coming weeks and months I had visions; I spoke in tongues; I saw Jesus bleeding for me on a cross when I closed my eyes and prayed; I saw the light of God.

Jackie had Bible studies in her trailer most evenings, and they became charismatic prayer sessions. I was convinced that Jesus would be returning any day now and taking us all up in the Rapture.[1] I was certain of it. I walked around looking up at the clouds and wondering when I would see His face.

What would it look like? How would it be that he would be seen everywhere at the same time? I hadn't made it to physics in high school... perhaps if I had, I'd understand a bit more how that would work, I thought.

Over the next few years as I bounced back and forth between Oklahoma and South Carolina I was in and out of cults, sects, and churches of fairly extreme varieties. I spent two weeks with the Children of God, also known as the "Family International" near Pike's Peak in.[2] I fled that cult one morning by walking miles down an icy road, before catching a ride into the safety of Colorado Springs where I caught a bus home. But no doubt my time at Joseph S. Carroll's Evangelical Institute (EI) in Greenville, South Carolina took the cake.

The EI was just down the road from Bob Jones University, the institution of higher learning affectionately referred to by the locals as "the Bijoux." I went to work at EI in early 1972 and was housed with an elderly couple who were really lovely people. They had no children of their own, and immediately adopted me with all the love, concern, and controlling behavior any good Fundamentalist Christian couple would demonstrate toward their own child.

Perhaps it was because I was still in the process of coming down off what had essentially been a prolonged LSD trip from 1970–1971. Perhaps because I was a recent convert to Christianity trying to hard not to think of songs from George Harrison's *Radha Krsna Temple* album (which my friends and I used to listen to as we tripped) that I couldn't help obsessing on them.[3] As George Lakoff reminds us, and as anyone who has had the experience of trying *not* to think of an elephant will know, all anyone in such a situation can do is think of an elephant.

In any case I began obsessing on the songs to the "foreign deities" and found it distressing. When I mentioned this problem to members of the EI, I was referred to the Reverend himself who informed me that I was possessed by demons and he made an appointment with me for the exorcism. I was alarmed but he reassured me that demon possession wasn't a really big deal, and mumbled something about it being no more problematic than "a common cold."

That Sunday we met in his office and the exorcism began, with Carroll and other elders laying hands on me and commanding the demons to leave me in the name of Jesus. Nothing happened.

"I don't think there's anything there," I said, more than a little flummoxed.

"The demon of lies!" the Reverend cried out, and they once again laid hands on me and commanded the demons to leave in the name of Jesus.

After a while they decided that my case was graver than they'd first believed and that it would be necessary to set another time for a more serious bit of work on my demons. I agreed, and returned to the house where I was staying, packed my backpack, and left.

I caught a Greyhound bus to Sumter, where I'd been baptized at the age of twelve as a Presbyterian, and met with the family minister there. After I told him the story, he stood up and said, "Well, they're probably right, you know." His demeanor changed from a kind, ministerial expression of concern to one of righteous godly wrath as he confronted the devil himself.

"If you were really a Christian, you wouldn't appear here with long hair! You clearly don't have the Light of Christ in you! Get out you hypocrite!"

As he shouted this he pushed me toward the door of his office and I left, bewildered, stumbling into the darkness outside.

I took a Greyhound bus back to Oklahoma and all along the road home I read a book on demon possession, a sort of "how-to-manual" for self-exorcism, just in case. And I tried to figure out my next steps.

It was my second foray that year into fundamentalist cults, and I stayed a little closer to home for the rest of the year. Fortunately, after a time my head began to clear and I went back to church with normal, slightly more down-to-earth fundamentalists. By now the Pentecostal Holiness and the Southern Baptists around the family in Oklahoma seemed quite liberated and friendly by comparison with the folks I'd been hanging out with in South Carolina.

I count myself fortunate for passing through most available phases of Bible Belt religion rather quickly. In Oklahoma I only briefly attended Tyler Assembly of God Church before I became a member of the First Baptist Church of Madill and, in addition, attended various non-denominational Evangelical churches. By the time I was coming to question most of the religion around me I had been sprinkled Presbyterian, baptized in the Spirit in the Pentecostal Church, and immersed in the First Baptist Church of Madill, Oklahoma. Through it all ran the thread of apocalyptic faith and a set of values that didn't square well with the world in which I lived—nor, strangely enough, with the churches I attended.

No one around me seemed to notice that latter fact. I lived in the region of the "Christian nation" with the densest population of "Bible-believing Christians" and it seemed that no one around me knew anything about the Bible. Somehow it eluded everyone that Jesus, were he alive at that time, would have been wearing his customary sandals, long hair and robe, and would have been out there with the hippies protesting the war in Vietnam. Somehow the Christians I knew didn't get what Jesus was saying when he stated "If you wish to be complete, go and sell your possessions and give to the poor, and you will have treasure in heaven; and come, follow Me" (Matthew 19:21). They seemed not to have read the Book of the Acts of the Apostles, or at least they had missed Acts 2:44–45: "And all who believed were together and had all things in common; and they sold their possessions and goods and distributed them to all, as any had need."

But that wasn't all. There were the other passages, powerfully impacting me but apparently ignored by my fellow Christians, passages such as the one in which Jesus rebuked a man for calling him "Master" because, as he said, "Call no man 'master' for you have only one Master in heaven." Then there were the many contradictions and problematic questions that people seemed not to notice, contradictions too many to note here, but which began to gnaw at my faith. To those around me it would have been blasphemy to have stated the obvious: that Jesus and his followers were anti-imperialist anarcho-communist revolutionaries attempting to overthrow the established order and set up a completely different way of life in the Israel of their time. It would have been blasphemy, and I would have been locked up in a mental institution anywhere in the region for stating the obvious. There was, it seemed to me, something seriously wrong with the people around me—or was it me?

During that time I was told the GED test was being offered at job training center where I was studying small engine mechanics, and on a whim I decided to take it. Two weeks later the guidance counselor called me into his office to give me the news. He said my scores indicated that I must have studied hard for the exam, and he congratulated me. I was shocked. I didn't know that you were supposed to study for the test. He said I'd done particularly well in reading and writing, and he asked me if I really wanted to be a mechanic, after all. I said no, that I really wanted to be a writer. He encouraged me to go to college.

In the fall of 1973 I started my first semester of college at Southeastern Oklahoma State University in Durant. I was the only "Jesus freak" on campus, and two or three years older than the other incoming freshmen, but I didn't care. I was there to learn and grow and find answers to the many questions I had about life.

The following summer of 1974 my friend from Dallas, James Elaine, invited me to join him and his church group on a study program for Christian college students to Switzerland. James and I had met at a Christian conference and as we were the only two hippies there, we became friends. I thought it would be wonderful to spend a summer with him and other Christians in Switzerland, so I applied and was accepted. I had just enough money for a round-trip ticket from Montreal to Zurich with a dollar left over. The route from Oklahoma to Montreal I could make by hitchhiking and I was certain I'd find something to eat along the way, but a dollar wasn't going to be enough.

My grandmother somehow had managed to save $40 from her Social Security checks and the sale of quilts she made, at $25 per quilt, and she secretly passed the money on to me so I wouldn't go hungry hitchhiking to Montreal and back. She didn't want the other grandchildren to know she gave me the money and she made me promise not to tell them because, as she put it, "they'd all be a-wantin' some money, and I ain't got no more to give 'em."

James and another artist named David Park and I spent our days washing dishes in the hotel, and evenings studying the Bible and Bible prophecy. The owner of the hotel was a Darbyite, or at least a dispensationalist, and he had a long map of time as taken from the bible up on the wall of his study that extended from near the doorway to the desk by the window at the far side of the room.[4] It started with 4004 B.C. when God made Adam and eve, and it ended somewhere in the near future, quickly moving through the Great Tribulation, the coming of the Anti-Christ, the Rapture of the Faithful when they rise from the graves to meet Jesus at his Second Coming, and finally, the coming of the Heavenly Jerusalem and the end of time. I no longer remember the old man's name, but he dwelt long on the map and studied the final section carefully, certain that the rapture would happen before he saw death. Now, more than forty years later, I believe, at last, he may have been proven wrong.

We took hikes into the mountains when we could, up steep paths through deep forests that led to alpine meadows from which we could see other mountains and valleys, dotted with villages. Once or twice I joined the Baptist youth on an evening of carousing in a local café where James's brother David practiced the only French he knew on the waiter, "une autre bouteille de vin, s'il vous plait!" We became so drunk we had to hold each other up as we walked back down the narrow streets to the hotel. On the way we slipped into a tent at a traditional Alpine music show and watched Swiss cowboys dressed in their traditional garb play songs in German and French, slapping their knees as they took elaborate steps in a strange traditional dance. We were discovered and thrown out into the night and we giggled loudly as we continued our way, with great effort, back to the hotel.

The evening studies were geared toward somewhat intellectual Baptists so we were introduced to C. S. Lewis (whose books I'd already read), Francis Schaeffer, Os Guinness, and others. We also had guest speakers visiting, and it was one of these, Dr. James Parker, "Jim," who had the greatest impact on me.

Jim only stayed with us briefly, but I recall his discussion of "radical Christianity" and the "radical discipleship" of people like Dietrich Bonhoeffer. He brought copies of two alternative newspapers: *The Post-American* (later changed to *Sojourners*) from the Sojourners community in Washington D.C., and *Right On* (later changed to *Radix Magazine*) from the Christian World Liberation Front (CWLF) in Berkeley, California. As I read through the magazines I became very excited. Here I met, in print, Christians who understood their faith as I did. There were articles by William Stringfellow, Dorothy Day of the Catholic Worker Movement, Phil and Daniel Berrigan, William Everson/Brother Antoninus, E.F. Schumacher, and many others. I no longer felt crazy, as I had for the previous few years, reading the Bible as a hippie in the Bible Belt and thinking I was reading out of a different book from the one everyone else had.

A few months later, back home at college in Durant, Oklahoma, I came across a stack of *Right On!* newspapers at the Intervarsity Christian Fellowship building. I took one and read the paper from cover to cover and then subscribed.

I was studying journalism at Southeastern Oklahoma State University and one day I heard a rumor that the ROTC would be moving in and occupying two floors of campus dormitories, likely displacing other students in the process. I decided to write up the story, so I went to the dean's office to see if I could get an interview. His secretary asked what I wanted to talk to the dean about, and I told her. She went into his office and returned a few minutes later to say he was busy and couldn't meet with me. I returned right away to the office of the school newspaper and a few minutes later Ken Nichols, the head of the Journalism Department came in and said he wanted to talk to me. He'd evidently just gotten off the phone with the dean, and told me I couldn't write the story. This was my second encounter with censorship in the educational system. I was getting the message loud and clear that "the press is free to those who own it."

By early summer 1976 I decided to drop out of college and hitchhike to California. My father didn't ordinarily give me much advice because he knew I probably wouldn't take it anyway, but on my final morning home, as I prepared to leave, he decided to do what he could to dissuade me from what he suspected might be a disastrous trip to Sodom and Gomorrah, or at least prepare me for what he thought I would find there. First he warned me to watch out for the transvestites of San Francisco, who, he said, were quite convincing until you felt the bulge under their dresses. When he thought I grasped the dangers of the transvestites, he turned to the second lesson. This one he'd doubtlessly learned when he was living in Oakland in the late thirties and it was based on the simple fact that Californians hated Okies. "You gonna find out when you get out there they gon' treat you worse than a dog," he finished.

"Dad," I responded, probably in a tone of mock exhaustion, "people in California will never know where I'm from. I don't have an Okie accent."

At that point he gave up. We loaded my pack in the car, I kissed my mother goodbye and my father drove me to the interstate where I would begin hitchhiking into my new life in California.

CHAPTER THREE

BERKELEY:
The Utopia after the Revolution

Fortunately, in 1976 a considerable number of people in Berkeley didn't yet know "the Sixties" had ended. Graffiti for the New World Liberation Front, "NWLF," sprayed in red on the wall facing People's Park indicated that some Marxist-Leninist-Maoist guerrilla activity was ongoing in the area, even if most armed revolutionary activity had come to an end with the dramatic, bloody attack on the Symbionese Liberation Army in Los Angeles two years before. There were still many signs of an active counterculture, like food coops, housing and worker cooperatives, and a lively cultural scene with many regular poetry readings, a number of repertory movie theaters, active café life and, of course, concerts and happenings, and everything else, at People's Park. It was, for me, a little paradise, the utopia I'd sought my whole life as I hitchhiked around the US, but never, until now, knew actually existed.

I had only the vaguest notion of the recent history of Berkeley, and even less familiarity with the recent history of radical Christian participation in what had been called "the Movement."[1] Aside from a handful of Baptist hippies, like James Elaine, most of the "Jesus people" I'd known up to that point were just fundamentalists or, at best, Evangelicals with sideburns, long hair and sandals. Until my arrival in Berkeley I'd been relatively isolated from the Left wing of the Jesus movement, and until I'd been introduced to *Right On!* by Jim Parker in Switzerland, I hadn't even known there *was* a Left wing. In Berkeley, I was soon to discover, there were hippie Christians, and early on many of them had been allies, if not collaborators, with secular leftists in what they had seen as a revolutionary process.

Certainly, the Left wing or, what one writer has called "the Moral Minority," of the Christian churches, was never granted a big role in North American society, and it certainly garnered fewer news headlines than did Jerry Falwell's "Moral Majority" and other right wing Christian groups.[2] Nevertheless, the acts of courage and protest of the "moral minority" were greater than their numbers, even if those acts were routinely dismissed or ignored by the press. There were, for instance, the radical Quakers, and many other radical Christians, who had made up the core of the Abolition movement of the 19th century, and had protested virtually every imperial campaign the US had engaged in from the Mexican-American War on. The Quaker American Friends Service Committee (AFSC), went on peace and human aid missions to Hanoi during the Vietnam War, putting the spotlight back on this small group on the margins of the Christian tradition.[3] The Social Gospel movement, which included the likes of Washington Gladden, Walter Rauschenbusch, and others, had become active in many progressive causes from the 1870s to the 1920s and left a legacy on radical politics in the San Francisco Bay Area. In 1933 Dorothy Day and Peter Maurin founded the Catholic Worker Movement to feed unemployed workers and engage in a struggle for peace and justice. Other Catholics, including Philip and Daniel Berrigan (the Berrigan Brothers), joined in the 1960s. The example of these and other "radical" and Left Christians began to take on a new sense of importance with the rise of the "Jesus People" movement in the early 1970s. New communities of Christians, often meeting in houses as "house churches" began to emerge as "free" or "liberation" churches.

These new church formations occurred in tandem with "the Movement" of the time, as Harlan Stelmach demonstrated in his fascinating work on the Berkeley Free Church (BFC).[4] Initiated in 1967 as the South Campus Christian Ministry (SCCM) by church and local businesses around Telegraph Avenue in Berkeley, the project was soon dubbed the "Berkeley Free Church" by the youths it served under the leadership of a young Episcopal priest named Richard York. Starting in June 1967 the BFC began its work in what had become a "full-fledged youth ghetto" by providing basic services to the hippies and countercultural youth who were flooding the area. Under its motto, "Celebrate life—Off the World Pig!" it became a significant institution of the emerging counterculture-New Left in Berkeley.

The ministry began as a paternalistic social welfare project aimed at controlling or mitigating problems associated with the emerging youth culture and so it provided a "crash pad," health and crisis counseling services, food, and referral services. Some of these "ministries" eventually were spun off into the Berkeley Free Clinic, Berkeley Emergency Food Program, and others. Alongside, or perhaps within, this context a church began to grow up, with John Pairman Brown joining as its resident theologian in 1968. Soon Anthony Nugent, who, like York, had been a community organizer in Oakland and met York in seminary, joined the "mission" as a co-pastor, although Anthony noted in an email to me that York "very much needed to control, dominate, be the sole 'leader.'"[5] In the wake of the struggle for People's Park, in which the Free Church played a key role, instigating, then mediating the conflict and, finally, serving as an emergency room for protestors wounded by the National Guard, the tensions between York and Nugent exploded. Anthony Nugent went off to form the "Submarine Church," leaving York as the sole authority at the BFC.

As a result of the internal splits and a coordinated program of repression on the part of the US government's COINTELPRO operations, by 1969 the fragmentation of the Youth/Anti-War Movement had begun in earnest and this was reflected in the BFC. Two currents ran increasingly in different directions, according to a quarterly report of the project directors of the BFC, with a divide "between 'mysticism and action, accommodation and confrontation, Utopian and revolutionary.'"[6] The "mystical, accommodationist, utopian" (hippie) side of what Stelmach called the "oppositional youth culture" inspired the growth of alternative spiritualities, the "back to the land" movement, and diverse lifestyle innovations throughout the following decades. The "activist, confrontational, revolutionary" current (New Left) flowed into burgeoning of the "New Communist movement" and an array of vanguard parties. That latter movement reached its peak in 1973—1974 from whence it began its slow decline.[7]

Into this context came the Christian World Liberation Front (CWLF) arriving in Berkeley in 1969 as a "ministry" of conservative Bill Bright's Campus Crusade for Christ. No doubt Bright hoped to convert much of the Berkeley Left to Jesus and the "American way," but the man he sent to organize the project, Jack Sparks, had different ideas—or at least he did once he arrived in Berkeley. The rather straight-arrow Evangelical ex-professor from Penn State quickly transformed into a long-haired, bearded "freak" indistinguishable, on the outside at least, from all the others who frequented the city. The ministry under Sparks also went "undercover" and appropriated all the trimmings of the counterculture—starting with a name that was designed to locate the organization amidst all the other "world liberation fronts."

One might have expected the BFC and CWLF to engage with each other, or cooperate in some way, given they both considered themselves "disciples of Jesus," but that wasn't the case. The CWLF had landed right in the middle of what Richard York no doubt saw as the BFC's turf. And even if the BFC was nominally ecumenical, York was Episcopalian, and certainly wouldn't have defined himself as "Evangelical" nor would he have had any desire to associate himself in any way with the right wing Campus Crusade for Christ.

There were clear differences in style and substance between BFC and CWLF, and personal and territorial rivalries kept the two groups of radical believers separate as each "church" continued on its own particular trajectory. York's BFC was far more integrated into the secular Movement as organized in Berkeley, and CWLF had, at best, an ambivalent and ambiguous relationship to the Movement it hoped to "save." Swartz describes a confrontation that might have been typical in the early years of the CWLF. He wrote "ahead of leftist activists in October 1969, CWLFers reserved the steps of Sproul Hall for a lecture by Chinese refugee Calvin Chao on the evils of Mao and the virtues of Christ." In response, the "inflamed antiwar activists and Maoists set up an amplifier next to Chao, threw rocks into the crowd, and set fire to the nearby ROTC Building."[8]

Nevertheless, despite the early hostility of the Left toward CWLF—which included a spoof flyer headlined "Jump for Jesus! Leap for the Lord!" inviting believers to join CWLF in a jump off the Golden Gate Bridge—there was also a gradual accommodation, and even, on some issues, a convergence, of the secular Left with the CWLF and other radical Christians. For an increasing number of CWLFers engaging with the radical community of Berkeley, the meaning of "witness" gradually shifted from its Evangelical definition of "saving souls" to the more socio-political meaning it had had for those associated with the Berkeley Free Church.

The CWLF had split the year before I arrived in Berkeley when Jack Sparks and other Campus Crusade leaders decided to move toward affiliation with the Orthodox Church of America. Those who remained regrouped as the Berkeley Christian Coalition (BCC) and began to organize themselves less officially as the House Church of Berkeley (HCOB).

I soon found a place for myself on the margins of the BCC community and the HCOB, right where I wanted to be. I was perfectly happy to hang out in the basement of Dwight House, especially on Sundays during occasional long afternoon HCOB meetings that followed morning worship services (the House Church was meeting at Dwight House at that time). I suffered through only one of those meetings, and afterwards I fled downstairs where I joined a small group of ex-hippie, recovering, and not-so recovering, drug addicts, alcoholics, and other denizens, refugees from Telegraph Avenue and the four corners of the American Empire. There in the labyrinth of the basement we smoked cigarettes and had long, wandering, intellectual conversations such as nothing I'd experienced in Oklahoma, or anywhere else for that matter. Sometimes a few of us would wander down to Telegraph Avenue and hang out in a café, drinking espresso, and then, of course, the conversations would become even more animated.

I learned about Dietrich Bonhoeffer and the German Confessional Church that resisted Hitler. I was introduced to Thomas Merton, and began reading Albert Camus, Soren Kierkegaard, and the other Existentialists whose books I found at Moe's Bookstore. With the help of new "comrades-of-the-cross" I was able to revise my ideas of what Christianity was and explore new, unfamiliar traditions and trajectories others had taken. Unlike the Christian circles I'd passed through in the Bible Belt, here questions, doubts, and challenges were welcomed, and even expected. My new Christian friends laughed at Fundamentalism, yawned at Evangelicalism, sneered at liberal Christianity, and proudly embraced a worldly-wise and radical Christianity.

I spent evenings with these friends watching double-feature movies of world cinema at the local theaters. I was particularly moved by the Italian films of the seventies: Fellini, Wertmueller, Pasolini, Bertolucci; the French New Wave; Vietnamese, Chinese, Russian, Czech: every night a new double-bill of the best films in the world, and the tickets were only $2! A few of the rowdier in the church—and I was immediately one of them—would have regular parties in their rooms at Dwight House and one or two of us would often duck out to smoke marijuana and wander in a daze through the University of California (UC) campus. Together we formed a subculture under the subculture of the HCOB.

HCOB was making a conscious effort to build a sense of community in the church, and to explore Christian alternatives to mainstream Protestantism. This led to an emerging interest of the community in Anabaptist[9] theology, which fit well with the anti-war, pacifist stance the BCC inherited from CWLF, although some notables, like *Radix Magazine* editor, Sharon Gallagher, came from families with some roots in Anabaptism. The interest in Anabaptist theology also was the result of a recent visit to the community by Mennonite theologian John Howard Yoder.[10]

Yoder and other Anabaptist theologians argued that the early Christian Church of Jesus and his followers had been radical and pacifist but that had changed with the "Constantinian shift" in 312 A.D. That was when the Roman emperor Constantine had a vision just before the Battle of Milvian Bridge in which he saw a cross above the sun and heard the words, "by this sign you will conquer." Although the shift from an anti-imperialist revolutionary religion of the colonized to a militarized, establishment religion of empire was gradual, with the Constantinian shift the Church had been subverted and perverted.

According to this narrative, there followed numerous attempts of believers to return to the original faith of Jesus, and these included the monastic movements, the spiritual and even the "heretical" movements of the Middle Ages. But only with the coming of the Anabaptists' "Radical Reformation," beginning with Peter Waldo and his followers in the late twelfth century, did a serious turn back to Christ's teachings occur in the West. This led to a crisis of authority as Medieval Christians asked what exactly constituted "Christ's teachings," and who represented them, but it also represented the beginnings of a radical political tradition in the West that would grow out of its religious roots and take distinct secular forms. As Norman Cohn wrote of the Medieval millenarian and apocalyptic movements' survival into our own day, "stripped of their original supernatural sanction, revolutionary millenarianism and mystical anarchism are still with us."[11] They certainly were with a few of us in the HCOB, even if the revolutionary movements of Christianity weren't yet on my agenda, and the same spirit was alive and well in Berkeley, even if expressed in the hip argot of the 1970s.

Radical Catholics, seekers of various sorts, gnostic mystics, and old hippies cycled through the HCOB as well as the collective households, either visiting or staying on for a while. This was especially true of Dwight House, which every imaginable form of humanity passed through, some of them saints, and true prophets and people of uncommon wisdom, depth, and compassion. But there were also the others, each with his or her own unique worldview, con, or delusion, depending on the person. Both saint and sinner found some corner of the House Church to rest in, although some may have never gotten far beyond the entryway. This was, after all, Northern California, a region that has always offered the tantalizing scent of utopia.

Chief among the many reasons I liked hanging out in the Dwight House basement was because that's where Karen Bostrom lived, a delicate woman with long, blond hair, a tough facade and a great, but wounded, heart. She would become my first wife in a relationship that, perhaps, was doomed from the start.

We married less than a year into my time in Berkeley, and I believe we were the first marriage to take place in HCOB. Within a month we'd began to encounter what I would only recognize much too late as insuperable problems. Less than a year into our marriage we went off for six months to live and work in Switzerland, passing part of the time at Francis Schaeffer's L'Abri.[12] By then I had a deeper affection for the secular philosophers Schaeffer criticized and a greater respect for their ideas than I did for Schaeffer and his Evangelical Reformed theology. I found myself challenging the Schaeffer dogma at every meal, and soon Karen and I left the community. A friend in Lausanne got us in contact with a local family who needed help tending their milk cows when they went up into the high slopes for summer grazing. I applied for the job and they hired me so I went to work in the mountains as a "cowboy."

I'd brought with me three books, and these would become my only reading for the next couple of months I worked outside of Villars in the high slopes: the *Complete Poems and Plays* of T. S. Eliot, *The Crooked Lines of God*, by William Everson/ Brother Antoninus, and a copy of *Slavery and Freedom*, by Nicolas Berdyaev. I had ample time to read and while the poetry of Everson and Eliot would become a form of devotion for me, Berdyaev would begin a new transformation in my heart and mind. His "mystical anarchism," as it has been called, was a particular comfort to me there as I passed hours of isolation in the high slopes of Switzerland: an idyllic context for a descent into hell.

The Russian philosopher had deeply inspired Peter Maurin, co-founder of the Catholic Worker movement, who had "indoctrinated" Dorothy Day with Berdyaev's "personalist socialism."[13] Berdyaev himself had referred to the personalists around the French magazine *Esprit* (Emmanuel Mounier, Jacques Maritain, and others) as being "the most interesting movement" in Western, Catholic Christianity, and "in Protestantism the most remarkable figure is [Christoph] Blumhardt." Christoph Blumhardt was a founder of Christian Socialism in Germany and Switzerland, an influence on the young Herman Hesse and close to the Anabaptist Hutterian Brethren.

Toward the end of his life Berdyaev believed that "the world is entering upon a socialist and communal period," but he continued to reject "the metaphysical untruth of collectivism, which denies personal character and the freedom of the creative act." For Berdyaev, the creative act was the greatest human endeavor because "in creative activity there lies a mystery which cannot be rationalized nor reduced to any form of determinism, nor in fact to anything coming from outside."[14]

Rejecting both communism and capitalism, Berdyaev insisted on a communitarianism based on respect for the individual's personality and *sobornost*, a Russian concept meaning "spiritual community or common life." He detested Russian communism for "leveling society" and reducing all human endeavor to the lowest-common denominator; he had an equal disgust for the selfish individualism of the United States, a country he refused to visit. Berdyaev's socialism had a Nietzschean side to it, and so he also had great disdain for bourgeois culture.

After years in the Evangelical tradition that advocated a certain passivity before God—since humanity can do nothing to save itself but "believe in Jesus"—and a distinctly negative view of "sinful" human nature, Berdyaev's optimism, his Nietzschean exultation in human will and his Orthodox universalism, was a great relief. It also presented itself as a path out of my emotional hell as my first marriage disintegrated.

I studied Berdyaev in the solitude of the chalet, looking out the windows occasionally to rest my eyes on, and marvel at, the enormous mountains and beautiful green valleys painted with cascades of wildflowers. I read Eliot and Everson, lingering especially over their religious works like Eliot's "Choruses from the Rock" and his "Four Quartets," and the marvelous devotional poems of Everson's *The Crooked Lines of God*.

My wife Karen had gotten a job in a school teaching children English, and she made the trip down the valley every day to work while I stayed at the chalet tending the cows.

Impossibly, we both were becoming more depressed in the wonderland of the Swiss Alps. This paradise of majestic mountains and rivers, serene forested slopes leading up to bare rocky crags and winding green valleys would have been the perfect setting for a romantic first year of marriage, except that now Karen had decided she wanted to return to California and file for divorce.

I followed her home and soon I was back in Berkeley where I picked up my old life again, now with eighty-five cents in my pocket, no work, no place to live, and even further out on the margins of the Christian community. Fortunately I ran into Marc Batko, a street theologian and translator of German theology, and he offered me the floor of his studio to sleep on until I could get on my feet.

I eventually put together enough part-time work that I was able to get a room of my own, and then I got steady work in Logos Christian Bookstore on Telegraph Avenue.

At Logos Bookstore I was introduced to a whole new world of theology. At first my job was simply to open boxes of books and stock the shelves under the management of the bookbuyer, a brilliant and likeable man a few years younger than me named John Young. He had long hair and a beard and he knew every book in the store and the whole field of theological writings. The bookstore was owned by an Evangelical couple from over the hill in the more conservative area of Walnut Creek, but John had very eclectic tastes and he had a special interest in the obscure areas of Patristic theology, Catholic Scholasticism, and Eastern Orthodox theology so he kept the second floor stocked with the "good stuff."

It was the Eastern Orthodox theology that most interested me as I continued to study the works of Nicolas Berdyaev. I explored Timothy "Callistos" Ware's history of the Orthodox Church, and then went on to read other modern theologians like John Meyendorff and Vladimir Lossky before plunging into the writings of St. Symeon the New Theologian's writings on "Divine Light" and Gregory Palamas's theology of the "Uncreated Energies of God," and other mystical notions central to the Orthodox church, but strangely paralleling ideas also found among Quakers and other "unorthodox" western mystics.

The Eastern Orthodox faith has traditionally been characterized as "optimistic" by contrast with the Roman Catholic and Protestant West with its emphasis on Augustine's notion of "original sin." The story of Jesus is framed in the West by Roman legalism: God offered his Son to pay for the sins of humanity in a legal process by which one life is offered to redeem another. In Orthodoxy the point is not to be "saved" but rather to join God in the work of continuing creation. The stress is put on humanity's divinity, the fact that we were "created in the image of God" and have within us a divine nature. Berdyaev summed up the Orthodox view by saying that humanity's "chief end is not salvation, but rather to mount up on the wings of creativity." Like other Orthodox theologians and philosophers, Berdyaev believed in *theosis* or "divinization," based on the idea proposed by the early Church Father Irenaeus: "if the Word (Jesus) has been made man (sic) it is so that men may be made gods." The Orthodox believes that through active co-creation, humanity finds what Aristotle would call its "entelechy" or end and meaning.

Meanwhile, I moved to Berkeley Way in Berkeley, thanks to Dave Smith, a UC philosophy student I knew from HCOB who invited me into a very affordable, but unstable and disastrously dirty and cluttered house. Upstairs and in the rear lived an ex-convict, we'll call Aaron, who slept on a table in the center of his room which was otherwise almost bare. On the two entrance doors to the room he had padlocks installed on the inside. Aaron was already in the process of moving out as I came in. Dave lived in a room just off the kitchen, and in the front lived one of the owners, Calhoun Phifer, a very affable middle-aged ex-Cal student who had worked for the Union Pacific Railroad for the past few decades. And what a very dear, delightful, and generous soul Calhoun Phifer was. On a weekly basis he cooked a huge meal for everyone and left the kitchen a complete mess. But the whole house was really a mess. The dining room was full of stacks of dishes: they covered the central wooden table, the bookshelves, and they had even begun to grow beside the fireplace, where burnable trash was incinerated. There seemed to be a greasy layer over everything in the common area, on top of which were several layers of dust.

Eventually Dave moved in two other Christian philosophers, Kevin Rath and Steve Lohrey. When Calhoun moved out, the four of us occupied the house, although other housemates were always coming or going, including an outcast or two from the streets or the House Church, and usually a guest or two occupying the living room. Our house eventually became known around our community as "Calhoun House" in honor of our gracious landlord, and little by little it took on its own identity as a "party house" where the wilder members of the House Church would come to drink, listen to music, and hang out or spend an afternoon drinking coffee and talking philosophy or politics.

I went to work for *Radix Magazine* part time as circulation manager. This was simply a fancier title for the work I'd done at BCC as mail clerk, since my *Radix* job involved mailing out the bi-monthly magazine. I also took it on myself as part of my job to promote the magazine through poetry readings and an occasional art exhibit in the community.

In fact, since my divorce the only thing that kept me going was creative expression in poetry. We had a small poetry group that had initially been formed around the HCOB, and we met monthly to work on poetry. There were some very talented writers in the group, including Fr. William Ruddy, who eventually introduced me to his friend, the poet William Everson, when we took a trip to Everson's home in Davenport, just outside of Santa Cruz.

William Everson (Brother Antoninus) by that time appeared to be far older than his sixty-seven years, with his white hair and beard and the tremor resulting from Parkinson's Disease. Be he was also very friendly and down-to-earth and patient and we quickly became very comfortable with each other. As we left I invited the old poet up to read in Berkeley and he accepted the invitation. For the occasion I produced a small pamphlet of poems from poets who were on the bill for that night's reading and called it *Poems of the Third Epoch*. Everson was curious about the title and I explained that it referred to the Trinitarian conception of history originating in Joachim di Fiores and developed in Nicolas Berdyaev as the epoch of the Father (the Old Testament period), the Son (the New Testament period) and the Holy Spirit ("the new epoch of creativity in a testament being written on the human heart"). As I wrote in a revised version of the pamphlet, I saw "these three epochs exemplified on a personal level in the career of William Everson."[15]

Only later would I discover the essentially apocalyptic, utopian and millenarian nature of di Fiore's idea and learn that Hegel, Marx, and Comte had all adapted this three-stage model of historical development to their purposes. Hitler, also, had based his idea of the Third Reich on di Fiore's conception.[16] In fact, this Joachimite conception pervades movements of the Left and Right all the way down to the present time, given the enormous foundational role millenarian thinking has in Western thought.[17]

Bill Everson and I became friends and engaged in a correspondence that lasted for a number of months as we both read through Berdyaev. I also spent many weekends at his cabin in Kingfisher Flat drinking wine and talking about poetry, theology, philosophy, Carl Jung and, of course, Nicolas Berdyaev.

I was brought out of this cosmic millenarian reverie one morning as I talked with Steve Scott, a Christian poet who had been part of both the Third Epoch poetry reading and the anthology I'd produced from it. As I babbled on about the theurgical and synergistic mysticism of creativity in Nicolas Berdyaev over a cup of coffee in a small café on University Avenue in Berkeley, Steve smiled indulgently. When I finished my spiel he said, "yes, good. And while you're at recreating the world, you might want to come up with a few fields of wheat to feed the poor." I felt my racing mind come to a complete stop as the words slowly entered my ears and dripped into my sinking heart. Yes. Of course. There are things poetry and art cannot resolve.

Scott's down-to-earth counsel roughly coincided with Daniel Berrigan's visit to Berkeley. He was to teach a course at the Graduate Theological Union and I decided I'd see if I could arrange to interview him for *Radix Magazine*. When I heard the class would deal with his exegesis of the *Book of Revelation*, I was determined to audit, no matter what. As it turned out, it wasn't that difficult to audit, since there were no police or bouncers at the door: all one had to do was go into the class, sit down, and imbibe the clear teachings of a great man.

Diminutive and quiet, peaceful and gentle, Daniel Berrigan was a lion in the sheep's clothing of priestly vestments. He spoke in a soft, matter-of-fact voice, and yet somehow projected to the back of the class where I sat. But most impressive was his understanding and insight into the book that had long fascinated and perplexed me. He started off talking about the need to take responsibility for the arms race. "If no one is responsible, no one is human," he said. "How will Babylon (and by this, he clearly was referring to the USA) be saved if that which is most human, that is, freedom and responsibility, is not invoked?" Faith, he said, is an unfinished drama in the *Book of Revelation*, and that Book cannot be closed as long as we're here.

"In the light of the Lord's coming, the end is not in the hands of the nuclear bomb tinkers, but in the hands of Christ." Babylon was an image of John's time, but it must be translated into our own time. The Book is unsealed, Berrigan told us, and that indicated that there are no sealed facts. We must keep the "book" open and use it to unseal the present.

"Cold, rational means lead only to a cold, rational utopia. Technique," Berrigan said, "is a spiritual invasion, a demonic, inhuman, a 'disposal' sense of time, a way of getting rid of problems, of 'resolving' problems, because you get rid of human activity. War is the dispose all (disposal), the way to get rid of problems because you get rid of humans."

Berrigan embodied the prophetic voice of the apocalyptic vision. While Hal Lindsey and the Evangelicals puzzled over their charts of the "End Times," and while they argued over whether the Rapture came before, midway through, or at the end of the Great Tribulation, Dan Berrigan swept the whole discussion aside to present the heart of the question: how do we propose to live in this world? What shall we do before the great inhuman machine, East and West, that devours humanity like Moloch and produces only a mechanistic simulacrum of human life?

Berrigan's class moved me ever closer to the concern, the challenge, that Steve Scott had laid out before me in the café: what about the poor? Is there a greater question to be resolved, for a Christian, or anyone, for that matter, than feeding the poor?

Around this time the BCC and HCOB experienced another split. Three households, calling themselves "Bartimaeus Community," decided to have a "common purse" along the lines of the first century church, in which all possessions were held in common. It was a painful parting, and it also signaled the beginning of the end of the community I'd come to Berkeley looking for. Eventually the various ministries of the Berkeley Christian Coalition separated and only the few larger ministries survived independently. Eventually the House Church and Bartimaeus disbanded.

Some of us had a sense that it had been a fatal error trying to "build a community" in the first place: community, if it happens at all, emerges out of natural sympathy and friendship as people go about their lives. David Fetcho, a poet who had been in both the House Church and then Bartimaeus, reflected on those projects saying that "In our youth we felt that we needed to mandate the structures of love and, as it turns out, love mandates its own structures. Those structures come into being organically over a period of time. And that was a lesson we all had to learn."

CHAPTER FOUR

FIRE FROM HEAVEN

The election of Ronald Reagan sent shock waves through what was left of the Left, and the Left was still a significant minority of the population, especially in the San Francisco Bay Area. After four years of the bland but somewhat endearing and moderate Evangelicalism of Jimmy Carter, many of us in Berkeley sensed that a brutal change was coming.

I was living in the basement of Calhoun House, the cheapest room in the house. The outer wall of the room still had the initials of one of the house's earlier residents, Steve Soliah, spray-painted on the wall. Steve was one of the survivors of the Symbionese Liberation Army and former lover of Patty Hearst. I remembered Calhoun Phifer telling us about the day the FBI came looking for Steve.

"I was coming home from work," he'd told us with a big grin on his face, "and saw these two men with dark sunglasses, black suits, and ties sitting across the street from the house in a new black car. They definitely weren't from Berkeley!" He laughed. "I went inside and mentioned it to Steve, and he started. His face turned white, and he ran out the back door." They eventually caught him, but such was the legacy of the house in which we lived in early 1981 as Ronald Reagan took the office of the presidency. Most of the residents of Calhoun House thought of ourselves as inheriting the tradition of revolutionary struggle, and in that moment our faith took on a distinctly apocalyptic hue.

One night in early 1981 I went to hear Carolyn Forché read from her book, *The Country Between Us*, on the UC campus. I didn't know Forché's work so I didn't know what to expect, a perfect set-up for the sort of surprise I got. I remember the sense of shock, confusion, and awe I felt as I listened to Forché talk about a far away country of El Salvador where the US was pouring in millions of dollars of aid to help the army slaughter its own people. The Salvadoran army was also being trained by US military advisors, so I felt ashamed and angry that I knew nothing and had heard nothing about what she was discussing; I also felt morally outraged, and morally obligated to do something. She read her poems about the military death squads, financed and directed by my country, each poem telling a story more gruesome and shocking, or painfully moving than the previous. It was a wrenching experience for me, and I came out of the reading shaken.

When I got home, I realized I didn't really know where El Salvador was. I found the country in the index of our house atlas, and I looked it up. It was in Central America, right next to that other country she'd mentioned where they'd just had a revolution: Nicaragua.

I'd already begun looking around for other poets beyond the Christian community to invite in to read at the *Radix*-sponsored events, and that led me to attend the Left Write conference in San Francisco about that same time. Among the poets I met there were Jack Hirschman, John Curl, and two others with whom I was to have closer and longer-term collaborations, Garry Lambrev and bob rivera.

Garry was a gay man who had spent many years in People's Temple. He was still recovering from the shock of that experience when I met him outside of Noe Valley Ministry early one evening after a day-long session of the Left Write Conference.[1] For some reason our eyes met and we began talking. Within a few minutes we discovered that we had a mutual passion for, of all people, Nicolas Berdyaev! Garry and I started talking about spirituality and politics, Berdyaev's personalist socialism, poetry, and became immediate and close friends—and we have remained friends ever since.

A week or so later Garry and I went to Talking Leaves bookstore for a meeting of a Union of Left Writers (ULW) that was emerging out of the conference. The bookstore lent its space to us for the meeting and it was also the place where Kush had brought the Cloud House to settle for a while. Cloud House was a regular open "round-robin" poetry reading that went on for over a decade, living up to its name as it floated around San Francisco like the characteristic fog that comes and goes, irregularly flowing through the neighborhoods and down the streets to lend its mystery to the Pacific city.

After the meeting I was talking with strangers—everyone there was a stranger to me—when a tall, dark-skinned man with a big bushy Afro and scarves around his neck, Hendrix-like, interrupted the conversation to contradict something I had just said. Eventually Garry and this new comrade, bob rivera (he refused the use of capital letters—perhaps because they were "capital"?) and I were engaged in an intense conversation about politics, spirituality, sexuality, and I don't know what else. Bob ended up in the East Bay either that evening or within a matter of days, and the conversation continued as he eventually moved into Calhoun House, on Berkeley Way, pushing what remained of the Christian community there still farther to the left.

Bob, Garry, and I formed the Rosa Luxemburg/Dorothy Day Poetry Brigade of the nascent Union of Left Writers that had emerged out of the Left Write conference, and eventually we held open poetry readings on Telegraph Avenue every Friday afternoon. I was familiar with Dorothy Day's ideas, of course, but Rosa Luxemburg was still a mystery to me. But not for long. I was moved deeply by her writings, especially after I read "You would have thought the servants of the Church would have been the first to make this task easier for the social democrats. Did not Jesus Christ (whose servants the priests are) teach that 'it is easier for a camel to pass through the eye of a needle than for a rich man to enter the Kingdom of Heaven?'"[2]

Around this time I changed jobs, which had the effect of further removing me from the Christian community in Berkeley. I began working as a night desk clerk at the Berkeley City Club, an elegant social club located in a Julia Morgan-designed building on Durant Avenue in Berkeley. Responsibilities were minimal so I spent three nights a week in an excited state of study, feeding my obsessive curiosity a steady diet of whatever it chose to devour. From ten at night until eight in the morning, with only two or so hours of security work, my job was to stay awake at the front desk—not always an easy thing to do during the blue hours before daybreak—and I took advantage of the time to read books on liberation theology, Latin American politics, and poetry. I started translating the poetry of Ernesto Cardenal and other Latin American poets, sitting at the desk all night with my

Spanish-English dictionary and my books, drinking coffee to stay awake. It was my idea of heaven.

In those all-night study sessions, I now added onto my list a number of revolutionary classics like Regis Debray's *Revolution in the Revolution*, speeches of Fidel Castro and Che Guevara, as well as histories of the Cuban revolution. I read Howard Zinn's *A People's History of the United States* and had my adolescent intuitions confirmed, that everything I ever thought I knew about my country was a lie. I felt a deep sense of shame and guilt: shame that I knew none of this, and guilt for having benefited from my childhood in the "warrior caste." I anguished over how to expiate the sins of my nation and I didn't have to look far. As I read Ernesto Cardenal's poetry and theology, my curiosity about the Sandinista Revolution deepened. Cardenal's book, *In Cuba*, increased my curiosity about what was happening on that island.

I became obsessed with Latin America, in particular, Central America, which was in the throes of revolutionary upheaval. I befriended a poet who had just arrived from Colombia, Rodrigo Betancourt, and we began translating revolutionary poetry together, and that was how I learned my first words of Spanish.

Rodrigo was an actor, a poet, an artist, and a revolutionary. He had personally suffered through the years of "la Violencia" in Colombia and had lost a sister who had been killed by the Colombian military alongside of the revolutionary priest, Camilo Torres. So I read Camilo Torres, and his words echoed from another side those of Rosa Luxemburg: "Why do we Catholics fight the communists—the people with whom it is said we have the most antagonism—over the question of whether the soul is mortal or is immortal instead of agreeing that hunger is indeed mortal?"[3]

That spring of 1981 Dave Smith returned to Calhoun House from a trip through Central America and brought back a green military duffel bag full of books. Dave's new awareness of the changes wrought by the potent combination of Christian theology and Marxist analysis that comprised liberation theology caught fire. Suddenly our house was studying and discussing the Sandinista Revolution of Nicaragua. We collectively began reading *The Gospel in Solentiname* series, and used it as the basis of what someone called our "Commie bible study." *The Gospel in Solentiname* was a collection in several volumes of transcripts of Bible studies Ernesto Cardenal conducted with a peasant community on an island of the Archipelago of Solentiname in Lake Nicaragua under the Somoza dictatorship. Through the reflection on the gospels the peasants began to understand their world more deeply as well as articulate the revolutionary vision of the gospels. Something catalyzed in me as I read these books and I found my "mission."

Suddenly my interest in the Orthodox theologians and mysticism was displaced by Roman Catholic liberation theology. I put aside Berdyaev's mystical anarchism, his religion of creativity, his theosophical conception of unconditional freedom and the ultimate value of personality, and began reading Gustavo Gutiérrez, José Porfirio Miranda, Dom Hélder Câmara and others who dispensed with theological speculations, no matter how profound, to focus on the practice of liberation, or as Gutiérrez might have put it, setting aside "orthodoxy in favor of orthopraxy." Certainly there were overlapping concerns between Berdyaev and liberation theology, but there were also significant departures. Liberation theology was far less skeptical of Marxism; indeed, it embraced it, often, it could be argued, uncritically. Berdyaev's starting point was interiority, spirit, subjectivity, personality, but liberation theology was all about the objective, external world of society. Ernesto Cardenal, who was becoming a new poetic mentor for me, called his poetry "Exteriorism," and it was a far cry from the Jungian erotic mysticism of William Everson.

Calhoun House was going through changes as the Christian philosophers graduated from UC Berkeley and Kevin and Steve moved out to get married. Of that particular formation, only Dave Smith and I remained. The house was big and growing as we colonized new spaces in the basement and built new rooms (literally) where there had been only boxes of the new landlord's massive book collection. The number of residents rarely went below six, but it reached a peak of fourteen when the house was completely full. And now a whole new group of people began moving in. Among them was Marc Batko, who was also a night desk clerk at Berkeley City Club (the Club). Marc could no longer afford to live alone in his studio apartment on what he made at the Club, so we welcomed him into Calhoun House, and I was glad to be able to return the good favor he'd done me by offering me a place to stay in his studio when I returned a few years before from Switzerland. He joined bob rivera and others who began to change the nature of the house back into a more overtly radical space.

Bob, when he wasn't building floats for a demonstration or painting placards for a protest, attending meetings of the recently formed anti-nuclear Livermore Action Group, or in his room reading and writing poetry, spent his days pontificating at the house dining table and I sat spellbound, usually accompanied by several other residents. In addition to being an extraordinary poet, bob's memory was phenomenal, despite all the alcohol, marijuana, and LSD he was able to put away. Bob could recount word for word whole conversations, and could as easily expound on the ideas of Georg Lukács as he could on the nature and aims of the Red Brigades of Italy or the German Red Army Faction, about the latter of which he inexplicably seemed to have much inside knowledge.

In those days the word "terrorist" had not been forced into vogue by the policies of the US national security state, presumably because the US government wanted to keep a focus on the enemy du jour, "communism." Bob, however, was the perfect combination of both, although mostly in theory. His Marxism-Leninism was detached from any party formation, allowing him to live an entirely anarchic existence and maintain an utterly independent ideological "line." His line, as I understood it, was "total revolution by any means necessary, moral or not," and in that way it was fairly indistinguishable from most other Leninist party lines. I found myself at once adopting him as a mentor, and also in a constant disagreement with him.

One incident in particular indicated for me the deep gulf between bob's views and my own. It was a sunny summer afternoon in 1981 and our house had moved all the living room furniture onto the concrete back-yard patio: the couch, two or three easy chairs, a table, and the television. We were lazing in the sun, late morning, and bob was talking about the forthcoming revolution as the joint was passed from person to person and we quietly listened to bob and sipped our coffee. At some point I had to ask bob the obvious question.

"When the revolution comes, what's going to happen to all the people who oppose it? That's probably going to be, what? Ninety percent?"

Bob's eyelids dropped and he looked at me with a cold squint and leaned back on the arm of the couch as he took a long drag on his cigarette. "They'll have to be eliminated," he said matter-of-factly, with a wave of his hand.

I protested, but the conversation turned to other problems that would arise when the revolution happened, or logistics required in bringing it about. The insanity, the cruelty, the utter self-righteous and blind inhumanity struck me and I knew then that eventually the two of us would part ways. But at the same time I found bob's perspective, while insane, in other ways well reasoned, even if I wondered about some of his assumptions. The utopia would be realized, he had no doubt at all. It was part of the "law of historical development." Those who were unable to meet the challenges of the future would be disposed of to allow room for the "New Man (sic)" of communism.

I found what I thought to be more humane and reasonable perspectives among the Liberation theologians and their advocates whose books I read. I found Fr. Camilo Torre's view reassuring: "I have given myself to the Revolution out of love for my neighbor."[4] I felt about bob the way I began to feel about all the secular political activists I met who were struggling against the economic inequality created by capitalism that the socialists, communists, and anarchists were attempting to resolve. As Jose Miranda put it, "ultimately the Marxists have been doing us (Christians) a favor by propagating the idea of communism in our absence—our culpable absence."[5] I was grateful to bob for having demolished my absolutist pacifism and for having shown me a way into the secular Left that I had yet to explore, but I often found myself shocked and disturbed by what I considered to be his more extreme views—and behavior. In the honeymoon period, bob served the purpose of challenging a house that was still predominantly Christian not only to give his Taoist views a hearing, which we did without hesitation, finding in Lao Tzu a very sympathetic and credible teacher, but also to look more closely at ideas current on the secular Marxist, and Leninist, left.

Meanwhile, I deepened relations with Christian left-ists and ex-Christian leftists. Among the former was Marc Batko, who introduced me to an entirely different current that flowed into the river that was carrying me away. Marc, a Jewish convert to Christianity, had a particular interest in the German theology of Jurgen Moltmann and other disciples of Ernst Bloch. While I found the translations difficult reading (Marc never quite got them into English) they inspired me to investigate an entirely different moment of Anabaptist history.

Ernst Bloch was a Jewish Marxist atheist of the Frankfurt School who, oddly enough, inspired a generation of German Christian theologians with his writings on the utopian vision of Marx, proposing the "principle of hope" as a meeting point for revolutionaries and Christians. Bloch's first book was called *The Spirit of Utopia* (1918) and it was followed by *Thomas Müntzer as a Theologian of Revolution*.

Thomas Müntzer was a contemporary of Martin Luther who started out as an ally in the Reformation, but his contact with the spiritualist Zwickau Prophets led him to advocate for deeper changes than Luther felt comfortable advocating. Müntzer became popular among the peasant class and his agitational sermons caused consternation among the princes, nobility, and his old ally, Martin Luther. Part of the so-called "Radical Reformation," which included the Anabaptists and an array of other spiritualists, prophetic, and apocalyptic movements, Müntzer was a principal organizer of the disastrous 1525 German Peasant War that ended with the armies of the nobility slaughtering thousands of peasants and then capturing, and executing, Müntzer himself.

Luther had played what many (including myself) considered to have been a shameful role in the slaughter of what he called "the murderous and plundering hordes of the peasants."

Luther was unequivocal in his opposition, directing in detail to the princes and their armies as to how the peasants should be treated: "They should be knocked to pieces, strangled and stabbed, secretly and openly, by everybody who can do it, just as one must kill a mad dog!" He went on to recommend, "dear gentlemen, hearken here, save there, stab, knock, strangle them at will, and if thou diest, thou art blessed; no better death canst thou ever attain."[6]

Müntzer was written off as a madman and a fanatic for centuries until he was "rediscovered" by Friedrich Engels who saw in him the precursor of modern communism. Ironically, Thomas Müntzer, the revolutionary Christian mystic, eventually became intrumentalized by the German Democratic Republic, part of the Communist movement that went so far to destroy religion that it sent many believers to the death camps of Siberia to be rid of the "plague."[7]

I discovered Christians for Socialism (CFS), a national organization with a very strong Northern California branch. In September 1981 I went to a gathering in Vallejo with Dave Smith, expecting to see people pounding the pulpit and calling for revolution in the name of Jesus. Instead it was a sedate group of nuns, one very friendly and gentle Presbyterian minister named Joe Hardegree, a quiet couple from Tracy, and a few other pretty average-looking people. There was a potluck and discussion about God's "preferential option for the poor" and the need to build a socialist movement to redistribute the wealth of the country and the world and we brainstormed a Christian Socialist creed.

We formed a Christian socialist study group and of the books we read I remember being particularly impressed by José Miranda's book, *Communism in the Bible*, and wishing his work would get a fair hearing in US churches. Both he and Geevarghese Mar Osthathios, the late senior Bishop of the Indian Orthodox Church in Kerala and author of *Theology of a Classless Society* demonstrated that both communism and a classless society were the bottom-line Christian positions on economics and social structures for the church and, by extension, society. The "world turned upside-down" that Winstanley the Digger and so many Christians before and after him foresaw was a vision reawakened in the 1980s and it inspired a few of us in Berkeley.

But we knew we were few. The mainstream Christian Church, after a brief opening in the late 1960s, showed signs of going with the mainstream secular culture as it took a right turn under Ronald Reagan. The sense of isolation I often felt helped me understand bob rivera's loner approach to politics, and it also gave me a real empathy for Garry Lambrev whose religious and political community had gone out in an apocalyptic fury. Dorothee Sölle expressed our feelings well in an article published in *Radical Religion* about that time. She wrote of "the dilemma of being Christians without a church and socialists without a party." But our marginalization was powerful, she said, reminding us "It is not the center from which liberation will come. It comes from the periphery. Christ was not born in the palace of Herod but in the stable. He did not grow up in the center of Jewish culture among the power elite but in the backwaters of Galilee."[8]

And our little "cell" of Christian socialists was going to become more isolated still. Sometime in 1982 the national office of CFS was closed down, as the director explained, due to "burnout." The Northern California branch made several valiant attempts to first relocate the national office to the Bay Area (the offer was refused) and then to keep the local branch going. All attempts failed and within a year or two of my joining the organization, it ceased to exist.

Caught up in a millenarian mania, I plotted ways to get the word out. I'd initially bought a proof press with my friend Julie Holcomb, but politics separated us and she went on to take the proof press and become a master hand-press printer. I had a vision to save the world so I started learning to print on a mimeograph machine, but never managed to get it to function well enough to print more than a dozen or so semi-legible sheets. I quickly disposed of the machine and several of us in Calhoun House began looking for alternatives. We had no resources: as a house we fed ourselves mostly by dumpster diving. But we had faith and a vision so we began compiling and editing articles for a small magazine we hoped to eventually print down in the basement.

My ex-wife Karen and I were giving our relationship "one last try" and she joined in the project, offering to contribute her skills as a printer. We finally found a printing press advertised for $75 and when a few of us went to look at it we found it under a tarp next to a garage, the image for a flyer for a demonstration for the 1976 UFW grape boycott still on the blanket. We took this as a clear sign we had to buy this movement press, and I didn't even try to bargain with the seller.

The printing press, in as bad shape as it was, seemed to be no problem for Dave Smith to fix and the challenge even excited him. Dave and I set to work, using rubber bands and pieces of pipe to replace springs and missing handles, and he sewed elastic bands together to make a conveyor table. It took weeks of hard work to get the machine running, and a month or two of long days working to print the forty-eight-page magazine. We had to raise the press up on a platform in the basement because the periodic winter rain would flood the area where we worked, and we often had to walk through two or three inches of water to reach our workstation. We solved that problem by making a path with milk crates to the platform holding the press. Bob rivera threw in his energy as art director, accompanied by my ex-wife Karen, and while Dave and I worked trying to fix the press, to get it, and keep it, running, bob and Karen spent the next several months of winter laying out the magazine.

Called *The Second Coming*, the editorial line was "Evangelical Marxist" since we were all former or current Evangelicals, with the exception, of course, of bob. The issue included solidarity statements with Nicaragua, articles by Dorothee Sölle that Marc had translated (and all of us had taken turns attempting to get them into English), poetry from the Rosa Luxemburg/ Dorothy Day Cultural Brigade, and others, and it ended with the statement from the Christians for Socialism Vallejo meeting. "Towards a Christian Socialist Creed" affirmed, among other things, "that change is the result of the linking of the variety of our gifts and struggles in a non-hierarchical sharing" and that "the world and all its wealth belongs to everyone, that we are stewards of the resources within our reach and that the means of production cannot be owned by any individual but should be administered collectively by those who labor."

The centerfold was perhaps the most controversial part of the magazine. It was a series of four illustrations by the Nicaraguan artist Cerezo Barreto and the first one was innocent enough: Jesus, with the dove descending on him and his Father's hands reaching down to him as his own great hands protect little black children. That, however, was followed by a giant Uncle Sam with a blood-stained napkin around his neck, devouring handfuls of black and brown people. That was followed by a Nicaraguan pietá and the sequence ended with the giant Uncle Sam menacingly towering vampire-like as if preparing to pounce on a Sandinista demonstration above which was held a banner in Spanish saying "The children of Sandino neither sell out nor surrender."

Needless to say, we gained few, if any, converts or supporters and the fact that we were supporting the revolutionary
cause of the Sandinistas, a cause that had been won by force
of arms, put us at greater odds with the pacifist Anabaptist
and Evangelical community in Berkeley, the only community
likely to be otherwise sympathetic.

Ronald Reagan had decided to go on an anti-commu-
nist offensive, declaring the Soviet Union the "Evil Empire."
Many socialists and communists I knew agreed with that assessment, but we also saw the US as no less evil an empire.
The anti-nuclear movement burgeoned under Reagan: he
ended up being its best organizer. We seemed to be ever closer to nuclear war as well as intervention in Central America.
Meanwhile, the entire culture seemed to be veering off toward the right in politics as well as in ethics and Jerry Falwell's
Moral Majority seemed to have captured the attention of
Christians in Middle America. The entire political scenario,
domestic and international, looked bleak, except for Central
America where revolutionary insurgencies offered some hope
for alternatives in a bipolar world, or so we thought. I expressed my sense of doom in a journal entry in late 1981:

> I watch my hands turn to ash.
> I hear the cry of billions.
> The stars roll up like a scroll
> into the glowing darkness.
> A black silk shroud
> for a can of Del Monte corn.
> A coffin for a box of Kelloggs
> Sugar Frosted Flakes.
> The Pepsi generation degenerates
> into a carbonated corpse.
> Capital and competition

are the whores in every bed,
the idols of every altar;
icons of these gods reside
in every mind,
in the eye of every heart
and each tv screen of the soul.
I watch my legs melt away.
The waste of autos fills my lungs.
My veins pump pesticides and preservatives.
The little I have left is a shriek.
And I screw my lips into a smile
to meet my dead friends at a party
where we'll spend the evening re-
membering what it was like
to be alive.

I was obsessed with activist politics, and I could tell even bob was beginning to worry about me. He suggested I take a break and gave me a copy of *Self-Portrait in a Convex Mirror* by John Ashbery to read. I didn't read it. I had more import-ant things to read than what I thought to be the obtuse, elitist and a-political poetry of Ashbery. I couldn't understand why bob would push such material on me. But he was worried, and trying to cool me down with some post-modern cold water. That was how worried he appeared to be.

I didn't have it in me to worry about myself. I could only think that I needed to act against the great injustice of the world somehow, the great insanity that had even engulfed the church. And I was sure that if we could raise our voices and speak out it would somehow make a difference. It had worked with the prophets of Israel, hadn't it? Or had it?

CHAPTER FIVE

THE SANDINISTA REVOLUTION:
y un Paso Atrás

In fact, our little Evangelical-Marxist magazine had been largely ignored. Our little group of activists, and the little groups of activists dispersed around the country were all being ignored. There were more important things going on for North Americans, and television told them what they were. Everyone knew who J. R. Ewing was; millions followed *Dallas* on television. Hardly anyone knew which side the US was on in Nicaragua or El Salvador—or even where those countries were. Moreover, they didn't seem to care much, either. That was the reality behind the world of television the country lived in.

The Cold War began to explode in the Central American Isthmus after the July 1979 Sandinista Revolution in Nicaragua. The Monroe Doctrine, which had conceived of, and supported, a major role of the US in the affairs of its neighbors for the previous 150 years, suddenly was called into question as civil and guerrilla wars, with the backing of Cuba (and therefore, the Soviet Union), savaged the region. At the time the situation was understood in stark black-and-white, Cold War terms—and for many, it still is. In those days I saw the Sandinista Revolution as a distinctly new breed of socialism that departed from Soviet orthodoxy by welcoming Christians and others into the process, something the mainstream press couldn't quite grasp. Only years later did I understand the Central American civil or guerrilla wars of those years in their greater complexity. At the time I held a legitimate, but limited, view of the situation: that the imperial power of the US was seeking to destroy national liberation movements, and I couldn't be a neutral observer. By the very fact that I was a North American and US citizen, I had an obligation to oppose US government support and involvement in the bloodshed.

The spirit of the Sandinista Revolution of Nicaragua was expressed in the popular slogan of those days: "Between Christianity and Revolution there is no contradiction." Christians filled posts at all levels of the Sandinista Government of Reconstruction: from the Ministers down to the base. I think the religious sensibility that permeated the revolutionary current had a humanizing effect on the process itself. The Sandinistas abolished the death penalty on taking power and avoided what would have been a certain bloodbath in the process. After the struggle that ended in victory for the FSLN on July 19, 1979, utopia seemed within reach in Nicaragua. The government of reconstruction called on the people to help clear the rubble and rebuild. What they began to rebuild were clinics, day-care centers, hospitals, schools, and cooperatives that formed on expropriated lands of the ex-dictator Somoza and his family.

Certainly the country was governed by a guerrilla group organized, as was usually the case, along "democratic centralist" lines—with perhaps more emphasis on the "centralist" than the "democratic." Nevertheless, many of us hoped the nine-man junta would ensure that there would be at least a degree of consensual decision-making at the executive level of government, while the people at the base, who had come into their own as a revolutionary class, were clear they would no longer tolerate dictators. Indeed, in the final days of the revolutionary struggle the people of the neighborhoods became their own "vanguard," though I wouldn't know that or what it meant until many years later.

I took a Spanish class at Vista Community College but a half semester into it I could wait no longer. I dropped out of my first semester of Spanish and started preparing for my trip to Nicaragua. I was determined to join the Frente Sandinista de Liberación Nacional (Sandinista National Liberation Front, FSLN) and fight to defend the Revolution. Months after the ink had dried on the pages of *The Second Coming* and the pages were collated and stapled, I left for Nicaragua, taking a drive-away car to Houston and flying from there.

It was 1982 and I arrived just a couple of days after Tomás Borge and Daniel Ortega of the FSLN comandancia had declared the revolution "socialist." I was ready, dictionary in hand, to defend the Revolution, and the first thing I did was look up Fr. Ernesto Cardenal, Minister of Culture. I'd exchanged a couple of letters with him and sent him copies of pamphlets and the one issue of *The Second Coming*. The Rosa Luxemburg/Dorothy Day Cultural Brigade had also done a poetry benefit for the FSLN and I'd sent him money for that. It couldn't have amounted to more than fifty dollars, but he graciously thanked us for the donation and the solidarity.

Cardenal politely received me at his office in the Ministry of Culture but my Spanish was confined to the present tense of a dozen or so verbs, so the conversation was, to say the least, limited. He recommended me to another ministry where he thought I might be able to work doing layout for a publication, a task that wouldn't require great language skills. Nothing came of that contact, not even an interview.

I wandered around Managua marveling at this strange country in the middle of a very promising revolution. The literacy crusade, begun under Ernesto Cardenal's brother, Minister of Education Fernando Cardenal, had brought down the rate of illiteracy from over fifty percent to around thirteen percent in just six months, a stunning success for which the nation was given an award by the UN. The Ministry of Culture was holding poetry workshops all over the country, teaching peasants, militia, prisoners, policemen, and anyone else interested, the art of reading and writing poems. The government was attempting to implement a free healthcare system, raising up daycare centers and schools and community centers all over the country, financed by international solidarity. As one person told me in those days, "You can travel all over Central America and only here will you find campesinos wearing glasses, because now they know how to read."

Toward the end of my month in Nicaragua I took a trip to Ometepe Island in Lake Nicaragua, got terribly sick and returned to Managua with a fever. I was staying with a young seminarian at an Anglican church, but it was a limited stay and I had no money and no ticket home. Eventually my friends in Berkeley, many of them as poor as I, raised money to send me a ticket to come home.

I was still sick and feverish and the trip through Honduras seemed surreal, especially as we drove through an intense storm, one that had been going on for nearly a week. I arrived, exhausted, in San Pedro. I crossed the street from the bus station and took the first hotel I saw, the Hotel oderno, the "M" in the name having burned out. The Moderno was anything but modern, but it served my purposes for a clean, cheap place to stay until my flight out the following day. In the hotel's café I met a Guatemalan schoolteacher who invited me to sit with six of his friends. They invited me to join them for a beer and I apologized when I ordered a soft drink because I was taking antibiotics for my fever. The person I sat next to was introduced to me as Victor and he was, at first, surprisingly cold and aloof. As I talked with the other teachers he listened closely and finally turned to me and looked me in the eyes.

"At first," he began, "I thought you were CIA. But now that I hear you talk I know you aren't. If you were CIA you'd speak better Spanish."

I wasn't sure how to take that (I still carried my dictionary with me wherever I went and referred to it often) but I thanked him and affirmed that I wasn't, indeed, CIA.

"We're all teachers. We're here from Guatemala for a conference of teachers," he said. Leaning toward me, he spoke more quietly in a confidential tone, "We teach the Indians in the mountains how to read and write. You know, in my country, it's a crime to teach Indians to read and write. Still, we go into the mountains to villages where mestizos are rarely seen. And there we see little children who are dying of starvation. And you know what that's like? To see children die of starvation?" He teared up as he stared at me and I shook my head. "They vomit worms before they die. And do you know why they die? Guatemala is a rich country. We grow all kinds of food but it is sent to your country. They die in my country, the children, because you eat their food. And you live in Disneyland, completely unaware of it."

I was speechless and so were my companions at the table. There was a heavy silence in the café, a heavy, anguished silence. Victor wiped the tears from his eyes and cheeks. Then, looking around at his companions, he raised his beer to toast. "But still, life is beautiful!"

I am haunted by that moment and cannot recall it without tears even now. It was as if I had encountered all of Latin America face to face in this one person, Victor, with whom I would spend only a few minutes on a rainy Saturday in an otherwise nondescript Honduran town and yet would remember him the rest of my life.

By the time I returned from Nicaragua I was moving toward theological agnosticism. I was still inclined to work with the Christians because I felt comfortable with their ethic and their culture of kindness, but I needed more space to grow than Christianity offered. Still, when I was offered a job—if it could be called that since the work paid nothing but room and board—working at a social justice ministry of Holy Redeemer Catholic Church in East Oakland, I took it. I was interviewed by the only other two staff of House on the Way over a cup of tea in a beautiful, sylvan valley right in the middle of the East Oakland ghetto. In the interview I'd told Betty Frazer, the resident counselor, and Fr. Richard "Dick" Schiblin that I was agnostic and I felt closer to Marxism at that point than to Christianity, neither of them flinched. They still hired me on the spot.

In exchange for printing the newsletter for the Church and House on the Way ministry, I had access to the Multi 1250 printing press. Once I managed to learn how to run the press I started printing small runs of poetry books and a new magazine that I co-edited with Marc Batko called *Poor Konrad*, named after the 16th century revolutionary German worker's conspiracy to "bind the strong man and take the kingdom by force" (Mark 3:27). We printed statements from the Nicaraguan churches translated by James and Margaret Goff in which they implored Christians in the US to work to stop the killing and acts of terror the CIA was directing against their country. And indeed, as time went on the US government increased financing to the Contra army that was wreaking havoc on the country.[1]

Once again, Marc and I found very little support for, or interest in, the issue of revolutionary Christians in Nicaragua except among a few of our friends. We felt it was nevertheless important to get out the regular statements from Nicaraguan churches and translations of Nicaraguan poetry and German liberation theology, particularly the writings of Dorothee Sölle and other Christian socialist theologians, as well as Ernst Bloch.

Nevertheless, the Sandinista process defined the word "revolution" for me and convinced me that there existed the possibility not just for individual searches for utopia, nor small utopian communities in progressive cities, like the House Church of Berkeley, but for large-scale social projects that could transform nations and peoples. I wanted to be part of that any way I could so I contacted Ernesto Cardenal, enlisting a Puerto Rican priest who lived in the Redemptorist monastery to help me write the letter in Spanish.

A few weeks later, in October 1983, the day the US invaded the tiny island of Grenada, I got a letter back from Ernesto Cardenal, inviting me to Nicaragua. Dick and Betty were supportive of my going to Nicaragua and they did what they could to help me organize my trip and find some funding. Another priest who was living at House on the Way, a real saint, Fr. Pat Leehan, gave me two hundred-dollar bills. "Roll them up and put 'em in your sock. You'll need 'em," he said. Pat was involved in the Sanctuary movement and had personally smuggled dozens of Guatemalan and other Central American refugees in his tiny red car with tinted windows. He was mostly deaf and had KPFA on in his room from early morning into the night and you could hear it blaring as soon as you walked into the upstairs area where House on the Way had its offices and living quarters.

Arriving in Managua, I stayed at Hospedaje El Molinito and immediately fell in with a group of ex-pats, internationalists and revolutionary tourists from the US By now the counter-revolution was in full swing and the Contra war was underway along the border, funded by the US government and cocaine dollars—though, in all honesty, both sides in the conflict were getting money for their war chest taking cuts from the cocaine going into the US to make the dangerous new drug, crack.

Soldiers and *milicianos* and *brigadistas* in olive green were everywhere but in Managua life went on as usual. In Gringolandia, a few square blocks of Barrio Marta Quezada near Tica Bus station, and especially at Comedor Saras (Sara's Café), you could find the internationalists guzzling beer and talking politics, frequently with Daniel Alegria at the center of the conversation. Daniel was Claribel Alegria's son and assistant to Tomas Borge, Minister of the Interior.[2] Aside from a good knowledge of English, Korean, and God-knows what other languages, Daniel was our contact for information and analysis of the political situation in Nicaragua. He knew everyone and everything about the country from his work in the Ministry of the Interior (MINT). When I say "our" contact, I mean most of the internationalists and tourists who passed through. Daniel was the unofficial Sandinista internal ambassador to internationalists. Besides that, he was funny and had the ability to state things clearly and poignantly. One morning as we discussed the US and international capitalism over eggs at the *hospedaje/comedor* known as the *casa con la puerta verde*, the house with the green door, he turned to me and asked, "Do you think most North Americans understand that everything they own is splattered with someone else's blood?"

My transition from Christianity to *Sandinismo* was by now fairly complete, although I still found (and continue to find) much wisdom and spiritual resonance in the Judeo-Christian tradition. Still, for all practical purposes, I'd made the transition from one set of symbols to another, much the way the original people of the Americas traded the names of their gods for the names of saints even while maintaining the original meaning and substance that nurtured their lives and cultures. Over time the new and old faiths and rituals blend together such that the convert is able to distinguish the two, and easily manage the dissonance that would overwhelm and befuddle anyone else.

I probably spent too much time drinking beer with Daniel and the other internationalists at Comedor Sara's but I did manage to get out of Managua from time to time to do interviews. On one such occasion I interviewed a number of young Christians who were picking coffee during the harvest, some from the traditional peace churches. I was struck by their sincerity and commitment but I was at a loss as to how to respond to them when they asked me about North American Christians and their views on the Sandinista Revolution. I didn't have the heart to tell them that most Christians in the US probably knew nothing of their struggle. Most, like me just a few years before, didn't even know where Nicaragua was.

CHAPTER SIX

A DREAM MADE OF RED STARS
AND BLACK ROSES

Toward the end of my time in Nicaragua I went to hear Ernesto Cardenal and Lawrence Ferlinghetti do a reading at the memorial amphitheater dedicated to Pedro Joaquín Chamorro, the founder of *La Prensa* newspaper who had been killed for running articles unfavorable to Somoza during the dictatorship. I was stunned by the beauty of Cardenal's translation of Ferlinghetti, and it struck me as I sat listening that I should translate and publish poems being written by soldiers, police, peasants, and youth involved in the poetry workshops being held all over the country under the Ministry of Culture.

I'd collected a large number of them, published in the popular magazine, *Poesía Libre* (Free Poetry), a publication of the Ministry of Culture that was printed on Kraft paper and bound with cheap twine. It was ubiquitous in Nicaragua, appearing even in the supermarkets where in the US one would find *The National Enquirer*. It sold for a few pennies and it had some really extraordinary poetry in translation from all over the world, and it also had copious amounts of poetry from the *talleres de poesía* (poetry workshops), a project of the Ministry of Culture that had become a national phenomenon.

I returned to the Bay Area and started translating poetry. At House on the Way I moved into the basement so I could be near the printing press. I wanted to master the craft of printing so I began sleeping on the worktable in the evening, right next to the wild animal I hoped to tame. Eventually the printing press submitted to my will and I embarked on my career as a printer. Only rarely did I get paid work, but I got in lots of practice printing small books of poetry, including *Flamingos in Gangland* by bob rivera, *Similitudes* by Eugene Warren, and my own first chapbook of poems, *Names*, a book I decided, a week after I printed it, wasn't ready, so I recycled the entire edition. I found paper in odd sizes and quality at a local paper discount store run by Sikhs, and managed to find other print shops where I could make paper plates that I needed to print with. I began printing for Witness for Peace, Pledge of Resistance, and other political groups, but my options, and my equipment, were limited.

For the 1984 Democratic Convention Dave Smith and I printed up a pamphlet titled "Commies for Christ" that featured Jesus on the cover, gazing adoringly at an image of Karl Marx. We passed out a few thousand of the pamphlets, Dave showing up in his suit and tie on his lunch hour to leaflet. He'd taken a job at Wells Fargo in the financial district to try to save money so he could return to Nicaragua and work with TechNica, a solidarity organization of tech workers. I didn't know how he dealt with the contradictions of having a job at a bank and working to overthrow capitalism at the same time, but that was his business.

Dave had to leave after an hour, but I stayed around for a hardcore-punk show with Dead Kennedys, the Dicks, MDC, and others. As the music ended, the audience formed a spontaneous demonstration that marched to the Hall of Justice where we demanded the release of a number of protestors who had been arrested on a march and tour of the bloody corporations of San Francisco that morning. When we got to the entrance to the Hall of Justice we saw that the exits were sealed off by uniformed police and we realized we had been trapped. Police on horseback charged into the crowd beating people with billy clubs and plainclothes cops emerged from the crowd and began jumping people and handcuffing them. Those trampled by police on horseback were later booked for "assault." In the chaos I looked around for an escape and saw one person I vaguely knew.

"Over this way, there's an alley!" he cried, also recognizing me. We ran through the confusion and he commented, "check it out: the plainclothes cops are all dressed the same. They're the big guys in flannel shirts and jeans. They look like lumberjacks." Sure enough, the cops were all dressed, as if in uniform, in plaid flannel shirts, blue jeans, and black jackboots.

We ran down the alley and then I remembered where I'd seen the man I was with. We'd met in the basement of a Catholic Worker house in Oakland where he had a printing press and was organizing a printing collective called "Red Star Black Rose Printing and Graphics." His name was Ben Clarke and he and I would eventually become close friends and comrades over the coming years.

A few other contacts came out of our leafleting the Democratic Convention. The most significant one was

Henry Noyes, the founder of China Books and Periodicals in San Francisco, who had been intrigued by the thought of Communist Christians and had gotten in touch through our post office box. He was a "young man" of seventy-four and had become politically active years before during the Spanish Civil War doing solidarity work with the Republic by raising money in England for ambulances. After getting his Masters at University of Toronto and his PhD at the University of London, he finally landed at the University of Missouri where he was head of the Creative Writing Department for six years. Somewhere along the way he'd become a communist, though exactly when, and how much of a "communist" he'd been, he guarded as a closely-held secret. He and his family moved to Chicago in 1945 where he taught in an adult school, but his defense of China and the Soviet Union got him fired. He went to work in a machine shop in Chicago where he became a union steward and, eventually, after being chased out of several jobs for his communist views, founded China Books. Eventually he moved China Books to San Francisco in 1960 and he began driving around the country selling Mao's *Little Red Book* and other publications from China. It was largely, if not exclusively, due to Henry's efforts that Mao's *Little Red Book* fell into the hands of the Black Panthers, and from there to a very large part of the Left.

Henry was a delightful, brilliant gentleman and we hit it off from the first time I met him at his house in the Mission shortly after he wrote to us at *Poor Konrad*. He had me pegged as an anarchist, probably because I worked at Red Star/Black Rose and had no party affiliation. I surmised that Henry was a Maoist, but we had an "ecumenical" anti-capitalist faith and both were far enough from party politics that our political differences served mainly as the basis for long and engaging conversations that we both seemed to find productive.

Henry believed in "united fronts" for building a revolution, and so did I, but his dialectical materialist perspective also helped me move beyond the less productive political views and tactics I'd inherited from the "idealism" of the Anabaptists and Evangelicals. Often in those circles the emphasis was on civil disobedience and acts designed to "witness" against social evils. Henry didn't find that approach to be of much value. "I only fight battles I think I can win," he told me. The idea of tying one's self up in legal problems to "make a statement" just didn't fit in with his pragmatic revolutionary perspective. It made sense to me.

Henry was there when I was living on a shoestring and needed a place to stay, or if I didn't have enough money for a meal he'd find something to cook up or invite me out to a local restaurant in the Mission. Though our friendship was tried much later after the Tiananmen Square massacre—which at first he denied, and then, incredibly to me, claimed was a CIA plot—he remained a friend and I still miss his bright optimism, his infinite curiosity, and his down-to-earth brilliance over a decade after his death in 2005.

Ben Clarke had saved me in more ways than just showing me an exit from the police riot at the Democratic Convention. Soon thereafter he began to send work my way from Red Star Black Rose and I made enough money to meet modest expenses while I lived at House on the Way.

Then on May Day of 1985 Gwen Gilliam danced into my life, introduced to me by a mutual friend I'd met in Nicaragua. Gwen was an exotic dancer in New York, and was just visiting the Bay Area to meet with her literary agent. She was only planning to stay around a few days, but we ended up at a demonstration in Berkeley against the embargo Reagan imposed on Nicaragua that day, and that evening she came back to stay with me at House on the Way. Given her

free spirit, her eccentricities, and her open and defiant honesty, it was clear to me there was just no way we were going to
live a problem-free life in the basement of a Catholic Church.
After a few days living together in the basement we briefly
moved into Dave Smith's apartment; we house sat for different people and stayed in a friend's vacant house as we looked
for something more stable. Then, by chance, as Gwen skate-
boarded through East Oakland looking for apartments, she
found a studio upstairs from Red Star Black Rose (RSBR).

I began working nearly full time at RSBR and in the
evenings I translated and edited *A Dream Made of Stars:
A Bilingual Anthology of Nicaraguan Poetry* (ADMOS).
Eventually a storefront space next door to RSBR opened up
and Gwen and I shared that space with Jim Martin who started working on a project called Flatland Distribution. It was a
strangely tranquil time in many ways, even accounting for all
the non-traditional facets of our life together.

Ben Clarke and I spent many hours in RSBR printing
and playing what we called "ideological ping pong" as the
presses ran. The game was an ongoing political argument
that ranged between anarchism, communism, socialism,
and points between. When we tired of arguing a side, anarchism, or communism, for instance, we'd switch sides in the
argument and begin the argument over again. By this method we would pass through a work day having argued any
number of contrary political perspectives, both pro and con,
and the time would pass quickly. It was only conceivable
because both of us found major problems, and virtues, in
all the radical Left perspectives, but neither of us found any
one of them problem-free. Speaking for myself, the sectari-
anism of the Left amused and also infuriated me. I couldn't
understand how people who were so far from realizing their
own utopian projects could be so dismissive of other ideas

of utopia. On the other hand, for my part I perhaps over-estimated the Sandinista's ability to carry out their revolutionary project with great success. RSBR was a great resting place but the peace of that oasis wasn't to last. There were too many shadows wandering in our midst, and I include my own as one.

By summer of 1986 I had finished the layout of ADMOS and put it on the press. I printed a thousand copies and it sold out within a month. RSBR decided it wanted to reprint the book, but problems were emerging in the collective, especially after it had expanded to include three or four more graphic designers. Political disagreements between collective members (framed as an ideological issue between anarchism and Leninism) and my own unresolved resentments toward the collective, about which I no longer even recall the details, all made it easy for me to decide to jump ship and take a job in Managua the following spring.

Dave Smith, now living in Managua, heard about a position for a translator in the Managua office of *Centro de Reportes Informativos Sobre Guatemala* (CERIGUA). He called me up one spring morning in 1987 and asked me if I was interested in the job, and since I was always happy to run away from problems I couldn't immediately solve in those days, I said yes. Within a month or so, I'd sold most of my possessions and was ready to leave.

I went overland to Nicaragua and arrived a month later, ready to start work at CERIGUA. I wasn't happy at CERIGUA, which, as it turned out, was a political project of the Guatemalan National Revolutionary Unity (URNG), a grouping of many revolutionary organizations and, like all Marxist-Leninist organizations, governed by a "democratic centralism" that was hierarchical, elitist, and directed top down. Still, I hung in because I didn't know what else to do.

One day I took the afternoon off from work and rode my little Yamaha 175 to the market to do some shopping. I'd just bought the motorcycle from an Italian who, I got the strong impression, had been part of the Red Brigades and now, after working a few years in Nicaragua, was on his way home. I loved the bike: it had cross-country tires and *"Tierra, Viento y Fuego"* (Earth, Wind and Fire) painted on a side cover. It kept me off the buses: slow, always overloaded with people and a perfect place for pickpockets to practice their art.

The market was the usual scene, like being in the jungle, listening to and watching all the bright birds sing and preen and flit about, and I was one of them. It was a beautiful hot day in Managua so the shade of the market stalls offered a cool respite from the afternoon sun as I wandered, called to by the market ladies to buy from them. As usual, I had very little money so I just continued walking toward the section where I hoped to buy some dried beans. Suddenly the voices around me stopped and all eyes turned toward two Sandinista policemen making their way through the market.

I felt a jolt of confusion. Here were the representatives of the state with which I was working in solidarity, policemen "of the people" who in earlier years had been celebrated and loved. Yet now the people in the market had fallen into a sudden hostile silence at their appearance. In that instant I recognized some contradiction I couldn't quite process. I therefore tried to put the incident out of mind, as I went on to make my purchase and ride down the Panamerican highway home.

I'd already seen a couple of instances in which robberies had actually been perpetrated by the Sandinista police—some of them had stolen batteries and tapes from journalists who were covering that year's celebration of the anniversary of the Revolution in Matagalpa, on July 19th. It was understandable, given the economic situation, that the Sandinista police, whose wages were proving inadequate, would begin trying to make ends meet by any means available. But the comandancia didn't seem to notice such problems, or if they did, they didn't seem to acknowledge them, or the growing dissatisfaction, expressed in the graffiti around the city.

But it was also true that the FSLN resembled very little of the original Sandinistas, named after the anarcho-syndicalist anti-imperialist "General of Free Men," Augusto Sandino. He had fought with the Liberals against the Conservatives, and then broke with the Liberals and led the first guerrilla war against occupying US Marines from 1927 until he drove them out in 1933. A messianic figure, he combined anarcho-syndicalist ideas with vegetarianism and magnetic spiritualism of a theosophical nature. Given Sandino's spiritualist anarchism, it's understandable that he was unable to pact with his Salvadoran secretary, the Communist Farabundo Martí, and as a result the two conducted simultaneous, yet unrelated, guerrilla struggles in the neighboring Central American republics. They were both killed within two years of each other. Martí was killed in the peasant uprising in El Salvador, along with thirty thousand others in February 1932. In February 1934, while in Managua to sign the peace treaty, Sandino was murdered by soldiers of the Nicaraguan National Guard under General Anastasio Somoza. Somoza went on to slaughter or disperse the remaining Sandinistas and take power as "president." He and his sons ran the country as his own private *finca* (ranch) until he was overthrown by the latter version of the Sandinistas, the FSLN. These latter coalitions of guerrilla fighters were all Cuban-trained communists with a strong Marxist-Leninist orientation. It was, in fact, a group of people with whom Augusto Sandino would likely have eschewed contact, given that the General of Free Men had separated with Farabundo Martí precisely over the latter's communism.

Gwen joined me after a few months and we were just starting to get settled in Managua together when I had a fairly serious motorcycle accident, breaking both wrists. It was five months into my time in the country, but since I could no longer work, and really wasn't interested in continuing on with CERIGUA, we decided to return home.

A couple weeks after we returned I heard about a job opening at another printing collective, Inkworks, so I took the splints off my hands (they had no material to make casts with in Nicaragua) and went in to apply for the job. I really wanted the work and didn't want any appearance of weakness to screw my chances of getting the job. I got the position of small press operator and I was welcomed into the Marxist collective despite a past association with the anarchists at Red Star Black Rose.

The freedom and the easy-going style of RSBR contrasted with the more "professional" Inkworks, which was afiliated with the AFL-CIO. Inkworks was certainly successful, but it seemed to me that basic questions were never raised. In the collective meetings there was always a discussion about how to expand the business, and no one seemed to pay attention to my question about why the business needed to expand. Was this Marxist collective simply incapable of questioning the logic of the capitalist system? Didn't anyone feel that they would prefer free time to more work? Most of the core people at Inkworks did overtime, and lots of it. After my six-month trial period I decided to leave. I went on unemployment and worked on some translations of Sandinista poetry, and eventually I was invited to join a partnership with a friend who was growing marijuana in Northern California. Suddenly I found myself living in Laytonville, or just outside of it, on a marijuana farm. It was a serene location on a little creek fed by snowmelt from the Sierras and between the tasks of carrying grow mix up the hillsides to well-hidden plots where the plants were installed, I read a translation of *Don Quixote* and planted a vegetable garden outside of the geodesic dome cabin where I was staying.

Within a couple of months I ended up back in Berkeley after a disagreement with my partners, wondering if marijuana was causing more problems in my life than I could deal with. That suspicion was confirmed when Gwen and I finally broke up in late 1989. After an emotional tailspin that led to a "bottom," I decided to get into recovery for marijuana and alcohol addiction. I started going to "Anonymous" or Twelve Step meetings.

I moved back to Calhoun House, but it was in a new post-political phase and it seemed the only thing that held the house together was the cheap rent and a collective love of marijuana. The exception to that were two straight-edge punks who gave me inspiration to look at my own life and modeled for me a sober lifestyle.

Thus began a long process of struggling with my personal demons as I found myself frequently slipping back into my old habits and just as frequently returning to sobriety.

The collapse of USSR was shocking, elating, and also quite depressing. Communism, most of us already knew, didn't work, but neither did capitalism. However, capitalism obviously functioned better than its enemy, and with the USSR gone the US could now do what it wished. The US invaded Panama and the long terrorist war against Nicaragua contributed to the defeat of the Sandinistas at election time in February 1990, although the Sandinistas shared responsibility in their defeat. Socialist insurgency gave way to the neoliberal economic model that had come to power with Reagan and Thatcher as the new orthodoxy.

Within a few years even "socialists" and "communists" would be advocating "lean, mean government" and neo-liberal economics.

CHAPTER SEVEN

WOBBLIES, ZAPATISTAS, AND CUBANS

I watched the collapse of the Soviet Union, the invasion of Panama, the defeat of the FSLN, and the first Gulf War between homework and classes at San Francisco State University. I worked and studied, supporting myself by odd jobs, mostly printing and cleaning houses. It was a depressing time, the emergence of the unipolar world under the hyper-US empire. Socialism had been cleared from the table in what seemed to be an instant and the "victory" celebrations lasted just about as long. Now it was time for the United States to take over, from the USSR, the task of designing a utopia of the future, and it was called "neoliberal capitalism."

Locally, these big international events were presaged by the demise of the Consumer's Cooperative of Berkeley (CCOB) in 1988. The Co-op had been an institution in the city since the New Deal years (1939) and grew to twelve stores and over

100,000 members by the time it closed. In addition to providing groceries, the Co-ops were community intersections. There were community billboards inside and someone was always tabling outside or nearby. This venerable Berkeley institution was a meeting place not just for shoppers, but also for members of the community and members of the Co-op.

The collapse of CCOB, due to mounting debts and internal faction-fighting, and a lackluster line of products—the chain's brand designs seemed to have been outsourced to Moscow rather than Madison Avenue—was a real blow to progressives in Berkeley, but it also was part of a whole process many of us recognized as a general decline of the aging "New Left" and hippie counter-culture. Worker cooperatives and community houses had begun to disappear and of the worker cooperatives only Inkworks Printing and a few dozen others remained.

Many socialist organizations and parties had already begun disbanding, some after doing good analysis of the shortcomings and problems inherent in socialist and communist models. But as the Soviet Union began to break apart, so too did the socialist parties that were left, until only a few small sects of Maoists or Trotskyists remained. Protests diminished in frequency and size as well as in militancy. There seemed to be a sense of defeat among people my age and older. And then I began noticing the circle "A"s of anarchism appearing all around Berkeley.

For over seventy years the big Marxist-Leninist Communist tree in the forest of the Left had overshadowed, and dwarfed all other variations of the Left in the world. Non-Marxist socialisms and the wide variety of anarchisms hadn't seen the light of publicity nor had room to grow for the enormous and monolithic hegemony of Communism. With the USSR removed, new discussions began to take place. Out of communism came the Committees of Correspondence for Democracy and Socialism in the US, the New European Left Forum in Europe, and other attempts to redefine communism, or at least find a new language to describe it in a way that would grant it some credibility after all the disasters it produced in the twentieth century. But more interesting to me were the initiatives that would emerge on the libertarian Left, and the most immediate one exploded in Oakland, California in May 1990. Literally.

When Darryl Cherney and Judi Bari were hit with a car bomb in Oakland I began paying greater attention to Earth First! and the Industrial Workers of the World (IWW), two organizations with which Darryl and Judi worked closely. I joined the IWW soon after and as I'd put a printing press together in the basement of St. Joseph the Worker Church (thanks to Father Bill O'Donnell), I was able to print up flyers for Redwood Summer the following year.

Redwood Summer was an interesting initiative that, due to my other commitments, I was only able to observe from afar. The activists developed a strategy to stop the clearcutting of old growth forests by combining the issues of labor and environmentalism, since the capitalists and traditional unions tended to divide the two issues and make them appear to be at odds. That was the logic behind the alliance between Earth First! and the IWW, and the tactics mostly involved tree sits and other forms of non-violent protests and blockades. It was an inspiring moment in an otherwise dismal scenario on the Left, and in addition to saving trees, organizing and transforming many young people into labor and environmental activists, it was a powerful signal that new radical forces were emerging from the interstices between collapsing communism and emerging neoliberalism.

At the time I knew very little about the IWW, other than the books I'd read on the early history of the union, in particular Eric Foner's fourth volume of his *History of the Labor Movement in the United States: Industrial Workers of the World, 1905–1917*. I knew the union had been decimated by the Palmer Raids under Woodrow Wilson and that it had survived only in a very small and weakened form—but it had survived. As a revolutionary industrial union, it incorporated socialists and anarchists, although, I would soon discover, socialists were a distinct minority in the contemporary IWW. The IWW had a strong democratic tradition; it was ethnically integrated almost from its inception and it was about the only union I knew of that was willing to incorporate all workers in the same organization: white, pink, and blue collars. Only police and bosses weren't allowed.

I started attending meetings of the local branch where I met Dave Karoly, at that time a young man just a few years out of college at UC Santa Barbara where he'd been a student organizer. He'd gotten involved in Redwood Summer and moved to Oakland where he'd started volunteering at the IWW headquarters which had recently moved from Chicago to San Francisco when Jess Grant was elected General Secretary Treasurer (GST) of the union precisely on that platform.

The IWW was flush in those days, thanks to money bequeathed the organization by old Wobblies who had recently died. The union was also experiencing a minor growth spurt as a result of Redwood Summer, and a few organizing drives around the Bay Area, so the energy was high.

The union, as I gradually discovered, was an odd mix of anarcho-punks, old union activists, and eccentrics of all kinds, and there might have been a sprinkling of average working Joes and Jills. The "One Big Union" wasn't very big with under a thousand dues-paying members, but it certainly was diverse, and it had a broad cross-section of the Left, including bob rivera, who had joined up a few years before when he moved back to Flint, Michigan where he was from. I edited the Bay Area General Membership Branch bulletin for a while, until someone complained about the surreal cartoons I included on its pages from my friend the Mexican artist Arnold O (also known as Arnoldo Pintor) and I turned the work over to someone else. It was a good lesson to me that even on the anarcho-syndicalist Left, art seemed valued only for its functional role and not for itself. I also participated in the editorial collective of the union paper, *The Industrial Worker* (*IW*), which included Dave Karoly and a mix of (mostly) anarchists and anarcho-syndicalists.

Dave Karoly was a mostly straight-edge punk who I first took for a cop when I met him tabling for the IWW at an outdoor event in Berkeley. His close-cropped black hair, body-builder physique, blue jeans, flannel shirt, and combat boots vaguely reminded me of the plainclothes cops who had jumped protesters at the 1984 Democratic Convention. But as I got to know him, I realized my first impression was mistaken and we eventually would commute on BART back to the East Bay after the *IW* editorial, or other union, meetings.

Together with the straight-edge punks who lived in Calhoun House, Dave and I occasionally went to punk rock shows at Gilman Street and elsewhere and they introduced me to Chumbawamba, Pennywise, NoFX, Lagwagon, and other bands that were growing in popularity in those years. Gilman Street was a drug- and alcohol-free, collectively-run space, and, even if I didn't always care for the music, I enjoyed being around the free-spirit rebel energy of the kids as my own generation disappeared into lives of accommodation with the system. I was inspired seeing anarchist punks picking up the struggle much of the older generation of hippies and yippies had abandoned. I didn't blame the older generation:

most people felt they had no choice, or else they made their compromises to be able to fight other fights they thought they might be able to win, and I completely understood, given that I had my own struggles in those days.

Dave introduced me to Pete Swearengen, a friend of his from college who was a poet and also interested in Liberation theology. Pete and I hit it off and, as he did design and typesetting. Pete suggested that he, Dave and I form an IWW printing collective. I thought it was a great idea because collectives tend to get isolated and "apolitical" when they aren't part of larger movements for radical change and the IWW had a venerable history of struggle that we wanted to be a part of. We used soy ink in symbolic protest of the invasion of Iraq, a clear grab for oil. Eventually Pete left but Dave and I continued printing in the basement of St. Joseph the Worker's Church. After struggling for a year or so, we managed to put together enough equipment and stable income to move out of the Church's basement. We eventually hung our sign for New Earth Press on Ashby Avenue, just down the street from where William Everson once lived and Mary Fabilli still resided. Coincidentally, after being out of touch with Everson for a few years, I reconnected with him to collaborate on a collection of interviews. It was his first book to appear in England, and the final book he would work on before he died in 1994.

In December 1993 I noticed a book on my shelf: *Poesía* by Eliseo Diego. I pulled it off the shelf and looked at the photo on the back cover. A kind face, I thought. I'd first run into Diego's work in Nicaragua at the International Book Fair when I was living in Managua and working for CERIGUA. I'd read one of his poems in the book when I picked it up in the stall and, even though I didn't understand all of it, I felt an electric shock run down my spine. It had been a while since anything like that had happened to me, especially from just reading a poem, so I'd bought the book and sent it home. Since then I'd translated and published a few of his poems. Now, looking at his face, a cigarette in his fingers with the smoke curling up in the air, I wondered if this smoker was still alive. If he was, I needed to meet him, and in that moment I knew what I would be doing for Christmas, or at least in the New Year. If he was still alive, I was determined to find the poet Eliseo Diego.

I called a friend of a friend in Mexico City whose sister had a travel agency and organized tours to Cuba. The woman, Adriana, agreed to set me up to go on a weeklong tour from January 1–7, 1994. I would pass my forty-first birthday on the island.

I flew to Mexico City and spent New Year's Eve with my friend and her family, and a few other mutual friends. We had the traditional turkey dinner and sat talking until late in the evening. Little did any of us know that at the moment we were talking, a group of armed guerrillas were taking five little towns in the distant state of Chiapas in an uprising that would spell the beginning of a new wave of resistance we today call the "Anti-Globalization Movement."

I flew out of Mexico City the following morning at 5 a.m. to Cuba. The story of the Zapatista uprising got very little coverage in the Cuban press because the Cuban government maintained good relations with Mexico's ruling Institutional Revolutionary Party (PRI) but half-way through my week on the island, as I tried to track down Eliseo, I read about the Zapatistas in a little two- column-inch story on the back page of the *Granma*. I didn't think much of it at the time because surely if it were significant the revolutionary government of Cuba would have made more of it, wouldn't it?

Cuba was in the middle of the Special Period and prostitution was everywhere. It was painful to see this one example of socialism left in this corner of the world so desperate to hold on that it was willing to rent out its most beautiful daughters for sexual tourists arriving from everywhere. It was clearly a relief valve for the government since whatever needs the Cubans had during the "Special Period" after the collapse of the USSR—and there were many needs the ration books didn't cover—could be obtained in the dollar stores, if one had dollars. So police looked the other way as the *jineteras* walked the streets looking for "boyfriends."

I got to know a former Lieutenant Colonel who had helped design, along with Ernesto "Che" Guevara himself, the "Many Vietnams" strategy of funding guerrilla insurgencies all over Latin America. "Eduardo" gave me his ration card. "I want you to take this back to the US so people can know what we're going through here. See?" He pointed out that they had received no cooking oil for two months, no matches for a month, flour every other month... "And we're supposed to live from this?" he asked. Eduardo, however, was doing fairly well by comparison with other Cubans because he worked for a Spanish transnational. He had cigarettes and ate fairly well and led a relatively middle-class existence.

One day Eduardo invited me to accompany him to the Museum of the Revolution. We went into the museum and looked around and then as we started to leave one of the security guards approached him and asked him for a cigarette. Eduardo glanced at me and furtively winked. "How long do you have to work to buy a pack of cigarettes?" Eduardo casually asked the guard as he pulled his cigarettes out of his pocket to give him one. The guard paused as he took the cigarette. "A day. It costs me a day's wages." Eduardo nodded slowly. "And an egg? How many day's wages is an egg?" The guard rolled his eyes upwards, calculating. "Three days wages, señor."

We walked outside and I expressed my shock and started to talk when Eduardo elbowed me and stopped. I stopped. And the man beside us stopped. Then, startled, the stranger walked on, casually, toward a park across the street.

"Watch him," Eduardo said, quietly. We stood and watched as the man crossed the park to the other side where a policeman in uniform was waiting for him. Eduardo and I turned and walked off another direction.

"You have to be very careful here about what you say. There are informers everywhere," Eduardo whispered to me as we walked back to his apartment.

Each day was another shocking and depressing revelation about how socialism didn't work, and how a police state did. I could bear the contradictions until early afternoon when I would return to my hotel room and take a nap because I felt exhausted.

One day the tour went to Varadero and my Mexican roommate, Alejandro, who had come for the sexual tourism, encouraged me to go along to the beach. I had ditched the tour almost as soon as we'd arrived in Cuba and I'd gone off on my own to try to find Eliseo and explore Havana without "intermediaries." But now, since I'd exhausted all my leads to find Eliseo, I thought a day at the beach would do me good, so I agreed to go.

The bus arrived in Varadero and pulled up to the hotel. Alejandro knew the routine: the state tour agency drove tourists from their hotels to other hotels with expensive restaurants in its attempt to extract every penny it could from the tourists in overpriced state restaurants. As we got off the bus, he pulled me away and we went walking down the street in search of a cheaper alternative for lunch. We found it a little less than a kilometer away, a post selling *medallones* on buns and a glass of lemonade for about fifteen US cents.

Medallones are little golden fried hamburger-like patties made with soy and other undefined ingredients. They're rather tasteless, but with a certain amount of ketchup one can manage to get them down, and they satisfy hunger.

We sat down in the public area and ate our lunch. Someone had a copy of *Granma* on their table that they weren't reading so I asked to see it. The man sitting at the table handed me the paper and that's where I saw the report about the Zapatista uprising on the back page.

We started talking with the man and when the conversation turned to politics, he suggested we leave. We walked down the street a ways and he looked around. He said quietly that he'd heard Fidel's daughter had defected to the US Was it true? I remembered reading about that just around the time I left the US a week or two before. I said yes, it was true. How had he found out about it if it wasn't reported in the papers? I asked him. "Radio Martí," he whispered. "I know someone who has a shortwave radio and he tells us what's happening in the world."

My heart sank. The radio station the US was funding to broadcast to Cuba was, evidently, the only trustworthy news source Cubans could access. We continued walking and eventually arrived at the big hotel where our bus was parked. The only way to access the beach, the man told us, was through the hotel. "It's a way of keeping us off of our own beaches. Only you guys, the tourists are allowed on the beaches of Cuba," he said bitterly. Looking up at the hotel he smiled ironically. "I was on the construction crew that built this hotel. And now they won't let me into it." Then he nodded and winked and said, "Watch." We approached the door to the hotel and a man in a suit guarding the entrance stopped us. He pointed to Alejandro and me and waved us in, then, pointing to our Cuban companion, he said, "but he can't come in with you." The Cuban man smiled as if to say, "See? I told you…" and then he waved and walked away.

My last day in Cuba I finally got in touch with someone at Eliseo Diego's house who told me that Eliseo was now living in Mexico and they gave me his telephone number. I arrived at my friend Luis Ballesteros's house early the next morning and called Eliseo. He invited me over right away.

There were helicopters circling the skies overhead in Mexico City. Soldiers stood on strategic corners armed with machine guns. The country had changed in the course of the week I'd been gone and everywhere people were talking about the Zapatistas and wondering if they, indeed, were planning to march on Mexico City to overthrow the "bad government"…

I found my way to Eliseo's house that morning and we became instant friends. We agreed to set to work the following day to translate his poetry in preparation for an upcoming reading at the Anglo-Mexican Cultural Institute. He insisted that I should join him at that event to read our English translations and he would read the Spanish original.

We set to work translating his poems that he already had in some form of English, an elegant, 19th century English so different from his own earthy and modern Spanish. In between work on poems we sipped sweet black coffee and talked about the Zapatista uprising.

Eliseo had a recent issue of a national magazine with images of the murdered Zapatistas, many of them fallen next to carved "guns" made only of wood, killed in battles in which they didn't have the possibility of firing a shot. Others had their hands bound behind their backs and had been killed with a *coup de grâce*. We silently leafed through the magazine, saddened by what we saw, and grateful to the journalist who had risked his life to get these shots.

I told Eliseo about my experiences in Cuba and he listened, nodding thoughtfully. Eliseo was a member of the Orígenes literary group and a Catholic who had gone with the Revolution. Nevertheless, the government had never quite trusted him and it recruited one of his children to spy on him. Eliseo told me the story. He said his son reported to the government on his father's comings and goings until finally, the young boy could no longer keep his dark secret to himself and confessed to his father.

"Dad, I've betrayed you; all these years I've been spying on you for the government."

Eliseo shook his head and smiled. "No, son, you haven't betrayed me. You betrayed yourself."

Eliseo told me the story as if it had happened to someone else, but I felt a deep sense of revulsion. In Cuba, a place that had once represented paradise to me, children were turned against their parents to be instrumentalized as spies for the State.

Just a few months before I met him, Eliseo had won the Juan Rulfo Award for Literature, which came with a significant cash prize, in addition to its great prestige. Eliseo was now settled in Mexico City and, as he no longer lived in Cuba, he seemed at ease talking about his homeland, which he still loved deeply.

"The problem with Fidel Castro," he told me, "is that he isn't a Cuban. He's a Spaniard through and through. Cubans have great heart and a great sense of humor. Fidel has neither." Eliseo went on to tell me of a cartoonist who had dared to publish a political caricature of Fidel early on in the Revolution. "And he was never allowed to publish again in Cuba."

I've told that story to Margaret Randall, and she sharply disagreed with Eliseo's assessment. I'm sure it's a problem of perspective, and I respect both views. But I'm also inclined to think they're both right: Fidel in all likelihood is charming and possesses a great sense of humor. In his deep arrogance and sense of self-importance, he only seems to lack the ability to laugh at himself.

A week later we had a good selection of poems translated for the reading at the Anglo-Mexican Institute and we read to a full house. It was the culminating moment of the trip to Cuba and Mexico, but there were other, equally great moments. I began collecting and translating communiqués of the Zapatistas. And I also spent time getting to know one of Luis's employees, a young woman named Patricia Luna, who would later come to the US and become my wife. I returned to Berkeley elated and I quickly deflated as I reentered the gears and rollers of working life at New Earth Press.

I did manage to get down to Davenport to see William Everson again during this time, as we were finishing up work on the book of interviews for the British publisher.[1] I wanted to read him some of Eliseo's poems since I thought he'd appreciate hearing the erotic and mystical verse of a fellow Catholic. But Bill was in bed and his mind and spirit were already moving somewhere between this world and the next.

I continued translating Eliseo's poems and we corresponded at least once a week about translations for the next month until I got a phone call from Luis, my friend in Mexico City, who told me that Eliseo had died in his sleep the night before. A week later I received a letter from the old poet, postmarked the day he died. In it was a revision of his poem, "From an Old Clown to his Son." I'd done a terrible job translating the poem, he said, and he had to do a major revision. I'd missed, he said, the theatrical context in which a clown was trying to pass on his art to the son, and in which he was watching him perform with such great anxiety:

AN OLD CLOWN TO HIS SON

1
Enter from emptiness, son,
where the folds of purple curtains
hide the shameless contraptions,
so useful, it's true,
the abandon of great curtains hung
like dead birds in the dust. Come along
from the shadows and make your bow
as if you were never to return.

2
You're in the midst of light. Before
you opens the enormous gulf of shadows
where there's certainly someone spying on you
with a thousand eager eyes. Sometimes
you'll hear him cough, laughing in secret,
and sneezing perhaps, or maybe shuddering:
But you'll never
ever really see. Bow,
then, like a stalk of cane in the wind:
but carefully watch the shape of the curve:
Everything is art in the end.

3
Now
what are you going to do? You've
finally escaped my care and it's almost
as if I were now the dark Leviathan.
I watch you come and go over the planks
but with an unquenchable apprehension:
are you sure

of the balanced weight of the balls
that you left flying in the air?
And the fish,
perhaps you've misjudged their strange humor
and they'll later change color.
Disasters,
minuscule catastrophes, who knows
what else?
(and yesterday
the invisible was pitiless).

4
But tomorrow
when the old women carefully sweep up
the little of today left in the cigarette butts
scattered through the wide wasteland
where there's never anyone: will it matter,
the thunder of glory or the silence
of the crumpled paper on a corner
beneath the dust of yesterday? No one knows.
And yet
it's necessary to do it all well.[2]

Through my brief friendship with Eliseo, and also from those years of friendship with William Everson, I learned a lesson in poetry, which applies well to life. Perhaps it won't matter, this work we do in life, yet, "it's necessary to do it all well."

Three months after Eliseo died in Mexico City, William Everson died at his home in Davenport.

CHAPTER EIGHT

DRAWING THE LIMITS OF UTOPIA

Ben Clarke and I began talking about putting together a collection of the communiqués from the Zapatistas. We set to work on *Voice of Fire* and managed to get out the first collection of Zapatista materials in English, because we had our own printing presses. Guillermo Prado at Inkworks did the layout and design and Global Exchange collaborated with some funding. *Voice of Fire* was published in August 1994 by three Left print shops of the Bay Area: Red Star/Black Rose, which by then was owned exclusively by Ben Clarke, New Earth Press, and Inkworks.

After my disappointments with Cuba, I found the Zapatista approach to politics refreshing, inspiring, and profoundly different. Their counter-manipulation of the press, their trickster approach to politics and their eclectic left-indigenous perspective were appealing to a whole new generation of people, like myself, who had lived and worked for a more just and humane world in the shadows of the Cold War, rejecting both the growing capitalist national security state and the Leninist *nomenklatura* of totalitarian communism.

I was particularly taken by the fact that the Zapatistas rejected the role of the vanguard and proposed an alternative to all that had come before them. In December 1996 when I was visiting La Realidad, the Zapatista community in the jungles of Chiapas, I met a Mexican woman who was active in the Zapatista National Liberation Front (FZLN), the organization that formed out of calls for solidarity the EZLN made when it was under fierce siege after their uprising in early 1994.

Teresa, who was visiting from her home in Mexico City, explained first the nature and conception of the EZLN leadership. She said that leadership among indigenous people in Chiapas is "based on the idea of the *cargado*, the responsibility to the community, that the one given the responsibility (*encargado*) must *mandar obediciendo* or 'rule obeying.' No matter how the media portrays Marcos he does nothing on his own." She went on to tell me that the EZLN "is primarily an indigenous movement. In a real sense it has more in common with the Civil Rights Movement of Martin Luther King than with the guerrilla movements in Central America in the 1980s. The uprising was about equal rights for the indigenous peasants, to say 'we're Mexicans too.' That's why you see the Mexican flag everywhere. It wasn't about 'taking power' because it isn't a vanguardist movement, in fact, it's anti-vanguardist. And it's more like a political force than a political party."

And as a "political force" the EZLN and its supporters are neither traditional indigenists, nor anarchists, nor socialists, nor communists. Not only had they taken on the name of a local Mexican hero of the Revolution, but they also paid homage to Ricardo Flores Magón, Lucio Cabañas, and many other lesser-known Mexicans. At the same time, the Zapatistas not only presented themselves as an "anti-vanguard," but they seemed to want to stand the very idea of "heroes" on its head by masking themselves and maintaining a strict anonymity, especially around a "main character" in their emerging drama, Subcomandante Marcos. In a touch that exposed the racism endemic to the Americas, the one obvious white guy was, notably, "sub" commander and the real "commanders" were all anonymous Indians! The mind-fucks, ironies, and parodies perpetrated on a spell-bound public seemed endless as it engaged with the "hologram" (as Marcos later referred to himself) that constantly underwent psychic shape shifts and eventually, many years later, died and resurrected (notably, without increasing rank) as Subcomandante Galeano.

The Zapatistas had begun their revolt at the moment NAFTA went into effect to protest, in advance, the destruction of the Mexican subsistence farmers. They had been driven to the rebellion because, in their words, "our people continue to die from hunger and curable diseases"—at a rate of fifteen thousand per year, the highest mortality rate from curable diseases in all of Mexico. As Marcos wrote, "Fifty four percent of the Chiapan population suffers from malnutrition; in the highlands and the jungle this figure increases to eighty percent."[1] Their struggle, then, was clearly regional, but the Zapatistas were anything but provincial. In fact, their internationalist sophistication was stunning, as was Marcos's talent for demonstrating parallels with, and linking to, other causes in the Americas and the world.

On the first day of the insurrection a reporter interviewed Marcos in the plaza of San Cristóbal de las Casas and asked him the reasons for the ski masks. "First, the main reason," Marcos responded," is that we have to guard against stardom, that is, to make sure no one is promoted over others... so we don't become corrupted. We know that our leadership is collective and that we have to submit to it. Now you're listening to me because I'm here but elsewhere there are other people like me talking with ski masks on. They call this ski mask 'Marcos' today and tomorrow they'll call it 'Pedro' in Margaritas, or 'Joshua' in Ocosingo..."[2] This was as close as a guerrilla army was going to get to good old down home American anarchism. At last, it seemed, a new wind was blowing through left politics, and it lifted up a fledgling movement of activists who would eventually find itself on the front lines in the battle against a globalizing neoliberal capitalism.

By contrast with the Zapatistas, the IWW seemed to be a weak and largely anachronistic network. My impression of the "One Big Union" was that it was in fact one very small association of fewer than a thousand, made up of aging lefties like me, the most vocal (or prolix) of whom apparently thought it more important to bring "charges" against one or another member or members than to organize workplaces; punk anarchists drawn to the historic "tool of struggle of the working class" but in many cases underemployed or unemployed, squatters, or otherwise marginal characters who preferred to remain marginal, which was why they gravitated to the union; those called "members of the IWW historical society," inactivists nostalgic for the good old days before, or immediately after, the Palmer Raids[3] when the union actually organized masses of workers; an odd assortment of anarcho-somethings, who seemed to fit in nowhere else but who found a welcomed embrace in the IWW, whose world headquarters were newly, and as it turned out, temporarily, relocated to San Francisco.

This odd collection of people was also overwhelmingly composed of men, and white men at that, but there were also a few great women, most notably, Melissa Roberts. She worked in the office for a while and did a great job of organizing the files, the databases, and anything else that needed organizing, and all with a brilliant and delightful sense of humor. She was, and is, one of the most delightful and talented people I've known, and she added an enormous amount of creativity to the union when it was briefly located in San Francisco. Melissa also came to work at New Earth Press toward the very end where I had the pleasure of getting to know her better.

I don't want to give the impression that the IWW was composed of nothing but cranks, weirdos, and oddballs, but it did seem to be a magnet for such characters. While I might have been just another one of the "cranks," and I felt very comfortable with the weirdos and oddballs, I couldn't help thinking most of the time how marginal we all were. Melissa was a creative artist in our midst, as was Jess Grant and others, so the union drew from a wide swath of the margins, but even as margins went, we were a select bunch.

My partner at New Earth Press, Dave Karoly, at his young age of twenty-four had astounded me for his independence of intellect, and his quiet, humble demeanor. At the same time, he demonstrated that he had no problem defying a whole group when it came down to a matter of principle. I saw him turn his punk ridicule on rock stars and big-shot artist-types and bring them down to the size of the regular Joes they were behind the costumes they wore. I also saw him defy a whole assembly as an individual standing on principle, and it amazed and inspired me.

The latter happened during the IWW convention in San Francisco in 1994 when Judi Bari and Darryl Cherney showed up to make a plea for money to pay legal fees in their case against the FBI and Oakland Police Department, both of whom had colluded to frame the two IWW/Earth First! activists on terrorism charges. It was an emotional plea and those present called a vote to give Judi and Darryl money from the union treasury. Everyone, except one, was in favor. Dave raised his hand, objecting that this was a decision that couldn't be made in the convention, according to the IWW charter, and making such a decision would be a grave error with consequences.

I had voted with the majority, but thanks to Dave I got a view on how public plebiscite democracy works, and how problematic it is. There was no private vote; it was done by a show of hands. And woe to those who didn't vote for our two aggrieved members! Only Dave held out, on principle, having dutifully studied the constitution of the union, unlike the rest of us. Voting in assembly, even an assembly of anarchists, cranks etc., invites groupthink, discourages open debate and critical thinking, and invites the violation of the "rules of the game" that the same group had agreed upon. And that's how the motion passed that would later bring on a new series of charges and countercharges and cause significant problems in the union.

Jess Grant, who once ran for the position of Sheriff of San Francisco (and lost), had become General Secretary-Treasurer (GST) and brought the headquarters out to San Francisco, had a more positive take on those years in the IWW. He said that "generation of Wobblies helped re-define/update the union for a modern audience." Those who thought of the IWW as a union for "manly men who worked in heavy industries" were taken aback by the work with Earth First! and organizing with "hippies or hookers," but, as he put it "We fought these trends by doing what we thought needed doing: organizing the unorganized wherever and whenever we could." He added that he believed in the Spanish saying that "'*El mundo cambia con tu ejemplo, no con tu opinion* (The world changes with your example, not with your opinion).'"

Dave and I certainly tried to be an example in our work and our shop that a few people could make a difference in their community. New Earth Press, in addition to being an IWW worker-owned and managed cooperative business that used soy ink and recycled paper, gave discount prices to political and community projects, and for a while we published a dozen or so books: New Earth Publications actually preceded New Earth Press by a year or so.

But it was a business, and "business" of any kind is a rather controversial activity in many sectors of the Left, especially the revolutionary Left where I spent most of my time in those years. As John Curl put it in the interview he did for my film, "worker cooperatives are basically small businesses," and most are, in fact, nothing more or less than business partnerships, like what Dave and I had: a few people who found it more congenial to work together rather than to "go it alone" or work for a boss.[4] However, unlike business partnerships and small businesses and corporations like New Earth Press (we were a "C" corporation), "worker cooperatives"are also susceptible to the other extreme of idealization.[5] In the IWW, we found, both the demonizing and idealizing of worker cooperatives and collectives were ongoing.

Some in the IWW criticized us for working in the safe refuge of a cooperative when we should have been engaging in the "class struggle" outside. From this perspective, we were "petit bourgeois" who had withdrawn from the real struggle of revolutionaries to engage in the "class war." This is undoubtedly a valid criticism and it has been borne out by studies of "cooperators" working at Mondragon.[6]

Nevertheless, such critics ignored the Wobbly proposal to "build the new society in the shell of the old," which was what Dave and I saw as the objective for collectively run businesses. We believed that worker cooperatives could be a model for the future, the "seeds of the new society." Nevertheless, I'm not convinced that worker-cooperatives are the cure for capitalism. Rather, they are themselves *capitalist businesses that produce commodities for sale on the market at a profit, just like any other capitalist business* and, as such, they don't constitute a "socialist" alternative to the capitalist system. This is a point worth stressing, because there is so much mystification of the "limited utopias" of worker-cooperatives, especially in the years since the collapse of communism.

The best example of that mystification is found in Raúl Zibechi's book, *Territories in Resistance*. There he argues that in recuperated factories and cooperative businesses labor can be "de-alienated in different ways: either by rotating tasks or because producers control the entire work process." Using the example of a local worker-run bakery, Zibechi says these "free producers" (contrasted with "workers as appendages of machines"), "although they sell what they produce, *they do not produce commodities*" (italics his). What is the magic that transforms, let's say, a cupcake that is a commodity, into one that is not? According to Raúl, the "non-commodity" cupcake is sold to someone known to, or friends of, the bakers, while the cupcake which is a "commodity" is "sold on the market." In this process, Zibechi believes, "hierarchies" are somehow eliminated. He goes on to tell us that in such businesses as the exemplary bakery "selling requires building social relations in the neighborhood" and that "political economy is not applicable to these kinds of enterprises." Finally, he asks "And what is produced?" and he replies, "what is produced is non-capitalist social relations, or non-capitalism."[7]

These few pages in an otherwise brilliant book are an infuriating tangle of verbal mystification, confounding, rather than clarifying, a process occurring *within* the capitalist market. The passage is reminiscent of theological arguments for transubstantiation, when the touch of the priest's magic fingers are presumed to transform a horrible-tasting cracker into the Divine Body of Jesus. In the same way Raúl would have us believe that the cupcake made by the fingers of a "free producer" at the worker-run bakery has thus been transformed into a "non-commodity" that exists outside of the time and space of a "market"—because it was sold to a friend?!

Worker-owned businesses operate according to identical restrictions as those imposed by the market on capitalist businesses: they must compete to get business; they must make a profit; they must pay themselves wages; and they do all that by *using capital* to produce commodities and sell them in the market. Worker-owned businesses' production and marketing processes must be as efficient as any other capitalist enterprise so they can be competitive. Efficiency at this level increasingly requires a specialization of functions in production since the janitor managing the business while the manager cleans the bathroom—or the manager programing the computer while the programmer manages the business—in a "rotation of tasks" is inefficient and probably not satisfying to anyone. They certainly aren't "free producers" even if it could be argued that they *feel* a *sense* of freedom (note the caveat *and* the qualification) when *some* tasks are rotated or made more flexible. In all likelihood the business that engages in such "task rotation" in an attempt to "break down" specialization or class structure in the workplace in extreme, or even significant, ways would only succeed in making itself vulnerable or uncompetitive in the marketplace. Certainly some flexibility and job rotation is possible, and some might be preferable, but how does that make workers "free producers" or "de-alienate" the work or eliminate hierarchies? And in what sense would they not "produce commodities"? What then, if not commodities, would they produce? Is not the cupcake, a thing made to be sold on the market, not the very definition of a "commodity"?

Both the traditional capitalist business and the worker-owned business sell their commodities by "building social relations in the neighborhood" since that's simply good business. The capitalist also may sell cupcakes to his friend, at a discount, even, but *that sale has taken place within the market*, and the cupcake was sold at a profit (even if at a reduced profit for a friend) and, as we noted above, is therefore a "commodity."

Raul's argument raises far more questions than it answers. For starters: what does he mean by "non-capitalist social relations"? What does he mean by "non-commodities"? And what does "non-capitalism" mean? Were the "non-commodities" produced by "non-capital," that is, without ovens or flour and money to buy the raw materials? As "non-commodities" do they therefore have no physical form?

All mystification and mythification aside, while there are certainly a number of options available to workers to make their workplace more flexible, democratic and less oppressive, at the top of my list would be the life of the petty bourgeois artisan, working alone or in the company of other small artisans. I'm willing to join James Scott in offering "two cheers" to the petty (small) bourgeoisie, which is why I still would advocate for worker-owned and controlled cooperatives/collectives.[8] The flexibility and control over one's own work process and work schedule; the care and concern that one is able to put into one's craft; the sense of responsibility one develops for all one's own acts; the fact that profit, or loss, accrues to none other than the worker him or herself; the sense of self-worth and dignity that comes from mastering a craft: all these gains are possible, though not guaranteed, working as an independent petty bourgeois worker or in the company of other workers in a worker cooperative. To this list must be added the sense of camaraderie and solidarity, and sometimes even friendship, which can emerge in a worker cooperative.

But I think it's worth repeating that worker cooperatives are capitalist businesses, even if some would consider them the ideal form of capitalist businesses. In a sense they replicate some aspects of the earliest model of capitalism as it organized itself when it emerged from feudalism around the "bourgs" or small towns that grew up in the shadows of the medieval castles (hence, the word, "bourgeois" or "one who lives in the bourg").[9] Free artisans and small merchants often found cooperative enterprises and mutual aid necessary for reasons of safety and convenience to carry on their work of crafting, buying, selling, and trading their wares.

This small "craft capitalism" is the sort of thing, I suspect, that many on the Left would hate to lose, and would, and do, defend before the onslaught of corporate capitalism as it seeks to take over the world down to the last corner of thought in the last consumer's brain. The small "mom and pop" family business, the "Mary-Joe-Jill-and Moe" worker cooperative (aka the local "small business partnership") is much of the Left's "secret pleasure" as they talk about a socialism that can't be smelled, tasted, or touched because there isn't yet a model for it. And so it becomes very tempting to propose these endangered small capitalist businesses as models, or part of a model, for socialism, despite the fact that Marxism has so stigmatized the term "petty bourgeois."[10]

Why are worker cooperatives so rare, and why do so few people find them appealing? At present, they number between 300–400 in the US and with 2,500–3,500 worker-owners and total assets at approximately $130 million.[11] Those thirty-five hundred workers in the US represent .0022%— that is, twenty-two thousandths of a percent—of a workforce of 157 million, or one out of every 45,000 workers. Even in the coop movement, dominated by consumer coops (92% of all coops) worker cooperatives only represent 1% of all the cooperatives in the US.[12]

This is not to deny that there are the success stories like Mondragon, the large multi-billion dollar cooperative of co-operatives in the Basque country of Spain that employs over eighty thousand workers. But even Mondragon is not all success, as the 2013 bankruptcy of the Mondragon subsidiary, Fagor, demonstrated. Moreover, to maintain its viability, Mondragon has found it necessary to organize itself along the lines of more traditional businesses, as anyone who has visited their headquarters will know. The buildings have a sleek, corporate look to them, indistinguishable in appearance, and feel, from what one might expect from visiting the corporate headquarters of Apple or Coca Cola.

And the cooperative hasn't merely replicated corporate appearances: it has also followed a fairly traditional corporate strategy for growth. While Mondragon is technically a worker-controlled cooperative, until recently that was only true in Basque country. Elsewhere in Spain until 2009 in its Eroski-brand supermarkets the workers were all employees. The workers I approached in one market weren't even aware their boss was a "worker collective" and didn't seem to notice a significant difference between working for a corporate or a "cooperative" boss. And that's still true of fully one third of the workers in Mondragon, such as those who work for the company in China, Morocco, Argentina, Mexico, Thailand, Egypt and other places where Mondragon has assembly or other plants.[13]

The subject of wage differentials in worker cooperatives is a hot and often fiercely debated topic and many see any differential as the opening mouth of the road to hell. Mondragon settled on a wage differential of 8 to 1,[14] which is actually fairly large by some standards, and double the wage differential between industrial workers and management in a country like Norway at 4 to 1.[15] This wage differential has led to internal class differences that were expressed in great conflicts in the past, such as the Ulgor strike of 1974 that many of the assembly workers in the Ulgor plant (later reorganized and renamed as Fagor, the cooperative business that went bankrupt in 2013) attributed to "professionalization" in the cooperative.[16] But without wage differentials larger cooperatives like Mondragon would likely be unable to retain quality managers.

These and many more contradictions that emerge as worker-cooperatives grow larger might explain why the model isn't more popular and why worker-cooperatives remain small, or dissolve at certain levels of achievement when the contradictions become severe and these "limited utopias" hit against the even harsher contradictions of the outside world of business, class struggle and conflicts between line workers and management.

A much more viable, but less glamorous, alternative to the most savage forms of capitalism (that is, the traditional workplace of a boss with employees or "wage slaves") is the ESOP (Employee Stock Ownership Plan). These hybrids between worker-owned and traditional businesses are more common business structures that have grown in popularity over the years as a result of government incentives and tax breaks.[17] But they're also not viewed as favorably on the left as worker cooperatives, perhaps in part because they're one model of employee ownership that even Ronald Reagan approved of, seeing in them "an intimate connection between employee ownership, nationalism and an identification with capitalism."[18]

ESOPs and worker cooperatives are concrete ways workers can improve their lives, when those options are available and viable. Internally they can provide greater freedom, flexibility, greater democracy, and worker empowerment for participants and shield them from the more brutal, demeaning and anxiety-provoking aspects of the capitalist market economy that is now a worldwide system. Nevertheless, neither ESOPs nor worker cooperatives are magical remedies to the problems of the capitalist system (much less "alternatives" to it), and they won't resolve the problems a majority of workers face in the "labor market" where people rent themselves out for increasingly lower wages and more insecure working conditions to capitalist enterprises over which they have little or no control. Furthermore, as many of my old IWW comrades and others on the far left would argue and as the experience of Mondragon demonstrates, ESOPs and worker-owned businesses inculcate a "bourgeois" mindset in their worker-cooperators which often leads to a growing distance from the plight of other workers. It's not likely, for example, that one will find many worker-cooperators in the movement for a living wage and other struggles where workers battle their bosses for a bit more of the pie. That's because worker cooperators and workers in ESOPs have a divided allegiance: in their space in the workforce they have to think like both workers and owners—but over the long term worker-cooperators generally begin to think more like owners than like workers. To function as a business the worker-cooperators have to internalize market values of efficiency, productivity, profitability, and apply these values to the exploitation of resources and labor, even if that labor is their own.

The real problem, I would argue, is not "capitalism" (we'd need another book to define that word) but how markets are structured, organized and, more importantly, what society allows to enter them. Karl Polanyi's ideas are helpful in clarifying the problem.[19] He says that the market has increasingly taken over more and more of the world and of human society and incorporated it into itself. Our situation now is that rather than having a society with a market embedded in it, we have a society embedded within a market. As such, we find ourselves using language, proposing alternatives, considering solutions, and doing all our planning, thinking, and even plotting our revolutionary activity, within the market. Even the values by which we measure or judge the market and society, and the world (the environment) are market values because all our measuring and judging is done within the market.

Markets do an effective job of distributing goods and services and I think they're better than any alternatives I've seen. However, as Polanyi also points out, the idea that they're "self-regulating" is utopian—I would say, laughable—and they certainly aren't the solution to every problem, as neo-liberals seem to believe. I think the problem is not that we have markets but that we don't design, regulate, limit, and control them effectively and we have allowed them to get so big that we have lost our society, our natural world, and even our humanity in them. The market has become a huge black hole that threatens to swallow everything on the planet. Until we have some social territory freed from the market (the university used to be one such territory, that is, until it was absorbed by the market), we have no "anti-environment" that would enable us to speak a non-market language to express non-market ideas and, especially important, establish non-market values, all of which could prove to be the lifeline to extract what we value from the clutches of the market. But the bottom line is that neither ESOPs nor worker cooperatives, for all their virtues, are that lifeline, firmly embedded as they are in that very market.

Intuiting all this, I came to believe that New Earth Press would never be more than a business, and I no longer wanted to be a businessman. Dave and I had a conflicted, but ultimately amicable, parting of ways and we sold the business in 2000.

I had managed to get my BA on my third pass through the University, so the way was now clear for me to go back to the University where I would, thirty years after starting college, finally set to work on a Masters degree in English. I went to work at Berkeley City College for the next few years as an English and ESL teacher.

Meanwhile, I met the woman who would eventually become my third—and I swear, final—wife, Marcy Rein, a Jewish Marxist from Upstate New York who had been living in San Francisco for a number of years. She had been part of the Marxist party, Line of March, until it dissolved after the collapse of the USSR. At the time I met her, she was the editor of *American Writer*, the publication of the National Writer's Union. Marcy was also doing 12-step work in her own program, so while our religious and political backgrounds were very different, we had the practice, principles, and traditions of the Anonymous programs to work from, and we found all our differences enriching. Her long trajectory in journalism and social movement work, especially in the queer, feminist, labor, and racial justice movements enriched my understanding of life, as my own work in poetry and Latin American politics I suspect did for her. We took our relationship a day at a time for a few years, but eventually we married. The wedding, an informal potluck at a park in Richmond, was a bittersweet day for me: it was held just a week after a memorial service for my friend Dave Smith, who had died just a little over a month before.

CHAPTER NINE

CHASING THE BOLIVARIAN DREAM

I finished graduate work in May 2003 so Marcy and I celebrated by taking a trip to southern Mexico. We went first
to Oaxaca and interviewed teachers in the *plantón* or occupation just three years before that situation exploded, gain-
ing Oaxaca world-wide attention. We stopped briefly in
Juchitán in the Isthmus of Tehuantepec and had some good
conversations with people about the gay and lesbian-friendly
Zapotec culture and the history of the COCEI (Peasant
Worker Student Coalition of the Isthmus of Tehuantepec)
activity in the 1980s. The visit was brief, indeed, as the area
was like a blast furnace, a not too uncommon condition for
the Isthmus. Finally, we headed into the cooler mountains
of Chiapas where we hoped to visit Zapatista communities.

In Oventic we were allowed into the community for a tour
of the school, but no further, as we had no contacts and had
made no prior arrangements. A teacher graciously showed

us the bilingual school with a big mural of Zapata painted on an exterior wall, and then we spent some time talking to a man from Mexico City who told us he'd been there over a year and still felt he was being kept at a distance from what was happening at the center of the community. Such was the security around Oventic in 2003.

There was, and remains to this day, an uneasy truce between the Zapatista communities and the government. As a result, the Zapatistas have been unable to expand and grow outward but have remained an insular force, withdrawn from the larger context of Mexican national life and only emerging dramatically in critical moments to let the world know they're still around.

I'd found a pamphlet in a bookstore in San Cristóbal referring to a popular education cooperative in a small town near the Guatemalan border so we took a bus to Comitán to meet members of the co-op. Antonio and Paula met with us and we spent a couple of hours talking about their projects, in particular, their attempts to educate communities about the Plan Puebla Panama.[1]

At some point the subject turned to Nicaragua and the Sandinistas, and Antonio mentioned that they had the files from the Sandinista Ministry of Education that Fernando Cardenal had sent out of the country to protect them from destruction. "The new neoliberal government was burning up all the books and papers from the Sandinista period," Antonio told us, "so they needed to get the papers somewhere safe."

It had been a while since I'd thought about Nicaragua. Like many of those who had spent years working in solidarity with the Nicaraguan Revolution and the revolutionary movements in Central America, I'd felt a great sense of disillusionment when the FSLN lost the elections of 1990.

The disillusionment came from seeing the people we'd come to qualify as *valiente* (brave) who refused to take "*ni un paso atrás*" (not a single step back) suddenly vote out the Revolution they'd brought about.

Of course, when I'd lived there in 1987 I came to understand why people would be willing to consider an alternative to the Sandinista Revolution. On one block where he lived, a friend told me, six families had lost sons defending the Revolution from the US-backed contras. The country was running on bald tires and you never knew when the blowout was coming. The US had mined the harbors in Puerto Corinto; it had blown up oil storage tanks; and with the help of the comandantes, it had wrecked the Nicaraguan economy: all this had happened because the little country had decided to overthrow a bloody dictator the US had helped bring to power fifty years before, or so I viewed it at the time, with my limited knowledge. It was all true as far as it went, but it didn't encompass the complexities of the situation. In the intervening years of the revolution thousands had lost their lives defending the process, and many thousands more would live their lives maimed or with deep emotional scars. Who were we, the solidarity movement of the US and the world, to be "disappointed" and disillusioned? But we were. Along with many Nicaraguans.

But worse still was the betrayal of the *comandancia* when the FSLN prepared to leave power. Sandinistas claim that what was known as the *piñata* was simply a hasty response to defeat and an attempt to ensure that many of the revolutionary reforms and redistribution of land and wealth be maintained under the new administration. And so land titles were handed out, they maintain, to cooperatives, poor workers, and peasants who had informally occupied lands confiscated from Somoza and his supporters after the revolution. However, it also is acknowledged that many ministers and comandantes and other previously trusted figures in the *Frente comandancia*, people like the Ortega brothers, Daniel and Humberto, and Tomás Borge, transferred money and properties from the state into their own personal accounts.

The ironies weren't lost on many in the movement who, in watching this process, recalled the line in the Sandinista hymn, "los hijos de Sandino no se venden ni se rinden ¡jamas!" which, roughly translated is, "the children of Sandino NEVER sell out nor surrender!" Nicaragua, it seemed, had surrendered and its leadership had sold out, it seemed, FOREVER. And much of the solidarity movement became disillusioned and closed the book on Nicaragua while a minority ignored all this and continued supporting the Sandinistas.

The following year, in June of 2004, I decided to reopen that book, mostly as a result of Marcy's encouragement. She'd mentioned at least once that she thought a trip to Nicaragua would help me resolve what she saw as a "political bitterness" that often slipped into cynicism. So when I finished my first year of teaching at Berkeley City College (then named Vista Community College) I went to Nicaragua to conduct interviews with Sandinistas and their critics. I hoped in the process to find out what happened to the Revolution that defined the 1980s for much of the world, and certainly for me.

For some, the electoral defeat of the FSLN and its aftermath signaled the end of the Revolution. Such was the view of Fr. Ernesto Cardenal who was Minister of Culture from 1979 to 1990. "The electoral defeat was just that. The FSLN could have won the next time around. But the piñata was the loss of the Revolution." The FSLN's later refusal to democratize the party structure resulted in the further erosion of support among many Nicaraguans who had participated in the revolutionary process.

Since the electoral defeat in 1990, there had been a number of attempts to democratize the party. One sector of the FSLN attempted to reform the party and make the comandancia more accountable to the grassroots, but without success. This sector eventually split from the party to form the Movement for Sandinista Renewal (MRS). A series of splits in the party and defections over the years left the FSLN weakened, but increasingly centralized: the Ortega brothers, Daniel and Humberto, former President of Nicaragua and Minister of Defense under the FSLN, respectively, and their allies swept in like vultures to consume what was left of the FSLN and convert it into a populist party under the direction of the self-appointed caudillo, Daniel Ortega.

In preparation for the trip to Nicaragua I bought a video camera and left to spend the summer interviewing some ex-Sandinistas and getting their perspectives on the past and present situation of their country. I first arranged an interview with Fr. Ernesto Cardenal at his Casa de los Tres Mundos.

To get to the Casa de los Tres Mundos I had to take a taxi and we hit some very rough patches of highway in between. It looked like the road had been intentionally destroyed and, when I asked the driver about it, he confirmed that it had been. "Every year, you know, the students have demonstrations and the police come and there's always a fight. The students tear up the pavement to throw at the police when they arrive."

We arrived and I went into the Casa and sat as Ernesto finished an interview with a group of European tourists. After they left he brought me into his office. I began by asking him what possibilities there were for some sort of revolutionary change in Nicaragua. "None. There's no possibility for revolutionary change in Nicaragua," he replied flatly, "especially not with the FSLN under the present caudillo dictatorship of Daniel Ortega." We talked a bit about other processes in Latin America and then, at some point, the aging poet mentioned his one hope at the moment was centered on the process in Venezuela. As he talked about Venezuela and President Chávez I became more and more curious. By the end of our conversation, I was convinced that I would have to visit Venezuela to see for myself what was going on.

I didn't know anything about Venezuela at the time, having been immersed for nearly three years in a graduate program that didn't allow me time to keep up with world events. But what Ernesto told me, and what he wrote in an essay I later read, piqued my curiosity.[2]

All I knew of Venezuela was what I'd seen in *The Revolution will not be Televised*, a controversial film on the 2002 coup that took Hugo Chávez out of power for two and a half days.[3] The most powerful scene was the return of Chávez on the night of April 13, 2002, the helicopter arriving in the darkness, its spotlight casting a celestial beam onto the expectant crowds. These images awakened the archetype of the returning hero, the savior of the people: Jesus rising from the grave, Osiris reemerging into life or the return of Quetzalcóatl.

In preparation for my trip to Venezuela I searched online and found some interesting links by which I got in touch with Franz Lee and Jutta Schmitt in Mérida, the capital of the state of the same name, tucked away in a valley of the Venezuelan Andes. They responded and invited me to visit them and I began making plans to spend Christmas break in Venezuela.

I caught a post-Christmas flight and arrived in time for the New Year's Eve fireworks over Caracas. The next day I took my video camera and went to Plaza Bolívar to do interviews. I found I had a knack for "cold call" interviews (likely a gift from growing up in the military), and by early afternoon I had filled three or so tapes. I remember in particular one interview with a revolutionary musician named Juan who entertained the New Year's Day crowd lazing on the benches in the warm sun with covers of songs by Ali Primera, the nation's revolutionary hero of the New Song movement. I asked him what the Bolivarian Revolution meant to him. At the time I was still having trouble pronouncing the term "Bolivarian" in Spanish, but he was happy to educate this gringo tourist. "Look, this isn't a revolution. It's a reform and it's a positive process, but we need to push it further."

This would be the beginning of a long discussion that I would have with Venezuelans for the next eight or so years. How deep was this "reform" and what distinguishes a "reform" from a "revolution"? How do you know when you're in one and not the other? And what difference does it make? The fact that Chávez had finally come to power as a result of elections further confused the question since "revolutions" throughout the twentieth century had been defined as armed struggles under the direction of vanguards that resulted in a "clearing of the table" with entirely new governments, bureaucracies and political classes.

My trip to Venezuela took place in a particularly bleak historical context. George W. Bush had lied to justify the invasion of Iraq. Like many, I was still outraged that George W. Bush had managed to steal both his first election and then his reelection without any mass expression of outrage.[4] I was horrified by the invasion and occupation of Iraq, particularly by the brutal attack on, and destruction of, Fallujah.

It was, then, a delight to be in Venezuela where a sense of hope pervaded the already optimistic tropical ambience.

During the oil bonanza that resulted from Bush taking Iraq out of production with a war, Chávez went on a massive spending spree, financing a number of social welfare programs that he called "the Missions." This was welcome news to those of us who had seen programs for the poor and marginal cut to the bone or dropped completely as part of the neoliberal program beginning with Margaret Thatcher in the UK and Ronald Reagan in the US. Now, after decades of neoliberal fundamentalism, and nearly fifteen years since the collapse of socialism, a left alternative appeared to be developing in Latin America, and in particular under President Chávez.

The former Lieutenant Colonel who won the presidency in 1998 had a "revolutionary" proposal for Venezuela. The first step was to draft a new constitution that, in the process, coincidentally increased executive power, eliminated one house of the parliament to make it a unicameral body and, through artful gerrymandering, gave his coalition majority power even with a minority of the votes.

At the same time that there were disturbing trends toward recentralizing power under Chávez—after a decade or more of decentralization in the wake of the 1989 "Caracazo" riots or "rebellion"—there were other trends that pointed the opposite direction. Chávez included, both in the new Constitution (which renamed Venezuela the "Bolivarian Republic of Venezuela") and in official rhetoric, a proposal for "protagonistic participatory democracy" to replace the representative democracy that many admitted was in crisis by the time Chávez came to power. Social movement activists and revolutionary figures emerged to celebrate the project of the "Bolivarian Revolution" and they were joined by massive numbers of people from the underclass who had never participated in the political system before. These contradictions, among many others, encouraged cautious optimism from many in Venezuela and the world that something new might be happening to challenge the neoliberal "TINA" pronounced by Margaret Thatcher years before: "There Is No Alternative."

Many who had struggled, sweated, and exhausted themselves for years to make a better Venezuela suddenly found their dreams, visions, and projects funded by the flood of oil money into state coffers and handed out by Chávez. The Bolivarian bandwagon passed through the country like a mythic caravan drawn by unicorns that left trails of money and promises of more magic to come in its tracks. Who could resist this dazzling spectacle in a world that was otherwise left out in the cold by the austere policies of neoliberal orthodoxy?

Then there was Chávez himself, a one-of-a-kind charismatic political outsider with a big "llanero" (plainsman) personality that many, especially the poor, believed could fix the problems facing the country. He hypnotized the world at the UN when he took the podium and denounced as "satanic" the presence of George W. Bush. Chávez inspired Latin Americans and anti-imperialists the world over when he proclaimed Bolivarian Unity against imperialist free-trade initiatives with projects like the Bolivarian Alliance for the Peoples of our America (ALBA), Union of South American Nations (UNASUR), Bank of the South, Telesur (a Bolivarian response to CNN) and others.

Were there contradictions? Yes, many. The biggest one was that this was all being funded by high oil prices and led by a military man, a former Lieutenant Colonel whose democratic credentials left something to be desired: he'd participated in a coup attempt against the Carlos Andres Pérez (CAP) government in February 1992. For that crime he'd served a light sentence and had been pardoned by CAP's successor, Rafael Caldera. At a time when all of Latin America was recovering, at last, from military juntas and olive-green presidencies, Chávez's government seemed a step backwards, especially considering the number of posts he began to give to military, or former military. But the promises he held out for deeper democracy and greater social justice also seemed to be cause for cautious optimism.

Perhaps I wanted to believe too much that I was seeing a revolutionary process, the "Pretty Revolution" that people were talking about. Given the reality I'd just left behind, of a country engaged in an illegal war declared by an illegitimate president, and given the absence of powerful and sustained resistance to executive criminality in the US, I was no doubt desperate to believe something, anything, that appeared hopeful. Yes, there were questions and "disconfirming data," but it has also been established that "when faced with disconfirming data, instead of relinquishing their theories, people continue to maintain them by modifying them to take account of the disconfirming results."[5] Now, over a decade later, I can see that's what I did: I followed my intuitions and began to assimilate the "confirming data." But we're getting ahead of ourselves.

My first impressions of Venezuela from walking around Plaza Bolívar in Caracas and talking to average people, most of whom were poor, was that the country had at last been blessed with a president who took the majority and its needs into account. The woman selling drinks out of a pushcart on the street by the church; the man selling balloons in the park; the man on the bench watching his daughter play around the statue of the Simon Bolívar mounted on his steed; the street vendors painting light poles and cleaning plazas; the popular initiatives of community gardens, community centers, and other hopeful projects confirmed the narrative they all offered in one version or another: this president was following in the footsteps of the Liberator (as Simon Bolívar is known) and Jesus, with his concern for the poor.

Certainly, if nothing else, Chávez had awakened dreams among the people of Venezuela. The question on everyone's mind was, what impact would these dreams have on the stark reality of the country with its dramatic inequality of wealth, high levels of unemployment, and rising levels of violence? Would there be more reforms, or would there, indeed, be a revolution?

I went on to Mérida by bus and stayed in a guesthouse a few blocks from Plaza Bolívar. Franz Lee and Jutta Schmidt and I met in a place called Café Magnolia, also known as "Café de los Churros" for its fried donuts. We found an immediate connection in Ernst Bloch and spent a long time talking and drinking one café marrón (Venezuelan cappuccinos) after another.

Lee was a nearly-blind, light-skinned black South African who had gotten his PhD under Bloch at the University of Tubingen. He'd moved to Guyana where he knew Walter Rodney, and then to Venezuela where he'd gone to work teaching political science at the University of the Andes in Mérida. Jutta was some twenty years younger than Franz and had been his student when he taught in Germany and eventually they married. Jutta was and is one of the most brilliant people I've ever known, and together they made a formidable team in the classroom as well as in their writings. Through Franz and Jutta I got to know Juan Veroes, an Afro-Venezuelan Chavista who became a close friend and introduced me to the Chavista Left in Mérida.

I was amazed by the many projects that the oil revenue was making possible, such as the educational missions that included the Bolivarian Universities, and various levels of adult education. *Barrio Adentro*, or "Inside the Neighborhood" was a program of clinics located around the country and staffed by Cuban doctors. There were community kitchens and cafeterias where for about $1 US you could get a nutritious, multi-course meal. Job training programs such as *Vuelvan Caras* subsidized people as they studied and then offered them small loans to start their own cooperative business. Out of this program came an explosion of cooperatives around the country, the number rising from under a thousand when Chávez came to power, to an estimated 150,000 or more by 2006.

The cooperatives, as I understood it at the time, were to be the foundation of "Twenty-First Century Socialism" (TFCS) that was going to be the socialism of protagonistic and participatory democracy. The cooperatives would be the training ground for the new society. As Chávez put it at the time, if people could run their own business, they could eventually run the country!

In addition to job training, loans, and credits to the cooperatives, they were also given preference for government contracts. Cooperative cafes began making lunches and delivering them to government ministries on contract. Agricultural cooperatives were given expropriated land to grow on. Media collectives received funding to provide programming for government television stations.

Of course, it all came at a price, and that price was autonomy and independence, because, naturally, the government appeared to be funding only those grassroots projects that supported the government, though at the time this seemed to be unproblematic since the government was, after all, funding grassroots projects.

In addition to the local grassroots projects emerging within the country, Chávez began organizing international initiatives, particularly in Latin America. ALBA (Alianza

Bolivariana para los Pueblos de Nuestra América, Bolivarian Alliance for the Peoples of Our America) was to be a counterproposal to the Free Trade Area of the Americas agreement and it would function as a mechanism to unite the countries of the region. The Sucre would be a common currency and there would be the Banco Del Sur, the Southern Bank, for low-interest loans to poor countries, and Petrocaribe to sell oil on easy terms to poor countries in Latin America.

All these programs brought Chávez into the limelight, where he clearly loved to be. My skepticism evaporated as I watched the *llanero* on *Alo Presidente* ("Hello President," his weekly variety-show that he emceed), promoting his programs, criticizing his ministers for falling behind in their duties, talking to ordinary people who called in, interviewing guests, regaling them with his stories, offering political reflections and tidbits of historical knowledge—and singing! Chávez, more than a politician or a president, quickly became a very sympathetic television personality and soon even his weekly program wasn't enough for him. His *cadenas*, or obligatory transmissions, became regular interruptions of all media, and there he would be, inaugurating a new industrial plant or visiting a cooperative farming experiment or *núcleos de desarrollo endógenos* or NDEs.

NDEs was a strategy to develop and integrate Venezuela's productive processes. I remember Angel Palacios, a filmmaker at Panafilms in Caracas, explaining it all to me one afternoon.

"The idea is you have a region suitable for growing corn. So right there near the cornfields you install a granary. Next to the granary you have a mill, and then you set up a place right there to make *cachapas* (Venezuelan cornmeal pancakes). The whole economic enterprise is a circle, all integrated and united in the productive process." I listened and watched as he drew each little enterprise on the back of an envelope, and I marveled at the beauty of it. Eventually, NDEs became NUDES, *Núcleos de desarrollo endógenos socialistas*, but they maintained the same elegant theoretical beauty through the transition.

I never actually saw a NDE or NUDES in action. The yucca processing plant that I first visited in 2006 on the southeast side of Lake Maracaibo wasn't yet in production. I was told that the plant was almost ready and would begin to process yucca for the agricultural cooperative "any time now." When I returned the following year, still not a gear in the huge plant was moving, and, in fact, the gears and everything else, showed signs of rust. A friend familiar with the project tells me that now, nearly nine years later, the gears still haven't yet moved a single tooth.

Certainly there must be a NUDES somewhere in Venezuela that function, if nothing more than because the government needs something to showcase. But I can neither confirm nor deny that. I can only affirm that the NUDES remain, in my mind and in the minds of many Venezuelans, an elegant theory.

CHAPTER TEN

CRACKS IN THE FACADE

So I returned home to spend a semester teaching at Vista Community College in Berkeley but I was so inspired by the possibilities of Chávez's plans that I prepared to leave in the summer to spend a year in Venezuela. Over the spring of 2005 I followed news of developments in Venezuela through online sources and I eventually began to write for a few of them.[1]

When I returned to Venezuela in early June 2005 I was welcomed with open arms by people I'd met earlier in the Andean city of Mérida. I told Juan Veroes that I needed a place to live and he suggested I meet a couple of people he knew. Betty Osorio and her husband Humberto Rivas had built a children's theater named Teatro Colibrí (Hummingbird Theater) not too far from the city center. They were both puppeteers, and had traveled all over Latin America doing shows for children when they were younger. Betty had gone on to get her doctorate in early childhood education and now taught next door at the University of the Andes (ULA). Humberto had his workshop in the same complex where they lived and there he made beautiful puppets and wooden children's toys. Their son was by then gone from home, but their daughter Xica lived in another space downstairs and was finishing up her law degree.

On the bottom floor was a large patio area, part of it bricked, and another part had fruit trees and one banana plant, now heavy with green fruit. There was a two story apartment next to Humberto's toy shop, and then along one side was Xica's apartment, and then along another side was the three-story theater itself. Above Xica's apartment was a vacant studio, which was for rent, and on the top floor, the fourth, was a tango and dance studio where the tango teacher, Nelson, also lived.

Betty showed us around and offered to rent me the studio, which I immediately accepted. I began moving in right away: I swept up and cleaned and soon had a simple but beautiful place to call home in Mérida, in addition to a lovely family of creative, revolutionary people, who really made me feel like part of their family.

Humberto was a musician, in addition to making his living as toymaker, with a big heart and a happy disposition. He always had a joke or two to tell, and every encounter began with a big hug. Betty was cerebral and a big talker. Indeed, it was hard to find ways into her monologues that often ranged from simple stories from her travels, to the theories of Habermas and Simon Bolívar and long, complex expositions on hermeneutics and ethics in the revolutionary process.

The studio had one window looking out on Pico Bolívar, the highest mountain in Venezuela. The mountain range ran down from each side of the peak and disappeared into the horizon. It was June, and the "tardes de San Juan" (Saint John afternoons) were spectacular: the low clouds coming in from the south caught on the peaks, then slowly rolled down the slopes until they disappeared into the valley.

Thanks to José Sant Roz, a well-known and connected writer from Mérida I'd met on my first trip to Venezuela, I was invited to participate in the World Poetry Festival of Venezuela. I spent a week doing readings in various parts of the country, for which I was paid the equivalent of nearly five hundred dollars. I was exhausted at the end, and I felt I'd earned my money. It was, incidentally, the only money I ever received from the Bolivarian government. All other expenses from my stay in Venezuela, my movie and my other solidarity work came out of my own savings and a few hundred dollars of donations from friends.[2]

I returned to Mérida and soon was moving through the Mérideña Chavista Left (the Mérida Left) as if I belonged there. A poet I'd gotten to know by his pseudonym, Poeta Simon Arado, introduced me to the community kitchen known as "The People's Café," which served up a good, multi-course lunch for the equivalent of one US dollar and that's where I met Malacara (Ugly), the Tupamaro.

The only space available in the cafe that day was right next to a table full of Tupamaros, the radical left group who took their name from the 1960s Uruguayan guerrillas, who, in turn, took their name from the last Incan ruler, Túpac Amaru. The Venezuelan Tupamaros made their reputation as armed revolutionaries who were the backbone of left resistance to social democratic governments of the Democratic Action. They'd had an uneasy alliance with the Chávez government that flared up into small conflicts at times, but generally they were allied with the Bolivarian process and saw themselves as its armed defenders.

Simon and I sat down, and eventually I got into a conversation with the Tupamaros. When they discovered I was a North American, one of them, a tall blonde man with no front teeth, but a wicked laugh, started talking to me in fluent English. I found out that his name was Malacara and he had grown up in a very poor family in Caracas where he'd joined the Communist Party as a young teenager. He'd been "adopted" by a wealthy benefactor and eventually had the opportunity to study ballet in New York. Now he was working with the Tupamaros of Mérida, who were under the leadership of a man named Matute, who seemed like a friendly enough guy. Malacara loved to talk, and he loved to talk above all about art and revolutionary politics. Malacara would eventually become a good friend because, like a handful of others including Juan Veroes, Betty, and Humberto at Colibrí, he was dependable and you could count on him when he made a commitment.

Part of the problem was that oil, known by many as "the devils excrement," had had a truly nefarious effect on Venezuelan culture, and that was according to the Venezuelans, themselves. With money bubbling out of the ground and a pipeline of dollars pouring into the government's hands as a result, the question on everyone's mind was how to get some of those "free" dollars.[3] Thus "rent chasing," that is, finding some way of getting a "subsidy" or *beca* (grant or scholarship) from the government when it was flush with money from an oil bonanza became a way of life. Certainly there were people like Humberto and Betty, and a few others I got to know when I lived in Mérida, who worked hard for their money. But the main source of income for the country, some 95% of the money that came into the country, came in the form of petrodollars.

One poet friend, José Gregorio Hernández Márquez, described to me how it worked, as Angel had done describing the NDEs, by drawing it out, this time on a napkin in Café Magnolia, which by now had become one of my haunts in Mérida. Jose Gregorio had been in the *Bandera Roja* (Red Flag), a Maoist guerrilla organization that eventually became a legal political party. When they split and went with the opposition to Chávez, José Gregorio left them. When I met him he was teaching elementary school and running a small publishing company, La Casa Tomada, which was mostly financed by the government.

"Look," he said, drawing a square and dividing it up by a number of vertical and horizontal lines so as to make eight little squares in the big square, "this is how it works. The government does a land reform. It gives people each a little parcel." He stuck his pen in each square, counting them out with eight stabs. "The people go there and they say, 'hey, we need to work this.' But do you think they'll work in the hot sun? No. They look for Colombians and hire them to work the fields. Or they find some way of selling off their parcel so they can party. That's how it is in Venezuela," he finished, pushing the napkin in front of me so I could assimilate his lesson.

I'd already seen this reality in the cooperatives. I spent many mornings sitting around one of the outdoor tables at the Café Paris Tropical in an alley off of Mérida's Plaza Bolívar. The alley was known as "Artist's Alley" because many of the city's painters worked there, painting and selling their work. Café Paris Tropical was one of two or three cafes near Plaza Bolívar where the Chavistas congregated to talk politics, and I could usually find Malacara there, or Poeta Simon. I would often be invited to sit for a while as I wandered through the alley on my way to or from the city center, and I listened to the dreams of the odd assortment of nouveau revolutionaries who would drink coffee as they described in detail the worker collectives they planned to organize when the financing from the government was approved. Much of it came to nothing, but a few of those cooperatives were financed, and then disappeared as quickly as they began.

Marcy came to visit me over the Christmas holidays and after a trip on a "pirate" bus (privately contracted bus) to Mérida, we went exploring the region, visiting cooperatives as we went. In one cooperative in Azulita we recorded the beginning of the collective breaking down and transmogrifying into a capitalist enterprise of the worst kind, with employees doing the work of the "cooperative owners." We found out about this only when we asked about why the office was locked, and the collective member took us into a room and began detailing the problems the collective was having. This was a process that, unbeknownst to us, was beginning to happen all over the country. By 2007, it appeared that "the majority of registered cooperatives [were] already inactive."[4] Even supporters of the Bolivarian government agree that by that year, "184,000 cooperatives were officially registered," but "only about 30,000, or 15 percent, were active." But as I noted, several years later,[5] According to the National Institute of Statistics figures, released "in a nonofficial capacity," there appear in 2009 to have been "47,000 collective associations, of which only 33.5% were active—some 15,745 cooperatives. And 75% of those were in the service sector."[6] Worse still, these cooperatives were used by the Bolivarian government "as a means of circumventing labor laws. Cooperatives that were not complying with the labor regulations received contracts from public institutions—a means of politically correct outsourcing."[7]

By March of 2006 I was ready for a break from Venezuela. I began the trip by flying to Montevideo where I visited the anarchist "Comunidad del Sur" (Community of the South) and interviewed Rubén Prieto. Rubén introduced me to Raúl

Zibechi, who I later visited and interviewed at his home. At a demonstration for a worker cooperative whose members had been arrested for occupying and producing at their abandoned workplace, I met Jorge Zabalza, a Tupamaro who had spent years in prison and now worked as a butcher in a working-class neighborhood of Montevideo. I spent one Sunday visiting and interviewing him at a local bar, where I had my first máte. I met some anarchists who had a magazine stand on the street and one of them, Pablo, took me to visit the Galpon de Corrales, a free community space that had organized a library, radio station, bakery, community garden, and café. I was surprised to hear that Pablo's group of anarchists had broken relations with Venezuelan anarchists to side with Chávez and the Bolivarian process because they felt the struggle against imperialism was decisive for Latin America and Chávez appeared to be the first leader in the hemisphere since Fidel Castro who had the courage to stand against the US.

I went to Buenos Aires on an overnight ferry and was present a few days later for the thirtieth anniversary of the 1976 military coup. The commemoration was marked by an enormous demonstration, at the center of which was a blocks-long banner carried by members of the families of the thirty thousand disappeared and decorated with the photos of the "desaparecidos."

I took a bus to Bolivia where I did interviews just two months after Evo Morales took the office of the presidency. One of the most powerful interviews I had took place at the Plaza Abaroa in La Paz with Pedro Portugal Mollinedo who opened up the Andean cosmovision as a means of illuminating a way through the modern political impasse from which all the world suffers.[8] He saw the political Left and political right as nothing more than the two hands of colonialism, and the government of Evo Morales as a continuation of the same colonial policies behind an indigenous mask. I would later come back to this interview for insight on how to understand the Pink Tide governments and their relations with social movements.

I spent a few days on the Isla del Sol in Lake Titicaca with a new acquaintance, Keith Richards, a writer and scholar of Bolivian culture and literature, and then I went on to Lima, Peru. By then I'd been on the road for two months and I was ready to go home, which in this case, meant Venezuela.

I got back to Venezuela in time for May Day and was surprised to learn of more changes that had taken place in my absence. Community councils were being formed in response to Chávez's initiative. They would be organisms of the "participatory protagonistic democracy" he'd promised the country to replace the "fake" representative democracy of the previous forty years of government. Chávez also promised that these councils would be the seeds of the future communal state.

I was on my way to other adventures but first I had to clean out my studio in Mérida. I ran into Malacara and he offered to help and in return I told him he could have my phone and everything else I was leaving behind. He arrived the next morning talking about how he thought maybe Chávez was being left in place by the empire to help build up Venezuela as a market for "all the goodies from the US" I shrugged. Could be, I said. I raised my own suspicions about the fact that so little prosecution for corruption was taking place. How was it that Chávez couldn't know about the corruption or could move so slowly to prosecute it?

"Cause it's payback time. You get it, man? All those Copeistas and Adecos who got him votes are now in the government and they're stealing just like before. And Chávez can't do anything about it because they got him in power.

It's the devil's bargain. You know, the thing with Fausto. You know Fausto?"

"Yeah. Okay, the Faustian bargain."

"Exactly. And I guess everybody figures that the people won't mind if they steal as long as the people are getting all the programs. You know, the *Misiones*."

He swept up the kitchen the way he did everything: quickly and efficiently. The Tupamaros were lucky to have him among them, I thought.

"I don't trust anything but passion," he said, leaning on his broom. "You know, you can't make a revolution throwing money around. It has to be a creative thing. People need a whole new way of seeing things. Like about money and materialism. People here need to get over the idea that everywhere is going to be just like the United States. There isn't enough to go around. Rather than flying all over the world they need to learn how to fly with their minds. They need to get free in their heads. Like you. And just like you, they need to learn this technology so they can learn how to fly in their heads." He continued sweeping, then as he swept the dirt into the dustpan he said, "You know I taught people how to fly, don't you? In New York when I worked at Alvin Ailey School of Dance. I learned it myself, just so I could teach people how to do it. You know Baryshnikov? I saw him do it. He came onto the stage flying, thirty feet and landing like..." he made a graceful move, one hand holding the dustpan high before his eyes and a foot extended behind him. He shook his head. "Incredible, man. And it's all passion."

I told him about St. Symeon the New Theologian and the Uncreated Energies of God as I cleaned the sink. How all the universe scintillates with the leftover uncreated energies of God.

He nodded and agreed. "It's like passion, right? I don't believe in anything but passion," and he shook his head as he put the broom in the corner.

I returned home and went back to work teaching at Berkeley City College, but Venezuela remained my focus and I returned the next year to work on two films.[9] Then in January 2008 my father died. We'd been in a long process of reconciliation and rapprochement, and no doubt dealing with the loss played a part in decisions I made to take off the summer and fall semesters from teaching at Berkeley City College (formerly Vista Community College). I spent summer and fall traveling through South America and gathering material for a book of interviews with Latin American social movement activists.[10] The trip would begin in Venezuela where I would meet up with another filmmaker, Ari Krawitz, who offered to help me with a film project I had in mind. From there I planned to travel through Colombia and Ecuador by bus, then fly to Buenos Aires and go overland to Paraguay and Bolivia to do interviews.

Ari and I joined Arturo Albarrán, a Venezuelan filmmaker who was working at the Ministry of Agriculture and Land (MAT) and others from the ministry who were promoting agroecology and organic agriculture among campesinos in the state of Mérida. I'd met Arturo the year before and had gone into the field with him, filming projects of the government-sponsored *Fondos Zamoranos* (Zamoran Funds, projects to fund community-based agriculture). I immediately liked him and trusted him, perhaps because he didn't need anything from me, so I didn't have to wonder about his motives in befriending me.

Arturo was a hard-working man committed to the Venezuelan peasantry and to agroecology, an ecological agricultural idea that accounts for socio-political dimensions of the problems of food production. He came from peasant stock and, under the presidency of Carlos Andres Pérez, he'd studied film and filmmaking at the University of the Andes as the government at the time was committed to giving scholarships to people from poor families. Arturo had come up politically in the CEPs, Popular Education Centers, and that led him to a left social movement perspective and commitment.

Ari, Arturo, and I went with others from the MAT to film meetings between government agricultural workers and campesinos in Aricagua. Through the meetings the people from MAT hoped to introduce the campesinos to a new government program emphasizing the use of ecological agriculture.

We rode in the Ministry jeeps up through the mountains and down into valleys where the vegetation looked like something out of a set for a film on dinosaurs. We arrived in the evening in Aricagua, and over the next two days Ari and I filmed as the MAT people talked and invited discussions about the new policies.

Ari and I traveled around Western Venezuela for the next month before I started out on my trip through Colombia. From Cúcuta I took an all-night bus to Bogotá and stayed there with Martha Henriquez, a school teacher in an alternative school who I'd met when she was in Venezuela the previous summer. She and her daughter Daniela lived in the north of Bogotá and they were just getting ready to go to Suesca for the week to go rock climbing, so they invited me along.

Martha supported the *Polo Democrático Alternativo* (PDA), the democratic left option of Colombia, which included former guerrillas of the M19 (Movement 19) like Antonio Navarro Wolff, Gustavo Petro, and others. Martha was more than happy to orient me to the ins and outs of Colombian politics and gave me contacts for people she thought I should interview for my book. Colombia, as it turned out, wasn't the drug den, terrorist, and guerrilla haven of its reputation in the exterior, or the scary, lawless place my Venezuelan friends warned me not to visit. I actually felt safer walking the streets of Bogotá than I did in Caracas, and the militarization of the country was far from evident in most areas that I visited.

Martha and I had a lot in common, but when the subject of the Bolivarians came up, we'd begin arguing. She despised Chávez and thought the whole Bolivarian process was a sham, and I couldn't understand why. We kept approaching an argument, but both of us felt it was better to remain friends and just avoid the subject.

One morning after breakfast Martha said she wanted me to meet a couple of her friends. "Laura has a story I think you'll want to hear," she told me mysteriously. We took a cab to Guatavita, a beautiful tourist town with lots of colonial architecture and white adobe buildings. We went to Ramón Valdez cafe, a new cafe run by Martha's friends, near the artisan market. Martha introduced me to her friends Sergio and Laura, and then we all sat down to talk over a coffee.

Laura had gone to Venezuela to study medicine on a scholarship the Bolivarian government was offering to poor people from all over Latin America. They were told they "would study in an institute with top quality equipment" but instead they were taken to a military base in Caracas and left in a building that she described as being "like a prison" with inaccessible windows, no library, minimal facilities, minimal security, and "nothing to read but Chávez's speeches." There were no phones, and when they went to use the computers they found there were only screens with no functioning computers. A little later Chávez arrived to inaugurate the program and "the red carpet was rolled out and white curtains were hung and we had to all wear red t-shirts with some slo-gan to Chávez written on them. He arrived, he spoke, and then he left. And the red carpet was rolled back up and the white curtains were taken down and things went right back to normal."

"Normal," Laura said, was so terrible that a month into the process, a month without lessons, teachers, access to books, computers or anything else that could be considered a "study program," a strike and a protest was organized that included everyone but the Bolivians, who didn't want to damage rela-tions between Venezuela and their country.

In the end Laura was able to get access to a telephone and get her family to send her a plane ticket home and she left after more than a month in what she described as "imprisonment."

We spent a bit more time with Laura and Sergio, and then Martha and I strolled around town a bit until the gray clouds, tinged a ruddy orange, slowly moved over our heads, threat-ening rain, and we caught a bus back to Suesca. All the way into Suesca I silently mulled over Laura's troubling story. I wondered if the white curtains and red carpet that had been brought out for Chávez might not be an apt image for the entire Bolivarian process with missions that never seemed to accomplish their goals before they were abandoned for other projects, and the buildings, the great projects, all inaugurated and then somehow forgotten and left to rust like the yucca processing plant I'd seen near Lake Maracaibo.

I spent the next three months traveling through South America and conducting interviews. In October, on my way home from the Southern Cone I made a stop for a week or two in Venezuela again and stayed with Marc Villá, a Venezuelan filmmaker and a friend who lived in Caracas. The last day, just before I left for the airport, it was raining and Marc was depressed. I asked him what was bothering him and he said that he was depressed about the situation in Trujillo with the father of our mutual friend, Eduardo Viloria, who was the governor of the state. Gilmer Viloria came out of COPEI[11] but joined the Chavistas early on and he had done a lot for the peasantry of Trujillo. He'd also been a great promoter of culture in the region, especially in the inaccessible mountain areas. Gilmer Viloria had sent cultural workers with books into those remote areas to read to the peasants, and he'd also set up small libraries and cultural centers around the state. I knew that for a fact, because I'd read there with his son Eduardo during the World Poetry Festival in 2005 and had seen what the cultural centers were doing in terms of publishing and organizing cultural activities.

But it was election time and Chávez had decided to put his own man in office there and had gone on the offensive campaigning against Governor Viloria, and even going so far as to slander him as a "traitor." It wasn't as if Viloria wasn't committed to the project of Chávez: he was. He simply maintained his independence, no more. But that was apparently unacceptable to Chávez who, like a good military man, needed to have everyone under his command. Marc called a cab for me and I left for the airport, still troubled by the news from Trujillo.

CHAPTER ELEVEN

A REVOLUTION IN THE REAR VIEW MIRROR

In 2009 I focused on Central America to begin doing interviews with social movement activists, first in El Salvador and then in Honduras in the wake of the coup that took Mel Zelaya out of power. The latter was a complicated situation, much more than many on the Left seemed willing to acknowledge. Mel Zelaya as Liberal Party president of Honduras, had proposed a referendum on amending the constitution as many other left presidents in the region had done. Coincidentally, most of those changes among the left governments had extended "popular power" as well as executive power. That had certainly been the case in Venezuela under Chávez, and something similar had happened in Ecuador under Rafael Correa, in Nicaragua under Daniel Ortega, and elsewhere, and now the same process was being proposed by Mel Zelaya, who was perceived by many Hondurans as being in the same camp with those other reformers who were viewed as "anti-democratic."

Latin America has a long-standing tradition of rule by *caudillos*, or strongmen who maintain themselves in power for far too long by a system of patronage to supporters. Since the peace agreements with rebels in the early to mid nineties and the dismantling of military dictatorships, many Latin Americans have been very cautious about the return of rule by caudillo. Liberal democratic reforms have been quite popular and they represent a great advance over the authoritarian governments of the past, of the Left or the Right. It was, in fact, thanks to these liberal democratic reforms, limited though they were, that autonomous social movements had space to grow and thrive in the region.

So when Mel Zelaya proposed reforms in the constitution, he might well have broken Honduran law. As *The Telegraph* reported, "The coup was triggered when Zelaya illegally ignored the Supreme Court and the congress who tried to stop him from calling for a constitutional referendum in a bid to extend presidential term limits." And, in fact, a six-member truth commission determined that both Zelaya and the military violated the law: Zelaya, for calling for the referendum, and the military for having sent him into exile, rather than allowing him to be impeached.[1]

At the time the nuances of this were lost on me, and on most left activists who went to Honduras to do solidarity with Zelaya supporters.

The following year I returned to Central America, this time spending a few weeks in Nicaragua. The FSLN had come back to power four years before, but under very different conditions than they had in 1979—and as a very different party. The Frente Sandinista de Liberación Nacional (Sandinista National Liberation Front, FSLN) when it came to power in

July 1979 organized its "vanguard of the vanguard" directorate as a coalition of nine "*comandantes*," (commanders) three
from each of the three "tendencies." Roger Miranda, former
aide to brother of Daniel Ortega and Sandinista Minister of
Defense, Humberto Ortega, in his book detailed the conflicts
and processes that went on in the nine-man directorate or
comandancia, during the years the Sandinistas were in power. On the positive side, the directorate as a group provided
a check on individual members that was ordinarily missing
in other Marxist-Leninist governments. No one person nor,
in this case, single faction, was able to unilaterally impose its
will on either the directorate or any subordinate organism or
branch of government, although the Ortega brothers, representing the *Tercerista* (Third Way) faction, maneuvered to gain
the loyalty of the entire Proletarian faction and one or two
members of the "*Guerra popular prolongada*" (Prolonged people's war, GPP) faction, headed by Tomás Borge.

Daniel Ortega, a man characterized as "lacking in grac-
es and personality," nevertheless was a cunning strategist and
politician, and back in 1984 he managed to win the candida-
cy for president among the directorate, and marginalize the
more charismatic and popular comandante, Tomás Borge.[2]
Daniel Ortega, of all nine comandantes, had the patience and
the will to take the mantle of Somoza and build a family dynasty that would eventually rule the country.

The Sandinistas, despite all their protests and denials,
were Marxist-Leninists in the mold of Fidel Castro. As such,
they considered "liberal bourgeois democracy" as something
of an obstacle on the path to socialist transformation. And so
the elections of 1984 that Daniel Ortega won with over 67%
of the vote, were described by one comandante as a "nui-
sance," but one "which disarms the international bourgeoisie,
in order to move ahead in matters that are for us strategic."[3]

Clearly, democracy in any meaningful sense was no more on their agenda than it was on the agenda of the elites of Washington. Indeed, for the "Vanguard of the vanguards," it was unthinkable that the people would lead.

That was certainly the conclusion one might come away with from reading Roger Miranda's book, *The Civil War in Nicaragua,* or Stephen Diamond's *Rights and Revolution: The Rise and Fall of Nicaragua's Sandinista Movement.* These two books, more than any others, filled in the gaps left by the official Sandinista narrative of the Nicaraguan Revolution, and they changed my own understanding of the Sandinista Revolution when I finally read them many years later.

Miranda's book was an insider account of the Sandinista comandancia: Before he defected to the US, he had been the secretary of the Minister of the Defense, Chief of the Popular Sandinista Army, and brother of then, and current, President Daniel Ortega, Humberto Ortega. Citing Miranda's book, *The Civil War in Nicaragua,* I wrote elsewhere that by the time of the Sandinista victory "the US had cut off aid to the Somoza government of Nicaragua and the government of neighboring El Salvador, hoping to defuse the violence in the region. When the Sandinistas took power, they immediately began to funnel arms to other leftist guerrilla groups in Central America, hoping to establish an eventual Castro-Communist Isthmus. That didn't go over well in Cold War Washington and President Jimmy Carter was legally obligated to end aid to Sandinista Nicaragua as a result. The incoming Reagan administration sent Thomas Enders to Managua to negotiate a peace agreement in which aid would be reinstated if the Nicaraguans would end arms shipments to the guerrillas in El Salvador (FMLN).

"According to Miranda, despite 'three detailed proposals' and two follow-up phone calls from Thomas Enders to the

Sandinistas, the FSLN Directorate never responded. Instead, Ortega and other Sandinistas went to Havana for advice. After Ortega recounted the details of the meeting, Castro told him, 'Don't negotiate.' Less than two months later, 'Daniel Ortega launched a bitter attack against the United States at the United Nations and the truce was off.'"[4]

The Contra War, then, was an avoidable war. And contrary to what we believed in those years of the Sandinista Revolution (1979–1990), it was essentially a peasant war—albeit with important sectors of it funded and directed by the CIA. It was, to be precise, a peasant and a proxy war against a Marxist-Leninist vanguard party with a millenarian vision of a "Liberated Central America," allied with Cuba, and the Soviet Union. This Sandinista "vanguard" played its part in creating the war by alienating the peasantry with forced collectivizations *a la* the Russian Revolution under Lenin and Stalin, arming the communist guerrillas throughout the region and following Castro's disastrous advice not to negotiate with the Reagan administration. And the US responded to what it saw as a Soviet incursion in its "sphere of influence" by arming the Nicaraguan "Contra" peasants.

In any case, the "armed resistance" in the form of "the first significant 'Contra' military attacks," according to Miranda, weren't carried out by Somoza's ex-National Guard nor by "counterrevolutionaries" of any sort. In fact, they "were carried out by frustrated Sandinistas under the leadership of Pedro Joaquín González [a Sandinista peasant]."[5] While it's true that former members of Somoza's national guard were counted among the Contras, "the maximum number of guardsmen in the Contras was only about four hundred," an estimate confirmed by "Sandinista spokesman Alejandro Bedaña."[6] According to oral history recorded by Timothy C. Brown, former State Department liaison to the

Contras, two of the eldest Contras were soldiers of the original Sandinista Army, and one had been a personal bodyguard of the "General of Free Men" himself, Augusto C. Sandino. The latter, Alejandro Pérez Bustamante, was by then too old to be a soldier, but he did support work for the Contras because he believed that "if Sandino had been alive during the Sandinista's revolution, he would have been a contra."[7]

The Contra war, while indeed funded by the US government, was a civil war that pitted thousands of disaffected campesinos against the Sandinistas and their urban supporters. Moreover, according to Miranda, the US aid to the contras was "only a small fraction of the amount of aid the Soviet bloc sent to the Sandinistas." In a section of his book entitled, "How to Provoke a Peasant Insurrection," Miranda argues that the cause of the war was the fact that "the Sandinistas reneged on their promises of political pluralism, a truly mixed economy, and international nonalignment, and pursued contradictory political and economic routes, with predictable results."[8]

In fact, the peasants weren't really on the Sandinistas' radar. Miranda says that "Somoza, the dictator, had been defeated mainly by urban workers and most of the middle and upper classes who had little sense of, or indeed true interest in, what the peasants thought and wanted. Somoza had kept the rural population poor mainly by denying them access to vast land holdings, but he allowed a largely free agricultural market economy in the countryside, which at least permitted subsistence living. The Contra War was fueled by peasant disaffection with the Sandinista government's step backward toward collectivization. The Sandinista leadership, influenced by the Cuban experience, didn't understand that what the peasants wanted was a piece of land and the resources to cultivate it. They didn't want cooperatives, production units in which peasant families worked together and share the produce of the land. The collectivization and other programs assured the alienation of the peasants, declining production, and in an agricultural country, a failed economy."

Miranda concludes that all this drove many peasants into the Contra army, making the Contra War a widespread rural insurgency so that "by 1987 Contra forces operated with considerable impunity in well over half the country."[9] None of this, however, negates the fact that the CIA recruited Argentinian fascists, fresh from the genocidal slaughterhouses of the dictatorship to train Contras in torture, terrorism, and other brutal criminal activity and bring the Sandinista government and its supporters to their knees—or, as then Secretary of State George Schultz said, "make them cry 'uncle.'" Nothing could justify the terrorist war the Reagan administration waged against Nicaragua in those years, but Miranda's testimony certainly throws that history into a new light.

Stephen F. Diamond is clearly more sympathetic to the FSLN and to a great degree he seems willing to accept the FSLN's narrative of the process, although he has a different understanding of its meaning. Diamond says that when the FSLN took power in Nicaragua, they had an extraordinary opportunity to democratize the country, but the comandantes refused it. The three tendencies, which had split from each other over strategy in the mid 1970s, had many problems to resolve in organizing a post-Somoza Nicaragua, but "at no time did any of the three tendencies ever surrender their perspective of becoming the vanguard in front of a mass movement... The idea of a mass movement...itself becoming the vanguard, or rather, training, organizing and selecting its own vanguard, was completely foreign to all three wings of the Frente."[10]

Some argue that the FSLN played a key role in the revolutionary process of Nicaragua and "earned" its place as the vanguard. While it's certainly true that the fledgling FSLN, with its membership of 500–1000 militants,[11] provided critical assistance at different points of the struggle, it's also true that in the major events of the struggle, the people were the key protagonists, often in scenes without any sign of the FSLN. Three major moments in the struggle demonstrate this fact. First, there were the "riots" in the wake of the killing of *La Prensa* newspaper owner and editor, Pedro Chamorro, in January 1978, when the struggle against the Somoza dictatorship "turned a corner" and some 30,000 took to the streets. The "mob" chose clear, strategic targets to attack, which were "key to the Somoza-dominated economy." Diamond points out that in this series of actions, culminating in a funeral where some 120,000 gathered to bid farewell to the journalist, "neither the FSLN nor the middle class opposition played a leading role."[12]

The uprising of Monimbó, an indigenous community southeast of Managua, a little over a month later represented "the most dramatic example of this mass opposition movement." When some 2,000 residents of the community gathered to rename their plaza after the martyred Pedro Chamorro, they found themselves quickly surrounded by National Guardsmen who lobbed tear gas and fired on the crowd. "Instead of fleeing in complete disorder, as the Guard had no doubt expected, the crowd resisted vigorously" with rocks and fireworks. The battle between the residents of Monimbó and Somoza's national guard went on for two weeks before the guard finally took the town and in the process killed two hundred or so residents. Diamond says "only a handful of FSLN cadre took part in the Monimbó uprising, and they were only sent in after events had begun."[13]

The most impressive action in which the people acted as their own "vanguard" began just a little over a month before the final victory when the FSLN carried out an action in the capital of Managua hoping to "sting Somoza and Carter, but not to win final victory." Stephen Diamond wrote "the populace of Managua surprised them. Thousands of "irregulars" formed their own militias and demanded a final confrontation with the Guard." What was to be a three-day guerrilla operation turned into a three-week mass uprising. The FSLN finally called the "*Repliegue*," or retreat, to Masaya, and the uprising subsided briefly. But the people of Managua continued to act as their own vanguard. Diamond writes that "when the official Frente [FSLN] forces reentered Managua on the 19th of July, they found the city already liberated. The population itself had done the job. A similar process took place in dozens of localities. As the National Guard withered in the face of the armed uprising, the population naturally took its place. This was not a passive mass, but a self-organized and armed populace that had thrown off the oppression of a brutal dictatorship."[14]

Humberto Ortega later reflected on the way that the "vanguard" ended up attempting to extinguish, rather than fan, the flames of discontent. He said, "we could not stop the insurrection... The mass movement went beyond the vanguard's capacity to take the lead. We certainly could not oppose the mass movement, stop that avalanche. On the contrary, we had to put ourselves at the forefront in order to lead it and channel it to a certain extent."[15]

Diamond speculates, "perhaps without the presence of the Frente, broadly based democratic institutions would have taken hold." Instead, the FSLN spent the next year disarming the people and convincing the real liberators of Nicaragua of their need for a vanguard. In large part, the Sandinistas were successful—except in the countryside with the peasantry, as we saw earlier. Throughout the entire revolutionary struggle, and into the "reconstruction" after the victory, the FSLN "confirmed its organizational principles as lying firmly within the Stalinist tradition."[16]

Both Miranda and Diamond believe that the FSLN National Directorate's hunger for power resulted in many missed opportunities. The insistence of the National Directorate on arming not only the FMLN in El Salvador—the sticking point in negotiations with the US—but also guerrilla insurgencies throughout Central America, from Costa Rica to Guatemala, was extremely problematic. The policy no doubt came out of an apocalyptic Marxist vision of a "revolutionary Central America," that was entirely un-realistic: during the Cold War neither Carter nor Reagan would have allowed such a thing. But the policy did have the effect of increasing tensions in the region, and it led to vio-lent backlashes against social and popular movements, and it cost the lives of thousands of innocent civilians. Diamond believes that "if the Frente had believed in democratic pol-itics, they might have taken the opportunity of the gener-al strike in the wake of Pedro Chamorro's assassination to organize new political parties and trade unions where open discussion of Nicaragua's future could have taken place. Such an organizing drive could have greatly altered the character of Nicaraguan politics—away from the inevitably violent and tragic confrontations with the National Guard, to a situation where, because the regime no longer held the political will of the population, it would no longer have controlled even its army. Then the military force of the regime could not have been stopped from simply withering away."[17]

We have no way of knowing if this counterfactual condi-tional view would have played out the way Diamond imagines it would have, whether, for instance, the Somoza regime would have simply "withered away" in the face of emergent democratic forces or not. Yet it most likely would have meant avoiding the regional war that cost 30,000 Nicaraguan lives and 75,000 more lives in El Salvador—not to mention those killed in Honduras and Guatemala. And a commitment to democracy and the strengthening of democratic institutions by the Sandinistas would very likely have had long-term positive consequences on Nicaragua's political culture and made it much more difficult for the reemergence of "Somocismo" in any form, including Orteguismo.

After Ortega lost his second bid for the presidency in 1990, and the rule of the Sandinistas came to an end, the FSLN underwent a number of splits, each one allowing Daniel Ortega to further consolidate his grip on power and eventually become the sole powerful caudillo of the FSLN.[18] He cut a deal with the right-wing former President Arnoldo Alemán, the infamous Pacto (Pact), to maintain control and power between their two parties, the FSLN and the Liberal Constitutionalist Party (PLC) and keep other parties out.[19] The Pact also helped Ortega avoid charges for the rape of his step-daughter, Zoilamérica Narváez. One agreement in the Pact resulted in a change in the electoral law that enabled a presidential candidate to win with 35% of the vote in a first round, and this had allowed Ortega to take the presidency again in 2006.

By 2010 Ortega had been in power three years, and the FSLN had become a relatively conservative institution, only slightly distinguishable from the other caudillo-led parties. The FSLN had been at the forefront of a conservative battle to impose some of the most restrictive abortion laws in Latin America—and Latin America is home to five of the seven most restrictive countries in the world.[20] The move was Ortega's way of ingratiating himself with the Catholic Church so as to regain power. Since that time, Ortega has gone on to rule the party, and the country of Nicaragua, as his personal kingdom. A later pact with big business, along with constitutional reforms eliminated his partner in the earlier pact, sending Alemán into obscurity and making Ortega effectively the new "King Somoza."[21]

When I arrived in 2010 I met a number of people willing to talk about the increasingly dark political situation in Nicaragua, but Ernesto and Fernando Cardenal, both of whom I'd interviewed and recorded in 2004, weren't among them. In response to a query for an interview, Ernesto wrote back an email, dated June 3, 2009. He said, "it wouldn't be advisable for us to talk about the political issues of Nicaragua because there's not a free climate for doing so" (my translation).

Cardenal's reluctance to speak on film was understandable given that, in relation to previous statements he had made about Ortega, including calling him a "thief," and "the betrayal of Sandinismo," the President had begun a campaign of persecution to punish the aging priest-poet. [22] Nevertheless, I found many others in Nicaragua prepared to help me understand the current political reality. Among them was former Sandinista commander Victor Hugo Tinoco, then a parliamentarian as member of the Sandinista Renovation Movement (MRS). Ortega, now effectively controlling most if not all branches of the state, including the judiciary, had maneuvered to revoke MRS status as a party in 2008.

Tinoco met with me in his office at the Parliament in Managua in January 2010. He started off talking about a basic conflict that has characterized the Left in Latin America and the world, saying "two theses have developed in the struggle within the FSLN since 1990. There were those who developed the opinion that the struggle for social justice wasn't compatible with civil liberties, so there had to be authoritarian thought married to the proposal of social transformation. And there were those who saw these [ideas] as complementary, that social justice can only be attained through a process that profoundly respects civil social and individual freedoms, and furthermore that social transformations are only sustainable over time if they are built and sustained on the basis of respect for civil rights and liberties."[23]

These words provided a framework within which I worked as I continued puzzling over the political process of Nicaragua, and it helped me understand the complex panorama of Latin American politics that unfolded before me as I conducted interviews for the book I was working on. Tinoco also mentioned the oil money pouring into Ortega's personal account from Venezuela, and this raised questions that I knew I would have to take back to Venezuela when I eventually returned, as I did a year later, with Marcy. Certainly, ALBA was strengthening the left governments of Latin America as it had intended, but what impact was it having on the *people* of the region? In Nicaragua its main impact appeared to be to enrich and empower an emerging dictatorship.

An old friend, Daniel Alegría, had introduced me to a friend of his, a taxi driver named Mario.[24] Like Daniel, Mario was an ex-Sandinista who had come to hate Ortega, and Daniel thought he'd be a good person to show me around Managua and re-introduce me to the country. He was right.

One morning Mario showed up at my hostel to take me somewhere. We'd been arguing about Venezuela for a few days, in a good-humored sort of way. Mario was convinced Chávez was a dictator just like Ortega and he distrusted his association with the military. I was arguing that things appeared to be mostly on a good course in Venezuela, but left the question open since we didn't yet know where things would end up. Despite our disagreement about Venezuela, we had common ground in our views on the situation in Nicaragua under Ortega.

Mario was smiling broadly as he stood in the doorway of my room while I got myself ready to go.

"So tell me, how is it that the country with the most oil in the world could be having electrical shortages?" he asked.

I stopped. "What? What do you mean?"

"Oh," he said, coming towards me to make his point," so you don't know about all the electrical outages in Venezuela?"

I didn't.

"Sounds like they're in trouble, to me, *compa*," Mario said, shaking his head. Then smiling slyly, he raised an eyebrow as if to say, "didn't I tell you?"

CHAPTER TWELVE

THE REVOLUTION THAT WASN'T

That winter Marcy and I returned to Venezuela. It had been five years since we'd been there together, although I'd visited the country alone just over two years before. We got a room at the Posada Alemania for a week. The posada had been recommended to us as an inexpensive option run by people one friend described as "critical Chavistas."

Once a week the posada hosted political discussions, and in conjunction with presentations by other guests, they asked me to present on what I'd learned doing interviews with social movement activists in Latin America. It was an informal setting and some fifteen or twenty people gathered around the table and nearby in the large outdoor patio for the discussion. After my presentation, there was, not surprisingly, a long discussion about corruption and then the topic of nationalizations was raised. This, evidently, was Chávez's new economic strategy for building the "Socialism of the Twenty-First Century" after the disappointing collapse of the cooperatives. Despite the propaganda widely disseminated on the Left in the US (and to which I contributed my share), by 2011 nearly all Venezuelans, including Chavistas, were well aware of the fact that all but perhaps a tenth of the 150,000–200,000 cooperatives funded by Chávez starting in 2005 were "phantom," fake or had simply disappeared.[1] Now Chávez appeared to be implementing the more "tried and true" approach to building the "Socialism of the Twenty-First Century," that is, by replicating the twentieth century model.

After listening to the discussion for a while, I entered the fray with a question. "We've just had this long discussion about the incredible corruption and inefficiency that we'd agree is pretty much everywhere in the United Socialist Party of Venezuela (PSUV) and the state, and as a result, nothing is functioning well in the state or the party. And yet you're suggesting that the best approach to building socialism is to nationalize more industries that are functional and profitable, and give them over to this non-functional and corrupt state? Do you see the problem there?" I asked.

There was a moment of silence before the man facilitating the discussion agreed that this was, indeed, a problem. And then, incredibly, the conversation went back to the need for more nationalization.

Marcy and I met up with Juan Veroes and he mentioned that a newspaper had been taken over by the workers in Mérida. The occupation had been going on for a few months already, and he offered to take us over to the offices. It didn't take much to convince us to go.

We met with Judith Vega, a reporter for the two newspapers produced in the building, *Cambio de Siglo* (Change of Century) and *Diario El Vigía* (El Vigía Daily). She told us that the owners of the paper hadn't paid the staff for four months, so one day after the owners left, the workers took over the business. They hung a "Worker Control" banner off the balcony of the second story, and began putting out their own weekly paper.

In an article Marcy and I later wrote about the occupation, we said that "Venezuela has worker-run businesses in many sectors, but this action [was] 'unprecedented,' according to Hugo Peña of the National Workers' Union (UNT), one of Venezuela's trade union federations. 'There are no other cases of a group of workers deciding to take control of a media outlet,' said Peña, Unete coordinator for Mérida."[2] You would think that this action would have received support from a revolution, and a revolutionary people, but so far only Alexis Ramírez, a PSUV member of Parliament and later governor of the state, had come by to bring some food and other necessities. On the multiple occasions we came to visit the occupation, we were the only people we saw in the offices other than the workers themselves and their family members.

As we did interviews we realized that the workers were feeling this isolation, and the vulnerability of being without salaries and dependent on donations. They were running their own workplace now, but that, apparently, wasn't what they wanted. One of the workers explained what they hoped would be the ultimate outcome. "We're hoping that our letters will arrive on the desk of the President [Chávez] and the government will come in an take over the business and make us employees," she said. "Worker control," it seemed, was just too daunting, certainly much more so than joining the growing hordes of "rent chasers" with their government sinecures. What was beyond doubt, however, was that the "Comandante" would be able solve the problem.

In our article, published in both Venezuelanalysis.com and *Correo del Orinoco*, the government-run daily, we ended by noting that "the workers wrote to the Ministry of Communications in Caracas early this year, explaining their situation and asking for a meeting. They are optimistically waiting for a response. Whether or not they get the needed help will be a test of the government's willingness to follow through on its rhetoric advocating worker control. 'We are sure we will get the support we need at a national level,' Vega said."

Juan Veroes took us to the office that his community council had arranged for him to use while organizing projects and applying for funds from the government. The main project now was to get a new roof put on the clinic next door to his office.

"It's really in bad shape," he said, shaking his head. "Every time it rains, there are leaks everywhere. You shouldn't have that in a clinic." So Juan had done the paperwork and he was hopeful that when the money came through, people in the community council would get the work because there was a lot of unemployment in the community. A little later he took us to a meeting of his community council but there were only a handful of people there and for some reason or other that wasn't clear to us, the meeting didn't happen.

I caught up with Arturo again, hoping for an update on the agroecological projects that he and Ari Krawitz and I had filmed two and a half years before. I did a short interview with him in the lobby of the MAT building and asked him if the new agroecological policies of MAT had been implemented and funding had come through for the small farmers doing ecological agriculture. He laughed. "Nothing. Nothing came of it. They haven't given anything to the small farmers and all the money is still just going to the conventional 'Green Revolution' agribusiness with pesticides and commercial fertilizers."

Arturo accompanied us to meet his friend, Mariá Vicenta Dávila, who had been doing community organizing, particularly among women, in the páramo town of Mucuchíes.[3] We interviewed Arturo on the bus going up to the páramo, and then did a couple of short interviews at an artisan's center before walking up to María Vicenta's house.

We stopped first by the vermiculture project the women had started under Mariá Vicenta's inspiration. They'd gathered compost from houses all around Mucuchíes and were hopeful that they'd soon be producing excellent fertilizer for the community. There was only one problem, and that was transport. The will was clearly there: the infrastructure had been built by the women's own hands, using rocks gathered from the mountain slopes, and money to buy cement drawn from the women's own savings. What they needed was a modest loan to buy a truck, and for that Mariá Vicenta had gone back and forth to Caracas, pleading with people in the government, as well as making presentations at the MAT in Mérida.

We sat down on a crudely-built wall and looked down on the dried up remains of the worm bins. It was in the back yard of someone's house and it occupied nearly the whole area. The women hadn't managed to get a singe bolivar for their project. The compost, then, stopped arriving when their truck broke down. The project came to an abrupt end, and the worms had all died.

Mariá Vicenta was visibly saddened by the experience and she referred to the problem obliquely in her interview with us a little later. As a Chavista, she felt that Chávez's "plan of the community councils is really good but that this plan shouldn't blot out those solid, grassroots organizations that have grown up locally," which she felt was happening. She complained about the problem of the "paternalistic attitude of dependence: do it for me, search for me, direct me." But clearly that attitude hadn't been there among the women with whom she'd worked on the vermiculture project. They had, in fact, displayed considerable independence, and from that autonomous space where they worked they asked only for a loan. But perhaps that's why they hadn't gotten it. Perhaps they were just *too* autonomous.

Taken together, all this information indicated a strongly top-down process underway in the country, regardless of the rhetoric of "participatory, protagonistic democracy." This became clear to us when we interviewed a young woman who was working at our posada at the time and who we'll call Ana Luz. One night when she and Marcy and I were alone in the kitchen Ana Luz told us about her experience as a grassroots Chavista activist. She and her fellow PSUVistas brought problems in the community to the attention of local PSUV directors, but it seemed to her that the concerns were never relayed any further up the chain of command. "Above the local PSUV is the state [of Mérida] bureau, and they are under the national bureau. That bureau is under the top ranks of the party, and then there's Chávez. So you see, nothing ever gets all the way to the top," she said. Then she added, wistfully, "if only we could get our concerns to the *Comandante* [Chávez]." Then she looked away thoughtfully, as if she was searching once again for how she and her fellow activists might be able to contact Chávez.

This fit the usual narrative on the problems with the "Revolution." From the beginning my friends—all my friends—had been complaining about the corruption among the ruling clique. I heard it so many times that I could almost predict when it would be coming up in a conversation, and almost the exact words: "Chávez is pure, but all those around him are corrupt." It was repeated so often that it began to sound like a single script everyone was reciting from.

While I was living in Venezuela I only rarely thought to question this "script,"—but I never expressed my thoughts on it aloud. The Chavista worldview, like that of most of the socialist left, is utterly Manichaean: Chávez and the Bolivarian "Revolution" represented for Chavistas all that is good, and aligned against it was utter evil: US imperialism, the oligarchy, the "*escuálidos*" (quislings, squalid ones), "*apátridas*," (stateless persons or traitors), Colombian paramilitaries, and citizens of the empire who disagreed with Chávez. In this, the socialists of the twenty-first century were only the slightest variation on the real socialists of the twentieth century. But while the latter made a clear ideological distinction between the messianic proletarian class and the evil bourgeoisie, the former based the distinction on loyalty to a single personality, the "Comandante."

I found the black-and-white thinking that lacked any nuance increasingly annoying, as well as the fact that no one wanted to raise the obvious question: Chávez ran the country so why is he doing nothing about corruption? This question would eventually lead to many others, but I would have to go outside of the Chavista circles to find the answers.

I had once raised the question about impunity, cronyism, and corruption under Chávez with Juan Veroes and he had shrugged and laughed, as if to say, "Isn't it obvious?" "You just can't go after your own family," he said. "Look, we're in a war here, a struggle to build a Revolution. If you start shooting people on your own side, where are you going to end up?" I argued with him and asked him where he thought Venezuela would end up if Chávez doesn't start getting rid of corrupt officials. Juan saw my point. "There will come a time," he said, "when Chávez can go after them. It's just not the right time now."[4]

It was the "Myth of the Fortress," as described by Leszek Kolakowski, in operation. The forces of the Revolution (in his myth, the Communists) "are in a permanent state of war with the old world; they are defending a fortress besieged on all sides by the forces of the old order. In this besieged fortress there is only one goal: to withstand the siege. And whatever furthers this goal is a good thing. In the besieged fortress every conflict, every dispute, is catastrophic, every sign of weakness a triumph for the enemy, every relaxation of the penal system a calamity," especially as concerns the enemy to whom no quarter should be offered. Kolakowski emphasizes this latter point, saying, "in a besieged fortress it is out of the question to seek allies in the enemy camp." And this fortress mentality results in two disastrous consequences. First, "it requires the besieged to perceive the whole visible world outside the fortress as the enemy, preventing them from swelling their ranks and so strengthening their forces, and cutting them off from all values and possibilities that lie outside. And within the fortress itself it creates a military hierarchy based on blind obedience and intolerant to criticism."

When the smoke of the battle one day clears and the besieged defender in the form of the rifleman emerges from the fortress back into the world beyond the reinforced ramparts, he sees the victims of what he thought were only his "defensive" volleys: certainly some of the enemy would be dead, but so would many friends. Worse yet, Kolakowski tells us, is the sudden recognition that the commanding officer who had led the "defense" of the fortress "enjoys giving orders so much that he would rather deceive his soldiers by inventing a siege than do anything to promote peace, for with peace his power would vanish. Power is dangerous; it wants to last forever, and the less it is controlled, the more easily it can maintain itself. This is why power—not just on a subjective whim, but by virtue of the workings of a historical mechanism—invents its own myths."[5] In Venezuela, I would come to discover, the "mechanism" was the oil wealth gushing out of the earth, and the myth would be the "petrosocialism" or the "Socialism of the Twenty-First Century" that Chávez would proclaim.

Marcy and I left Venezuela after a few weeks, returning home with a sense of uneasiness about the whole situation in the country; we were particularly concerned about the verticalist nature of the PSUV that Chávez had founded a little less than four years earlier.

I returned later that year, in August, passing as I usually did through Bogotá to Cúcuta, and then going on to Mérida by bus from San Cristóbal. I landed at Teatro Colibrí and after spending time with Betty and Humberto, I went off to see what had happened to the worker occupation of *Cambio de Siglo* and *Diario El Vigía*.

Arturo joined me and we walked with our cameras over to the office where the banner, "*Control Obrero*," still hung from the second story of the building. Inside we found only two of the workers left, as all the others had moved on. Judith and her partner agreed to do a follow-up interview. Judith said she was disappointed that, despite all their efforts, Chávez hadn't responded to their call for help. She clearly didn't understand why. I asked her if she thought Chávez had read our article about the situation in *Correo de Orinoco*, and her letters to him. She nodded. I asked her what she felt that said about Chávez and the Bolivarian project. She shook her head and then looked at me as if to indicate she didn't understand the question, but she said nothing.

As always, I went looking for my friend Juan Veroes. We met up at the Café Paris Tropical and sat at a plastic table under an umbrella in the shade of the jacaranda trees and drank *café marrónes* and caught up. I asked him how things were going on the project of a new roof for the clinic. He laughed and waved the question away. Then he said it had been approved by the national government, but as the money went through the state governor, the latter awarded the work contract to friends—a company that was run by a COPEIista.[6] No, he said, shaking his head, the unemployed people of the neighborhood had gotten no work out of the project.

A few days later Arturo and I went to do an interview with a Uruguayan couple, friends of Arturo's who were living in Barinas. They had received a tract of land along with a number of other people when Chávez expropriated a large finca in his home state of Barinas. Now Ignacio and Jimena Birriel were in a struggle to hold on to their finca, a thirty-three hectare plot they called Mama Pancha. They were about the only ones who were producing on their land, and they were using agroecological methods in the process.

The hundred or so other families, Ignacio explained to us, lived in the hills of Barinas; they were middle class folks, most of whom never even came by to visit their parcels. Ownership of the land was dependent on both production and residence, so only Ignacio and Jimena were legitimate owners of the land. Now the others had formed a community council and were in the process of selling the entire plot of land, but Ignacio wouldn't go along with it. "It's illegal," he said. "We were given this land to produce on, not so we could turn around and sell it." I asked how they could manage to sell the land if to do so was illegal. Ignacio smiled wryly and said, "by bribes. The government of Barinas is controlled like everything else, by mafias."

His community council would not allow him time to speak before it, and when he did manage to speak at the meetings, they refused to record his statements. He was essentially eliminated from the record.

Then someone set fire to his land. His crops had been destroyed. Next, their neighbor, who had left his own parcel fallow, but on whose parcel the community well was located, refused Ignacio and his family water. Ignacio went by night to the well and furtively pumped water out. Then the well was poisoned. Finally, in recent days he'd received death threats. A group of armed men had arrived and threatened his life.

His house was a palm *choza* or hut with no walls and within ten or so yards off the road. It was night, and we sat in the hut drinking coffee under a single light bulb as he explained his situation. Every car that drove down the dirt road made my heart race, especially as Ignacio would stand and peer out into the darkness to try to identify the passersby.

Ignacio's situation appeared hopeless to me, but he managed to hang on for a couple more years before he and his family suddenly left, presumably back to Uruguay. I don't know what happened to the *finca*, but with the departure of Ignacio, what little production that had been undertaken on that massive estate came to an abrupt end.

In early 2012 Marcy and I went to Chile, Argentina, and Uruguay to gather the final interviews for our book. In Montevideo we planned to meet Raúl Zibechi, who had promised to write a foreword to our book. I particularly wanted to sit down and talk with him about social movements in Latin America, as I knew I would be doing a major part of the "theorizing" for our introduction. By the time we met him at his apartment, I'd had plenty of time to puzzle over the main question I wanted to ask him, and I posed it almost as soon as we sat down for coffee in his kitchen.

"What do you see as the main problem confronting social movements in Latin America today?"

Without hesitation he replied, "Oh, well, the progressive governments, of course."

I was baffled by the response. "How so? What do you mean?"

He looked at me as if he thought the answer was obvious. "These new left governments are all following in the footsteps of your 'War on Poverty.' You remember that, don't you? It was the policy of the [Lyndon] Johnson administration, designed by the architect of the Vietnam War, Robert McNamara. The idea was not to resolve the problem, but to design a way of hiding it or keeping it quiet. You may recall that McNamara went on to become the president of the World Bank and there he applied the same 'solutions' all around the world. So this current crop of left governments is doing the same thing here. Welfare programs are developed out of new income from extractivist industries, but the real problems aren't addressed by this approach because they've problematized poverty and not wealth."

Our meeting only lasted a little over an hour, but by the time Marcy and I left, I felt Raúl had opened up a whole new vista on the interviews. Over the next few months as I translated and we edited the transcripts, we found themes emerging that confirmed, over and over again, Zibechi's critique of the left governments, a critique that some felt he was hesitant to apply to Venezuela.[7]

Marcy and I wrote a review for NACLA of a book co-written by our friend Roger Burbach and two contributors to our own book, Michael Fox and Marc Becker, in which the writers considered the changes of the Pink Tide governments as experiments in "Socialism of the Twenty-First Century."[8] We wanted to give the book a good review, but found much of the thinking, with the exception of Marc Becker's chapter on Ecuador, muddled by an inconsistent definition of terms (such as "socialism"), wishful thinking and an uncritical acceptance of the line of the governments of the region, especially the Bolivarian government. It was becoming increasingly apparent to me that the term "Socialism of the Twenty-First Century" had little or no content in the Latin American context, especially if one worked from the traditional Marxist definition of "socialism" as a "new mode of production." Not only did the predominant mode of production in Latin American countries remain capitalist, with the exception of Cuba, and to some degree, Venezuela, none showed significant signs of moving beyond economies based on extraction by transnationals. The new model of "development" after the import-substitution model had died, and with it, any hope of national industrialization.[9] In Cuba, a state capitalist model that the Bolivarians appeared interested in replicating, had developed under the rubric of "socialism,"but it had nothing of the "Twenty-First" century about it.[10] Cuba, it seemed to me, was a decidedly twentieth century Marxist-Leninist holdout that was only slightly more appealing than North Korea or Vietnam. And Venezuela now seemed to be going in a similar direction, with even fewer prospects for success, judging from the increasing chaos in the country.

The "Pink Tide," then, was characterized by a post-neoliberal capitalist economic model propelled by extractivist industries working to inflate and supply a commodities boom and states that allowed some of the wealth from the sale of those commodities to "trickle down" on the multitudes neglected throughout the "neoliberal nineties." But did a greater role for the state and increased welfare policies constitute "socialism" in any sense? Was this not the clearest example of what Zibechi meant by "problematizing poverty and not wealth"?

I thought over Raúl's critique of the governments of the region and wondered about Venezuela. I wondered, and I considered all the contradictions as we finished up our review and as I rewrote my introduction to the Venezuela chapter of our book. And on the day that I finished another, probably the seventh or eighth complete rewrite of my Venezuela introduction, I got a call from a friend telling me that Chávez had died. I knew then I would have to return to Venezuela before I finished writing my introduction.

CHAPTER THIRTEEN

LOCKED OUT AT THE BORDER

There were a number of changes that enabled me to come at the problematic of Venezuela and the Bolivarian process from a different angle in the Spring of 2013. First off, something I had discounted, but later came to see as crucial, was the fact that I had been teaching composition and critical thinking at Berkeley City College. I imagined my class might have had an impact on my students; I had no idea that it would transform me and how I saw the world. In my first critical thinking class I had taught students to begin with a working thesis and then assemble evidence to support it. I chose readings that offered my perspective on the world, and that formed my own, and students', expectations of what the final essays would look like, both in form and content. That simplistic approach got me through the first semester, but I found it boring—and also dishonest. It was what Paulo Freire called the "banking model of education," in which the teacher puts the ideas in the students' heads, and the students give them back with a little interest. There is no dialogue, no broad discussion, diversity of opinion, nor clash of viewpoints. In my defense I could argue that the ideas I offered the students were likely different from what they were accustomed to in their educational system thus far, but now I'm not even so sure of that, given that many of my students had grown up in liberal/radical Berkeley. In any case, the "banking method" was the way I'd been taught, and that was clearly the reason for my having hated school so much that I took decades to finish my studies. And like the abused that grows up to be an abuser, I was teaching as I had been taught.

The second semester I brought readings with contrary perspectives into my critical thinking classroom, and I introduced students to opposing viewpoints that I had them debate. As time went on, I tried to sharpen contradictions, encourage students to explore contrary points of view, and come up with their own perspectives. That was great for my students, but as I looked at my work with Venezuela, how well had I implemented my own approach to "critical thinking"? In my film I'd certainly raised questions at the end, but I also had ended on an upbeat note, celebrating the Bolivarian "Revolution." In my articles I'd done the same, which was why they were so widely published and disseminated. I'd gotten lazy in my writing and thinking, as I'd discovered in my own classroom.

Unforeseen events had made it possible for me to leave teaching in the summer of 2011, and it had been a great relief as I'd found the contradictions of the "educational system" too great to deal with any longer. I realized as much when I opened my first class that spring semester by telling my students that the university was definitely no place to get an education, but the ideal place to accrue an enormous debt. I suggested if they wished to get an education they might try getting a card at the public library three blocks away, and spending their time there. At the end of that semester, I managed to get laid off and went on unemployment for a year or so, during which time I was able to dedicate myself completely to work on Marcy's and my book.

As I did my research in preparation for my next trip to Venezuela, patterns began to emerge that I hadn't seen before, almost certainly because I hadn't looked for them. There was, for instance, the scandal at FONDEN, the development fund constantly filling up with cash from oil sales, and constantly being emptied out, where billions had gone missing and the accounts were all hidden.[1] FONDEN is the entity, funded by the state oil company *Petroleos de Venezuela Sociedad Anónima* (PDVSA), that funds development and social programs. It operated as a secret corporation with Hugo Chávez at the head, and directly under him Finance and Planning Minister Jorge Giordani (who was later dismissed from the government by President Nicolas Maduro) and other trusted government ministers. Funds came and went, but a great part simply disappeared from what some have called "Chávez's piggy bank."[2] As Francisco Toro pointed out in an August 2011 report, at the time "42% of public spending was secret" and, unsurprisingly, US $29 billion of US $69 billion dollars had gone missing.[3]

There were the "mega-projects" that were never built, or were abandoned half-way, but which in either case cost hundreds of millions—even billions—of dollars, like the national paper company, *Pulpa y Papel, CA*, the "vanguard socialist business." That project today remains a fenced empty field with a cleared space and nothing else, which alone has cost Venezuelans more than half a billion dollars.[4] No doubt much of the enormous amount of missing money went into foreign bank accounts of government officials, and as patronage to Chávez supporters in the community councils, as later reports showed.[5]

All this was just the tip of the iceberg of corruption in the country, and it had been increasingly clear to me that Chávez must have known about most, or all of it. And now Chávez was dead, but the mysteries continued. Worse yet, all those corrupt people who surrounded the "Comandante," as the Chavistas themselves characterized them, would now be in charge.

Any analysis of what was going on in Venezuela under the Bolivarian "Revolution," like it or not, had to start with Chávez. He was as crucial a part of the narrative as Jesus is to the *Gospel of Mark*. I didn't want to acknowledge that for the longest time, but as I puzzled over what was happening in Venezuela this much became clear to me. So this time around I started with Chávez himself, and I found the biography by Cristina Marcano and Alberto Tyszka a particularly interesting and enlightening study on the man behind the public mask.[6] Their work as opposition journalists was fair, but critical, and certainly a far cry from the adoring propaganda of the government that fed the popular mythology about Chávez.

While left media in the US was uncritically applauding the Bolivarian "Revolution," and denying, or minimizing the problems of the country, *Reuters*, *The Economist*, *The Guardian* and other mainstream ("bourgeois") media were putting out some damning reports on Venezuelan government policies, and I found these enlightening.

Noam Chomsky had once said "My impression in general is that the business press is more open, more free, often more critical, less constrained by external power and external influences," which was how he explained why he read the *Financial Times*.[7] So I began focusing on the business press, and it immediately became apparent that in the nation supposedly building "protagonistic participatory democracy" it was practically impossible to get information on the Venezuelan government's finances and when information was available, it was frequently incoherent and contradictory, as cooked books usually are.[8]

Secondly, I began looking at all the information I was finding from a different perspective, that is, not so much on how it supported what professed to be a "socialist" or "left" state, but from the perspective of what encouraged and nurtured "organized civil society" or social movements. Marcy and I had spent the previous year assimilating the interviews of social movement activists from all over Latin America, and their testimony had clarified for us a left alternative that was quite distinct from anything in the Marxist, socialist, or communist traditions. A social movement perspective proper was emerging for us that, while as yet inchoate, was distinctly its own.

The emerging social movement perspective also fit with my own view of the world that was shifting and growing as a result of reading about and observing indigenous social movements, reflecting on my own experiences, and working in the Twelve Step programs. This all went into my personal preparation for a return to Venezuela, but my recovery process was central. I'd had a relapse on marijuana nearly four years before and had returned a year later to a recovery program with a greater sense of humility and willingness to "work a program." In Anonymous programs this requires open-mindedness, a desire to focus attention on one's own comportment and, above all, honesty. I began "working the steps," that is, methodically undergoing a process of self-examination with a sponsor, guided by the Twelve Steps.

I'd just finished this process and now felt more aware and open-minded. In the Anonymous programs we are called to "practice these principles in all our affairs, and when we are wrong, to promptly admit it." The idea that "our common welfare should come first;" that "our leaders are but trusted servants; they do not govern;" and that Twelve Step groups "should be autonomous except in matters affecting other groups or [the program] as a whole" and the entire Anonymous organization "…as such, ought never be organized," all fit well with the emerging social movement political perspective that I had found so compelling.

With all this preparation, I left for Venezuela on April 9, 2013, planning to meet my friend Marc Villá in Caracas and go with him and his media collective to record the Presidential election that pitted Hugo Chávez's handpicked successor, Nicolas Maduro, against Henrique Capriles Radonski. As critical as I felt toward the Bolivarian Process, I still supported it and its candidate at the time.

Capriles had run against Chávez just six months before and lost. Chávez and his followers had pulled out the stops as Chávez referred to his opponent, Henrique Capriles, as a "pig," among other things,[9] and others, like Chavista commentator Mario Silva, suggesting that he was a homosexual, and a "Zionist" Jew.[10] In fact, Capriles was a fairly moderate (and, incidentally, straight) democrat who had made his reputation in 1999 as the youngest member of Parliament and as mayor of Baruta and governor of Miranda. The queer baiting of the opposition was quite an ugly feature of the campaign with Chavista assemblyperson Pedro Carreño leading the charge in the National Assembly itself, and others following, with accusations that the "drug addicts" of the opposition were leading "a gay prostitution ring." Carreño made these charges as he had images of men hugging projected on a large screen in the

National Assembly. All this was accompanied with the usual qualifications of the opposition as "extreme right-wing" (*ultraderechistas*), "fascists," and "oligarchs."

Nicolás Maduro, ten years older than Capriles, also of Sephardic Jewish ancestry and raised Catholic, cleaves to a peculiar mix of New Age and Marxism-Leninism. While Maduro is a follower of Sai Baba, he also has a very long history in the socialist Left, specifically in the Marxist-Leninist "verticalist" faction of the Socialist League that emerged when the party split in the mid 1980s.[11] Maduro had played a number of roles in the Chávez government, as member of the National Assembly, then as Foreign Minister before becoming Vice President from 2012–2013. If Capriles offered the possibility of a return to the bygone days of Venezuela before Chávez, Maduro's history indicated a possible hardening of the process under a man who not only believed in the strong leadership of someone like Chávez, but also very deeply in gurus and vanguards, and therefore top-down command structures.

I usually route my trips to Venezuela through Bogota to avoid the hundreds of dollars in taxes the Bolivarian government lays on air travelers to Venezuela: Bogota turns out to be half the price, even including a round trip flight to Cúcuta. From Cúcuta it's a couple of hours negotiating the border and six hours from San Cristóbal to Mérida by bus, so the travel time is nearly the same, or less, as a route through Caracas. What I hadn't counted on was the fact that the Venezuelan government would inexplicably decide to close the borders nearly a week before the elections.

Arriving in Cúcuta, I hailed a cab and an old man who introduced himself as Gerónimo loaded my suitcase in his trunk as I climbed in the back seat. I told him I was on my way to the border and he said it was closed.

"What do you mean, 'closed?'" I asked.

"Si señor," he said, "the Venezuelan government closed it yesterday [Tuesday, April 9th] for the elections on Sunday. But we'll go and see if we can get you across the river. I have a friend who can do that."

"Why did they close it off?"

"Because Maduro doesn't want Venezuelans to go in and vote."

"You mean the Venezuelans living in Colombia?"

"*Exacto*. He knows they'll vote for Capriles, so he's locked them out."

"How does he know they'll vote for Capriles?" I asked.

Gerónimo shrugged. "Well, if they left Venezuela, they probably didn't like that process, right? So they'll go back to try to vote out those scoundrels."

I had no better theory to propose, among the many I would encounter in the next few hours, so I left it there.

At the DAS (Colombian immigration) they refused to give me an exit stamp. The official smiled and said, "Sir, if we give you an exit visa you're stuck, because the Venezuelan office of immigration on the other side is closed until after the elections." I asked him why he thought Venezuela had closed their border and he shrugged. "They do things. Lots of strange things. I don't know why. All I know is what they say, that they're closing the borders for the elections." He shrugged and smiled again.

Gerónimo offered to help smuggle me across, but I decided not to count on the generosity of the Bolivarian National Guard if I got caught. Gerónimo took me back into town and on the way I decided to go to Pamplona rather than spend time in Cúcuta.

Cúcuta, when included in guidebooks, which is rare in itself, is described as "hot and dusty" and the writers go on to emphasize that "there's really no reason to visit" this chaotic border city other than to see the ruins of Santander's mansion near the border. Pamplona, on the other hand, was once described to me by a dear friend as something like a smaller version of Mérida, tucked away in the mountains.

I arrived in Pamplona and got a hotel room and immediately called my friend Marc Villá in Caracas to let him know I wouldn't be arriving as planned. Marc, being an independent sort, is quite willing, in normal times, to question everything. But these were not normal times; this was electoral season and his theory of why the border was closed was even harder for me to swallow than Gerónimo's. We found each other on chat.

"The government has locked up the borders," I wrote.

"No, it was the CNE (the National Electoral Council)."

I didn't buy that. They don't have the power.

"Why?" I asked

"Because of the paramilitaries along the border. They're trying to keep them out so they won't come to Venezuela to vote."

"Come on man. You don't believe that do you?" I wrote. "Do you really believe the paramilitaries take out visas to cross the border?"

"Some do," he replied.

Close the border to stop a few dozen Colombian paramilitaries who want to vote in the Venezuelan elections? That assumes paramilitaries had such a commitment to "democratic processes," or to messing with them, that they would be willing to try to cross borders just to vote—in another country's election, no less! It was all mind-boggling. I decided it was time to find a more credible theory for the sudden closure of the Venezuelan border nearly a week before the elections. I went a block down to the central park of Pamplona, the center of the city, and arrived just in time to buy the last copy of the local paper, *La Opinión*.

The border closing was front-page news. The lead article announced, "The border closed until Monday" and beneath that read the headline, "Supply of Gas is Guaranteed." The reference here was to the black market gasoline from Venezuela, where it sells for around US $.25 per gallon, which is smuggled across the border and sold all up and down the highway outside of Cúcuta for a few dollars a gallon—but still less than the actual price in Colombia, which is higher than the US price. Such is the special nature of a "black market" that has near-official status in Colombia.

I called Juan Veroes on Skype to get his take on the situation with the border closure. "Yes, they caught thirty Colombian paramilitaries," he told me earnestly. I replied that when I saw their faces and had their names, I'd believe it. And besides, there were problems with the story.

I asked him, "when you go to vote, do they ask you for your *cedula* (national ID card)?"

"Yes, and you have to be on the rolls with your address and it all has to match up," he said.

"So do you think the Colombian 'apatridas' are on the rolls? Do you think they have *cedulas*?"

"No, of course not."

So much for that story.

AFP reported that Maduro closed the borders with Colombia and Brazil due to a US plot to use Salvadoran hit men to kill him.[12] This seemed on par with many of the other "plots" that Maduro "uncovered," such as the one in which the US "infected" the late President Hugo Chávez with cancer.[13] Then there was the plot Maduro supposedly uncovered that the US was sending hit men to kill Capriles and blame it on the Chavistas. Like the dozens of plots Chávez claimed to have uncovered, however, the evidence, if it ever was present-ed, was always thin and controversial and never up to the level of reasonable proof. Still, Maduro knew, as Chávez did, that creating paranoia rallies the masses around the flag and brings out the voters for you—if they think you'll defend them from the enemy you've created. It certainly worked for Bush with all those Al-Qaeda "sleeper cells" supposedly wandering zombie-like around the US just waiting to be activated prior to the 2004 elections. Maduro, and Chávez before him, apparently counted on the same tactic working for them.

In Pamplona I watched the election from a distance. I even pretended to work. I wrote a bit; I recorded an interview with the rector of the university, strolled up and down the streets, though my "strolling" sometimes felt more like "pacing." I attended a couple of Anonymous meetings and made friends. And I searched the papers for some indication of when the government might open the border, but there was nothing but speculation, and little of that.

On Sunday, April 14th, the day of the election, it was pouring down rain. The dry vegetation covering the mountainsides welcomed the drought-breaking downpour, but I was anxious to get to the bus station and I faced the common traveler's dilemma in this part of the world: walk the five blocks to the bus terminal when the weather allowed, enjoy the stroll, and arrive refreshed, or pay twice what the locals would pay to have a taxi drive me there and arrive cranky and in need of exercise. I waited for a break in the rain and walked to the terminal.

The terminal was nearly empty. It was, like many provincial terminals in Colombia, neat, clean and orderly, a sharp contrast with stations on the other side of the border in Venezuela. I quickly found a *colectivo*, a van hoping to fill up with passengers for the trip to Cúcuta, and I took my seat, the first client. Soon we were on our way, descending the mountainside from the cool heights into the balmy valley.

Descending on San Jose de Cúcuta one is immediately struck by the number of trees in the city, a fact that is immediately lost on the visitor on entering the city itself. While it isn't the chaos of most of the cities of its neighbor, Venezuela, it's a busy, hectic border town on one of the busiest borders of South America. The name, Wikipedia tells us, comes from the combination of the saintly Joseph (Jose), the father of Jesus, and the Barí native word *cúcuta*, meaning "house of the goblins." There is surely plenty of the latter lurking in the often-sweltering streets of this burgeoning border city, but most of them are employed trafficking contraband from Venezuela into Colombia.

But the contraband smuggling, the black market currency deals, the tanks of cheap gas, all came to an abrupt halt from April 9th until the morning of April 15th. Food rotted in the trucks, money exchanges closed their doors and the supplies of cheap Venezuelan contraband dwindled, and then the floodgates opened again.

CHAPTER FOURTEEN

THE ELECTION

I watched the election results that Sunday evening, April 14 from a dark room smelling of Pinesol in a cheap hotel in Cúcuta where I fell asleep with the television broadcasting live updates. Sometime around midnight I woke to discover that Maduro had won the presidency. The vote had been very close, just over 200,000 votes, a 1.5%, margin. Capriles was calling for a recount, and Maduro promised he would have one.

And so, I thought, the process that Chávez had initiated would continue in some form, somehow, for some time. But with such a close margin, I knew the country was in trouble. Only in the morning, when I finally crossed the border, would I have the faintest idea of just what that meant.

The day started early for me. I was up at six to get to the border, but I didn't manage to leave my room until seven. I went to the terminal in Cúcuta to change money and prepare to cross the border. Although the prices vary somewhat between the money changers, I settled on a friendly woman who took the time to explain the mathematical logic of the change to me; to write the numbers down and do the calculations a few times so even this mathematically-challenged poet would have some clue to what the numbers meant. I had traded millions of pesos for thousands of bolívares, but I still felt rich.

I asked her how the border closing had affected her and she replied with anger in her voice, "well, imagine losing a week of work. You see from the calculations I make that we work on small margins. I'm not wealthy. And this closing really hurt bad. Thank God I was able to get over here [from Venezuela] today." I asked her what she thought of Maduro winning and she volunteered, "Look, [the PSUV] is ruining Venezuela. People are afraid to invest there because they're afraid they'll lose everything and that the government will take it over. And look at what happens when it does take over: it doesn't take care of the businesses it nationalizes. It runs industries like PDVSA in the ground. And people are suffering. Imagine losing nearly half the value of your money in devaluation, and then having the highest inflation in the world. My aunt was going to buy a house here in Colombia and she went to Venezuela and bought a business and two houses. It shouldn't be that way. It wasn't that way before. Venezuela was doing well. It's gone to hell and Maduro is going to continue the destruction."

I thanked her for her opinion, stuck twelve thousand or so bolívares in my pocket, and returned to my room to pack and head to the border.

The line between Colombia and Venezuela is invisible but dramatic. The streets of Cúcuta bustle with activity but there's a clear order to things, unlike Venezuela, which always feels chaotic, and yet relaxed; where the motorcycles ride with or against traffic and pass on shoulders, between cars and even over the sidewalks; people jaywalk and manage to cross the dangerous streets any way they can. After passing through the various checkpoints I put my head down and went straight to the bus stop.

I caught a bus to San Cristóbal and from there transferred to a bus headed to Mérida. The bus was already full, but I found a seat in the back where an animated and angry conversation about the election was underway. The five men and one woman all had purple little fingers, indicating that they had voted, and from what I gathered of the conversation, they were all in the opposition. I say "from what I gathered" because my ear, as always, was having difficulty adjusting to the Venezuelan accent from the Colombian, and I also had difficulty focusing on the words with music blaring out of the two speakers on either side of the back of the bus where I sat.

One of the travelers, the most angry and loquacious of the bunch, was animated and would have appeared fierce were it not for the smiles that appeared spontaneously as he spoke.

"We've got to take this into the streets and let Maduro know that he's president 'por ahora,'" he said, referring to Hugo Chávez's famous words after his failed 1992 coup when he said he'd failed to take power "*por ahora*" (for now). The speaker smiled slyly, and continued. "We've got to let them know that we're not going to tolerate their fraud. They've got to recount, vote by vote."

Another person mentioned he'd heard about ballot boxes that had been thrown away in the state of Barinas and another wondered aloud how many people had risen from the dead just to vote for Maduro.

The proclamations and protests continued as the bus started and the driver put on the road music track, a non-stop series of *cumbias*. This is the borderland, and Colombian *cumbia* is something everyone here can dance to, or in this case, conspire, with. Once the engine started, between the music and the rumbling diesel, I lost track of the conversation and pretended to sleep. I occasionally considered intervening but thought better of it since I had little to contribute and didn't want to break up what seemed to me to be a friendly political conversation, even if I didn't necessarily share the politics.

As we left the outskirts of San Cristóbal and moved further into the state of Táchira, an opposition stronghold with a Chavista governor, I saw the driver get on his cell phone. At some point, he took a turn off the road. The Spaniard sitting next to me said, "wrong move. This road is *estancada* (blocked)." He was also calling a number to find out which roads were not blocked by the *guarimbas*[1] that were now rising up in nearly every city in the country. The bus returned down the road we'd just left, made another turn and soon had taken three or four different roads and, at the advice of someone on the other end of the cell phone, had again changed direction.

We finally hit the guarimba in Coloncito, a little town on Highway 1, the Panamerican highway, near the border of the state of Mérida. Up ahead was a huge demonstration and blockade, huge for a small town like Coloncito. We got off the bus and, while the driver conferred with the passengers about what to do, I went off to a small nearby shack to get my cup of coffee for the day, in hopes of killing a caffeine headache. I returned with my coffee and a brownie and quickly ate my breakfast as the driver carefully made his argument that they should return to San Cristóbal. The Spaniard interjected that the roads into San Cristóbal were also blocked, but the driver seemed to think he could make it back to the terminal. At last, after some discussion, it was decided that now was a good time to find a cafe to have lunch.

We drove past the guarimba down an open road, and stopped at a roadside cafe/filling station where I invited the Spaniard to a *cafe marrón*, an espresso with just a shot of milk. My headache disappeared as the sweat dripped off my nose. The Spaniard, it turned out, was a professor of chemistry at the University of the Andes in Mérida, and had once been a Chavista himself.

"I supported the revolution. It did some great things, like helping poor people get an education and come out of poverty. Those were some good programs. Several years ago I started to see how the inflation was destroying the country, how Venezuela was going in debt even with all its oil wealth. How is that possible? Such mismanagement, such corruption and impunity. I couldn't support that any more. So I've gone over to the opposition."

We walked back to the bus and I decided to stay and try to find a way to Mérida. A young man, who introduced himself as Luis, joined me and we watched the bus pull away, leaving just the two of us. We gathered our baggage and started walking toward the guarimba and the road leading to Mérida.

The crowd was energetic, even angry, but not threatening. As we approached the other side, I stopped Luis. "Luis, would you mind if I got out my video camera to record some of this?"

"No. Go ahead. I'll watch your stuff."

I thanked him and walked into the crowd. I recorded the national guardsmen, facing off with the crowd, then turned for a pan of the crowd. Almost immediately a number of demonstrators approached me and asked who I was. I looked at them and froze up for an instant. What should I tell them? How would they react? Would they tear me up in an instant?

"I'm a gringo from the United States," I said.

To my relief they celebrated. They patted me on the back and spoke into the camera. "We're here to call for a recount. Capriles is President! He won the election."

After a few minutes I returned to Luis and we continued down the road, interviewing people as we went, some Chavistas, some Capriles supporters. We walked and as we walked my shirt soaked with sweat. Sweat dripped in my eyes and ran down my glasses as I walked faster, trying to keep up with Luis. We tried to get on one bus that was turning around, but it was full and pulled away. And then, at some point, a man in a jeep said something to Luis and Luis asked where he was going.

"I'm headed to Mérida," he said. "You need a ride?"

Luis and I thanked him and as the conversation continued and he loaded our baggage in the rear of his jeep, he smiled and said, "I'm happy to have people from the opposition with me! Get in!"

The driver, whose name I didn't get, drove fast, passing everything on the road. As we entered El Vigía he found his way up hillsides on dirt roads and got us around the guarimbas while I interviewed Luis.

"I used to be a Chavista," Luis said. "I mean, there were great programs that helped the poor. But this process has polarized the country. It's not possible any longer to have a dialogue. We've got to resolve this problem, but the *oficialistas* (Chavistas) attack the middle class. I'm in the middle class. I work hard, but I get nowhere. We have the highest inflation in the world. With the devaluation, it's impossible to live. Our salaries barely make our living expenses. And we're all in this situation. The opposition is really growing for those reasons."

"We help all these countries, building hospitals in Argentina and Bolivia and we spend all this money giving oil to countries while our own economy is being destroyed. This shouldn't be happening. We have all this oil, but it's being wasted, and being used by these corrupt people. And it has to stop."

Over the next hour or so as we sped towards Mérida, Luis continued to explain why he'd joined the opposition. He talked about the closing of businesses in the country and the destruction of small business owners, the middle and working classes. He asked, "If from one day to the next the government can come in and expropriate a business, who's going to invest when there's no juridical guarantee of property?" Certainly the government was giving the poor "a kilo of flour, a kilo of rice and a kilo of corn" where previous governments had done nothing for the poor, but at what cost? What was this teaching the poor about initiative, and doing things for themselves? It was keeping them poor and more dependent than ever on the government. And was this even sustainable in the long term? The government was expropriating land that was under production and giving it to the poor who did nothing with it because they didn't have the means since the government had nationalized other businesses like Agroisleña, the major producer of fertilizers, and other agricultural products in the country (now nationalized as Agropatria) and they no longer produced the needed inputs for agriculture.

The driver then introduced himself as Ricardo Uzcátegui and I asked him if he'd always been in the opposition. "No. Before there was no opposition. There were COPEIistas and ADecos, but we were all Venezuelans. The country wasn't divided as it is now."

Luis said that the night before when he went to vote in San Antonio where he lived, the National Guardsmen at the voting booth told him they opposed the Bolivarian process. And they'd told him that the Chavistas had lost the presidency because former supporters had stayed home or gone over to vote for Capriles. Luis talked about the illegal use of state money to pay for Maduro's campaign. "We all paid for his campaign," he said, indicating Ricardo, the other passenger and himself. "And then there was the abuse of the cadenas [obligatorily broadcasted presidential transmissions] that blocked out Capriles's few campaign broadcasts. And all the free airtime Maduro had on government television, which is now most of the television. If you go into the small towns, unless you happen to have cable television, all you have access to are the government stations. So they're creating an ideology, and a fanaticism of a single point of view." Luis continued talking and I recorded and listened, and Ricardo and his partner agreed and threw in additional details to Luis's narrative and missing pieces of the puzzle of the Bolivarian Revolution fell into place for me one by one.

We passed a thermoelectric plant that, Ricardo explained, was owned by the Chinese. "They're going to be administering everything. They're taking over everything: the teleférico (aerial cable car or ski lift) of Mérida, everything."

The texts were coming in all this time, fact mixed with rumor and, based on that mix, unsubstantiated extrapolations and conclusions. Were ballots being destroyed? I didn't know. But Luis assumed it to be true. "And if Maduro is so sure of his victory, why is he burning the physical ballots?" He looked down at his phone again.

"They're inaugurating Maduro now. I just got a text," he said. And so, I thought, there would be no recount after all. Or if so, it would now make no difference. Maduro had been scheduled to be sworn in four days after the election, but they moved it ahead to the day after to guarantee his taking the office. After all, the winner in such a situation is the one who's sworn in first.

Ricardo left us near a trolley stop where we hailed a cab that took Luis home first, then headed for Plaza Bolívar where I'd take a room before getting in touch with Betty and Humberto. I knew if I called them, they wouldn't let me stay in a posada but would insist that I stay at their house at Teatro Colibrí. Tonight I wanted to be alone, and ready to record whatever happened as the night went on.

The taxi got within eight or ten blocks of Plaza Bolívar after moving around various guarimbas, and at last I let the taxi driver drop me at a place from which I could walk the rest of the way. I passed two or three guarimbas where students were burning tires and waving flags, their faces covered with scarves. I moved through their midst and they raised the wire that crossed the lanes of the Avenue of the Americas so I could pass.

The guarimberos seemed to be having a good time, and the police just sat quietly in their jeep and watched. Everyone obviously had the same script. I walked the familiar streets of Mérida, pulling my suitcase behind me and headed up Avenida 2 finally arriving at the Posada Alemania. There was a new person at the desk, a man a few years younger than me with a beard and glasses, named Marco Castillo. He checked me in and I went to my room, dropped off my pack, and immediately set out to go back to Plaza Bolívar to record the *cacerolazo*[2] and the Chavista demonstration. As I prepared to leave, Marco warned me against going. "There's likely to be violence. It's very dangerous out there tonight." I thanked him for the warning and left with my camera. I stopped by a street food vendor to get an arepa since I hadn't had much lunch nor any dinner. While I ate a group of Chavistas came by and began throwing rocks at a window where people where banging on pots. Then they moved up the street menacingly toward the fires. I finished my arepa and walked across

Plaza Bolivar to see what was happening at the Chavista event. Compared to the guarimba in Coloncito, this group of Chavistas was a distinctly less friendly crowd, something I hadn't expected. Then, at the edge of the park I ran into the "Poeta" Simon. We talked and several Chavistas came up to greet us. They were friendly and I began to relax. Suddenly, there was a commotion and I turned to see a large contingent of Chavistas charging up the street towards another group of people protesting with cacerolazos. Simon started to follow, crying out, "we've got to stop them! They're going to destroy the city!"

I put my hand on his shoulder.

"Don't they have a right to protest? Is it now illegal to protest in Venezuela?"

"No, no, it's just that they want to burn the city down!" he replied angrily.

"Simon, they're lighting tires and trash on the street. There's no danger of fire. They're just angry and want to protest."

He stopped, then nodded and dropped his gaze. After a moment he said, "You're right. People say they want to burn down the city. But really a lot of these people are bourgeoisie, and if they set fire to the city, they'd burn up their own shops. It doesn't make sense, does it?"

CHAPTER FIFTEEN

AFTER THE ELECTION

In the morning I stopped by the front desk of the guest-house and talked with Marco.

He said that the night before he'd seen Chavistas on motorcycles attack and beat a group of protestors. One of the Chavistas was carrying a pistol. This attack was corroborated later by a Chavista friend who acknowledged that "people in red t-shirts" were attacking people, and they even attacked her ordinarily a-political landlord, who was holding a sign calling for peace, splitting her scalp open with a rock. My friend, however, didn't want to acknowledge that these violent people in red t-shirts were "Chavistas" even though we both knew that in Venezuela only Chavistas wear red t-shirts.

Both Marco and I suspected these "motorizados" or motorcyclists were Tupamaros, and I tried to imagine Malacara participating in such activities. I drew a blank on that

image, but I also knew that he was fully capable of joining in if he felt obliged to defend the "Revolution" from
the "counterrevolutionaries." The fact that the "Revolution"
might have won by fraud and, in the name of "protagonistic and participatory democracy," have violated the principle of democracy, would be a trivial problem compared to
the defense of the "Revolution": in fact, the history of most
revolutions shows that every imaginable crime can be jus-
tified by revolutionaries. Somehow the Chavistas managed
to justify their beating of the opposition parliamentarian
of Mérida, William Dávila, the day after the election and
during a session of the National Assembly. And no doubt
they also missed the irony of their calling him "fascist" as
they beat him.

In a bad sign for the "oficialista" Chavistas, the dissatisfaction began spreading to all sectors of society. As Marco pointed out, cacerolazos were taking place all over the country and
"not only in 'bourgeois' neighborhoods, but also in Petare
and 23 de Enero," that is, in traditional Chavista strongholds.

Rumors and suspicions abounded, and with good reason.
Capriles, in a news conference, claimed that over three thousand "irregularities" had occurred in the elections. According
to the opposition leader, these included 535 damaged voting
machines; 1,176 voting centers where Maduro received more
votes than Chávez had and one where Maduro received 1,000%
more than Chávez had. "Who can believe that Maduro had received more votes than Chávez when nearly a million Chávez
voters voted [this time] for Capriles?" he asked. Capriles went
on to claim that witnesses were pulled by force from 286 centers that represented altogether 722,983 voters. He went on to
say that there were "assisted votes" affecting 1,479,774 voters
and that more than 600,000 dead people, including people
over the age of 100 (and even some over 120) had voted.[1]

Chavistas and their supporters proclaim the Venezuelan electoral system to be "the best in the world," quoting, or misquoting, Jimmy Carter who, in the case of this election, praised *the voting machines* used and the fact that they functioned well, but was more guarded on other aspects of the elections themselves. In a final report on the 2013 Venezuelan presidential elections released in May 2014 the Carter Center said that "while the Venezuelan population, political parties, and candidates generally have shown confidence in the performance and integrity of the automated voting machines when counting votes, such trust is not automatically transferred to the particular conditions under which the vote took place, or to the capacity of the system to ensure that every registered voter can vote once and only once."[2] The report also noted "a number of inequities in campaign conditions, both in access to financial resources as well as in access to the media, which reduces the competitiveness of elections."

The English version of the full report, which in May 2014 was promised "in the coming months," has yet to appear, but the Spanish report has been released.[3] The full report noted a congruence between the electronic and the paper receipts, something the opposition never felt was much of an issue. What concerned the opposition were allegations of multiple voting, especially at the moment when the Internet went down just as the polls were closing. At that moment, many in the opposition allege that Chavistas were brought in to vote a second, or more times, which was why the opposition was more concerned with an audit that would match fingerprints to votes. The Carter report acknowledged that the CNE had done a biometric (analysis of fingerprints to check for multiple voting) but that "unfortunately, this audit didn't have the expected effect of publicly dispelling doubts and questions raised by the MUD (Democratic Unity Roundtable)" because no one in the opposition was allowed to attend that audit to verify the results.[4] The Carter Center acknowledged the fact that the Internet had gone down for nearly twenty minutes just as the polls closed, but they attributed no importance to the fact.

The Bolivarian government admitted it shut down the Internet "for three minutes," (although it was widely reported that the net was down for twenty minutes) just as the polls were closing, supposedly to stop hacking attacks on government Twitter accounts. Spanish journalist Emili J. Blasco published his account of what happened that night in *Bumerán Chávez*, based on the testimony of Leamsy Salazar, Hugo Chávez's, and later Diosdado Cabello's, bodyguard who defected to the US in January 2015. According to Blasco's account, Capriles had been ahead in the polls all day, but when the Internet inexplicably shut down in Venezuela (he mistakenly says it was at four p.m.), things began to change. Salazar told Blasco about his experience with Cabello in a secret location where top Chavistas sat with computers and monitors watching the elections, calling squads of the faithful out to vote "with false identification cards (*cedulas*)." The falsification of the vote was coordinated with the CNE and other agents, including future vice president Jorge Arreaza, and it also required the shutting down of the Internet so as to "better manage with greater guarantees the complex volume of data fed into the informational system parallel to that of the PSUV." Blasco wrote that "this final operation of Chavismo required time, and so a little before six in the evening, when the electoral centers should have closed, the CNE announced an extension of the voting time until eight o'clock, where needed."[5]

This account raises many questions, and it is also questioned, not only by Chavistas (most of whom know nothing about it) but also by solid opposition analysts like Juan Cristóbal Nagel, co-founder of, and writer for, the website, *Caracas Chronicles*. While he recognizes Blasco as a "well-sourced" Washington journalist who "has a reputation—at least in my book—for getting things right,"[6] he sees contradictions between Leamsy Salazar's account and that of Eugenio Martínez, aka "Puzkas," an opposition expert in the Venezuelan electoral process. Nagel concludes "What nobody disputes, however, is the anomalous spike in Maduro's votes in voting centers that stayed open until late. Both Blasco and Puzkas, as well as the MUD technicians, acknowledge that this was the crux of the issue. This is the heart of Capriles' claim of fraud."[7]

We may never know the answer to this mystery, but there is a ring of truth to the charge that Chavistas have been organized to engage in multiple voting in close elections. The issue came up again in the December 2015 National Assembly elections when the CNE again illegally extended the polling hours in areas of the country and witnesses saw people lined up who had already voted, as was clear from the indelible ink on their pinkie fingers.

Regardless of what fraud occurred that day, Maduro slipped into the presidency on what in the US would have been a hanging chad in Florida. In fact, he seemed to think he'd won a mandate and was apparently insulted that anyone would question his skimpy margin of victory. He continued on his tack of insulting and denigrating the increasingly diverse opposition, which now clearly included people who had voted for Chávez just a few months before. He said that the United States was behind the opposition's "plot" to refuse recognition of his victory, and that "we won't negotiate with the bourgeoisie." Meanwhile, Capriles called for calm. It was Bush and Gore all over again, but *al tropical*. But in this case I no longer knew who was playing Bush and who was playing Gore.

I left the hospedaje the next day and I walked through Mérida, avoiding the places where I'd once hung out with all my old Chavista friends, like the Café Paris Tropical. I didn't call friends, like Malacara, and I dreaded running into him or other acquaintances because I wasn't sure I'd be able to keep my thoughts to myself.

And my thoughts were changing. All the doubts I'd had over the past few years were being confirmed and I felt myself slipping into neutral and slowly moving in reverse to all I'd ever thought. Gear-tooth-by-gear-tooth, I watched myself going over the past few days, and all the hints over the years that had indicated to me the questions I was only now beginning to allow into my conscious mind. I asked myself how I missed this before, both the utterly partisan morality and the underlying authoritarianism of the Bolivarian movement? The experience reminded me of my first doubts about the divinity of Christ, which led to the next questions: "and if x is not true, what about y? And then we have to look again at a…"

When I called Betty and Humberto later in the day, I found that Betty was out of the country at the time, but Humberto insisted that I come right over with my baggage. "We have a room ready for you, brother! Come on over." I walked over and stopped at the newsstand to buy papers. I bought *El Comercio*, *El Nacional*, and *El Universal*, all opposition papers. I didn't bother to pick up the Chavista press. I stuffed the papers in my bag and walked over the viaduct to Teatro Colibrí.

Humberto greeted me with a big smile and a hug and took my suitcase into their house. Each time I'd arrived at their theater complex, they took me closer to the center of their home. This time I got the room next to theirs in the main house and then Humberto fixed coffee for us. Soon his sister-in-law and a friend of hers, both of whom were visiting from Barinas, came in and we all sat in the kitchen drinking coffee. The subject, of course, turned to the elections, and I was relieved to see the discussion was good-humored. Humberto was a Chavista, but a very critical one. Betty's sister was in the opposition, as was her friend, and to their angry comments about the fraud, Humberto made casual, friendly jokes and came back with smiles and more jokes. That was how Humberto was: an actor, puppeteer, storyteller, musician, in short, an artist and trickster to his core. With his many tricks, jokes, enactments of hilarious situations he'd passed through in his life, or tragedies he recreated as comic incidents, he had us all laughing and, for a time, forgetting the tense political moment.

Arturo came over in the afternoon and we went into the theater to look at some video clips for a movie we were working on about Occupy Oakland. Instead, Arturo and I ended up talking for far too long about the election, and I soon found myself in an argument with my friend. Arturo was defending Maduro, for whom he had voted, against the "fascist" Capriles. Just a week before I would have been listening and agreeing, though with some reservations. But now I was getting angry, especially when I heard Arturo repeating the same propaganda about Capriles, the "fascist" who represents the "oligarchy" and the "Empire [of the USA]."

"Arturo," I said, pleading, "Listen to what you're saying. What do you mean by 'fascist'? Last night the opposition was demonstrating peacefully, yes, with road blockades and little fires to stop traffic, but it was peaceful. And yet I saw Chavistas throwing rocks at them, attacking them. Who's the fascist there? And Maduro and all these corrupt people in the party who you know have been robbing the country blind for years with impunity, and have amassed fortunes, yet you call people in the opposition the 'oligarchy'? The Bolivarians have indebted the country to China, Russia, and to Chevron, and given them concessions to mine and drill and take out the wealth of the country, and you call Capriles an imperialist?" At last Arturo saw my point, and we dropped the talk of elections agreeing that they were all *malditos politicos* (damned politicians) anyway, and we got down to work.

That night the cacerolazos in Mérida were drowned out by a downpour that cleaned the air and left behind a dramatic silence. The next evening, the cacerolazos were back even more loudly, accompanied by fireworks. Betty's sister and friend excused themselves after dinner so they could join in the cacerolazo, and Humberto good-naturedly wished them a good time as they departed with pans and spoons to go to the roof.

I then learned a tangible lesson on how one can look and not see, listen, and not hear, that which is entirely visible and audible. I'd gone to the supermarket the first day back in Mérida and noticed that the shelves were full. Everything was very expensive, but I found what I was looking for. I returned to Colibri and reported I didn't know what everyone was talking about when they discussed shortages. All I saw were full shelves.

I should have known better, having lived in Nicaragua in the '80s. One would think I'd be more observant. One image in particular sticks in my mind from Nicaragua, 1987: a supermarket with a whole aisle of Worcestershire sauce, an item no one in Nicaragua had probably ever even tried.

A few days later I told Humberto I was going shopping and he asked if I could pick up toilet paper. Sure. No problem, I told the nonchalant trickster, who thanked me with just the glimmer of a smile as he went into the kitchen to make coffee. Betty was gone and he was living on fruit and coffee.

I went into the Yuan Yin Supermarket where I always shopped, asked where the toilet paper was and was told by an employee, whose job it was to scrape gum off the floor with a long-handled scraper, "no hay." I immediately began looking for napkins. There were two brands, located near the dairy where cartons of yogurt "hecho en socialismo" competed with the Táchira "capitalist" brand, and both brands populated the front of long shelves that were nearly bare behind the display.

Suddenly, my eyes opened as I walked down the aisle of mayonnaise, a long row of jars punctuated by a stack of pasta, and turning down another aisle of more mayonnaise and mustard, the other side of that aisle bare but for a few random bottles of salsas, soy sauce, and, of course, Worcestershire sauce.

Nothing had changed. But what just a few days before were the full shelves of a supermarket, I noticed today were nearly bare. Now that I could see behind the display, and now that I could understand the meaning of two aisles of mayonnaise, I began to understand how the deception worked. Certainties vanished suddenly like a card up the magician's sleeve and I needed someone to orient me in this strange world I thought I knew. So I decided on my way back to Colibrí to get in touch with Marco at the posada and see if I could take him out to dinner.

Back at Colibrí I unloaded what I bought on the table, and apologetically showed Humberto the napkins, saying there was no toilet paper. He smiled and shook his head. "It doesn't matter. Oh, and by the way, was there any flour?" I said I didn't notice and he shook his head again and repeated, "it doesn't matter."

I'd seen Marco a couple of times already, stopping by the posada to talk to him and get recommendations for people to talk to, books to read. I was already reading Damian Prat's book, *Guayana: El Milagro Al Revés*, having bought the last copy available at Librería Temas. Between the daily newspapers I'd managed to read a couple of chapters and had decided I needed to go to Guayana to interview him. Marco had also suggested that I get in touch with his friend Rafael Uzcátegui at PROVEA (*Programa Venezolano de Educación-Acción en Derechos Humanos*, Venezuelan Education-Action Program in Human Rights) in Caracas. Rafael also was an editor on *El Libertario*, an anarchist newspaper. I recognized PROVEA as a group my friend Arturo had volunteered for, and still highly respected. I also recalled that *El Libertario* had sponsored an independent World Social Forum of Caracas in 2006 that I hadn't attended because, at the time, I was convinced by the Bolivarians that they were being "sectarian," and, after all, were just a bunch of "bourgeois" youth who would rebel against anything.

I met Marco at a mall a few blocks from Colibrí. I invited him to Chinese food that was mediocre at best, but a relief from the usual fare of meat, rice, and yucca or plantain. We sat down to eat in the large dining hall and he began to tell me his story.

Marco joined the revolutionary communist Party of the Venezuelan Revolution (PRV) when he was sixteen. The PRV, split from the Venezuelan Communist Party in 1966, was a political organ of the Armed Forces of National Liberation (FALN), the guerrilla movement of the time. Marco made oblique references to having been part of the FALN, but we never pursued that subject since the present situation dominated our discussions. He did mention that he later went into the military where he served in military intelligence until 1993.

"You were in the military when the coup happened," I noted.

"Uh huh."

"What did you think of the coup?"

"I supported it. After the bloodshed in '89, the Caracazo, most of us did."

I paused. "That was Carlos Andrés Pérez, wasn't it? Acción Democrática. Part of the Socialist International…"

Marco nodded. The irony wasn't lost on him. "Exactly. In fact Cuban intelligence informed Pérez that a coup was in place as he was returning that night." The irony wasn't lost on me. While the Venezuelan socialists were sending the Army into the streets to shoot anti-austerity protestors, Cuban intelligence was collaborating closely with that government and would play a significant role defending it against the future leader of the "Bolivarian Revolution."

"The G2 (Cuban Intelligence Agency) has always played a complex, dual role here in Venezuela. Just like the United States. It's interesting how so many these days scream about US interventionism and interference, but what other country has allowed its sovereignty to be trampled on, opening its arms to a foreign government and allowing it to come in and direct policy as we have with Cuba?"

Marco drew a circle with his finger on the table. "So a movement starts here and it comes around and then becomes what it opposed in the first place."

"That's a Greek idea. It's known in Greek philosophy and drama as 'enantiadromia' and it's based on the Chinese idea of yin/yang, that anything reaching its conclusion turns into its opposite," I said.

"Yes," Marco said, "that's what's happened with Venezuela, all this resistance to US imperialism has turned into a wholesale selling off of the country to China and Russia, and other international capitalist countries, and turning the direction of the country over to Cuba."

I prodded him. "My friends in the US, my wife in particular, would ask, 'well, why would you want to invite US imperialism back into the country in the form of Capriles?' How would you respond to that?"

Marco smiled. "I told you I voted 'nulo' (no one, null). But really, on one hand you have an increasingly authoritarian variety of so-called 'leftists' who are on a witch-hunt against anyone who disagrees with them. They're destroying the nationalized industries, and selling them off to the Chinese and Russians, as you're discovering in Prat's book. They're destroying national capitalist enterprises that are the source of jobs for the people. They're giving small subsidies to people to buy their loyalty. They're buying up television stations, and have control of radio all over the country, where they broadcast their propaganda. Who would you rather go up against? Them or Capriles? We could deal with Capriles, and keep him in line. But these people [the Bolivarians] don't listen to us. They're arrogant and cynical and utterly corrupt."

"I'm sure my wife will also want to know how the Left plans to organize an opposition."

Marco shrugged. "We'll see if it manages to mount an opposition."

We moved down the hall to find a quieter place to talk than the large open area surrounded by food stalls. Everything was starting to close at 8:30. We found a table outside of a closed coffee shop and sat down for a few more minutes.

Marco told me he'd recently received a death threat.

"By whom?" I asked.

He shrugged. "I don't know. The Tupamaros, I think. But they don't say who they are."

"What are you going to do?" I asked.

He smiled wryly. "I take a 'zen' attitude toward it."

I thought of the Tupas I knew, like Malacara and Matute. They didn't seem like killers, but then again, I never could have imagined Chavistas chasing down people in the opposition, beating them up and throwing rocks at them.

On April 23rd the government began "militarizing" Corpoelec, the national electricity company, stationing military in installations to guard them against "vandalism and sabotage." Vice president Jorge Arreaza announced the measure, while Jesse Chacón announced conservation measures for the state to undertake.

Damian Prat had a different take in his April 24th 2013 column in *Correo del Caroní*. Prat saw the current situation as a political ploy by Maduro, "a 'McCarthyist' campaign of persecution of the workers accusing them of phantasmal acts of 'sabotage.' That's the government's way of avoiding responsibility for the black-outs, the disguised rationing, and the disastrous electrical service." He talked about the four thermo-electric plants that were bought for millions of dollars to deal with the problems in 2010. "Millions of dollars and bolívares were spent and the plants never functioned." Of the two he mentioned, one was painted red and the other wasn't even painted. They didn't provide enough power to "light a light bulb." "They were announced by Chávez himself, by Alí Rodríguez, the cabinet where Maduro and [Elías] Jaua sat [now President and Foreign Minister, respectively] and then-Minister [Rodolfo] Sanz, to be producing 800 MW in a few months that Sidor would use, and also free an equal amount of MW... toward the National Electric System."

Prat went on to write, "Persecuting workers, sowing terror, laying-off workers. That's what they're announcing. All this to hide their irresponsibility. Even the Chavista union leaders repudiate this ugly maneuver. For weeks they've rejected these accusations firmly and with clear arguments. They've said what we all know already: the cause of the problem is the absence of any investment or maintenance; the causes are the pathetic directors and the high officials put in office by the government; the poor state of many substations and installations in the cities. And we would add: for the nearly zero real investments (much money, the whereabouts of which is unknown) in generation plants and national transmission lines. For the destruction of [nationalized electric companies such as] Edelca, EDC, and Cadafe in the super-bureaucratic monster, Corpoelec, *summa cum laude* in inefficiency."

I was, at this point, half-way through Prat's book, a shocking tale of corruption, inefficiency, ideologized ineptitude, neo-Soviet bureaucracies characterized by servility to "El Comandante" who, according to Prat, had the Midas touch in reverse as he turned productive industries into dust as soon as he nationalized them.

While Chavista commentary dominated the five or so state television stations, the two or three private channels remaining were cautious in lending airtime to either side. I decided to try to watch the press conference Capriles had called for that night (April 24th) but he wasn't allowed to speak: the conference was interrupted by a "public service announcement" from the government in which it broadcast inflammatory images, literally, of fires, and supposed acts of violence by the opposition. Among these were the charges that Integrated Diagnostic Centers (CDIs) had been attacked and set aflame. In an interview in the opposition paper, *Tal Cual*, director of PROVEA Marino Alvarado claimed to have "used three direct sources" for its investigation into the supposed arson attacks: "people working in the centers, patients, and neighbors of the installations. A close examination of the information offered by public media was done. And, finally, [examination of] photos taken by people sent there."

According to Alvarado, none of the clinics were burned, even if five were "attacked" by "cacerolazos" and rocks were thrown and windows were broken and, in one case, a rocket was fired at a center. Alvarado went on to condemn those attacks but he also called for a dialogue with the government, but one that "had the minimal conditions of respect."

Chris Carlson dutifully repeated the government claims in an article he published at Venezuelanalysis without mentioning that PROVEA came to other conclusions. Communications Minister Ernesto Villegas accused PROVEA of "protecting fascists" and being itself a "fascist rearguard," without, of course, addressing the issues.

Throughout this time the blindness and intransigence of the international left press was the most disturbing for me. After initially publishing one or two pieces at one of my usual venues, I found it impossible to publish anything else. Even Upsidedown World, where I'd published a number of articles in the past, rejected my articles and decided instead to publish a pro-government article written by a San Francisco writer about the elections, based on government sources. I was told my firsthand articles from on the ground were, "not what we're looking for." When I asked what that meant, I received no response. I was getting a taste of what was to come.

It was beginning to look as if the messianic cult of "El Comandante" was unraveling badly, and with it, the Bolivarian Revolution. But there was another element of the Bolivarian Revolution. It was Humberto, and all the people like him.

Thursday night Humberto and I headed out for what he described as the *arepa de pinga* (the best arepa). Up above the Plaza Bolivar and near the Charlie Chaplin statue, was a hole-in-the-wall family business with a line out the door. "Artists, drunks, police, intellectuals, poets, everyone comes here for their arepas," Humberto told me as we got in line.

I could see why. I ordered *pollo frio* (cold chicken) with yellow cheese and it was delicious. We accompanied this with cups of *guanábana* juice, the first I'd had on this trip.

We left and Humberto drove us around Mérida slowly. I told him about the book I was reading, *Guayana: el milagro al revés* and he said he knew about the problem. He told me about a friend of his, a candlemaker who had a business he inherited from his father, who started it after fleeing Spain after the Civil War. "They produced eighteen tons of candles in a workshop. Then Colombians managed to get the paraffin from PDVSA and my friend couldn't stay in business. He managed to scrape by but now only produces three tons of candles a year."

Humberto pulled over to allow cars to pass. He was, after all, just driving. You can do that in a country where gas costs $.25 a gallon. He rolled down his window, lit a cigarette, and when all the cars had passed, he pulled out again and we were driving slowly through the night, down streets I'd never seen before.

"There are twelve of us boys in the family. My mother is seventy-two and she still works, getting up every morning to make empanadas. Of the twelve of us, only four are worth anything. The rest don't want to work."

"They're all unemployed?" I asked.

"No, but they do as little as possible to get by. They're all gifted mechanics, carpenters, and so on, but they don't want to work. They get just enough money to buy cigarettes and alcohol and they spend their time in that. And that's my country."

"I know about all the problems of my country. But to go back to the way it was before the revolution? My uncle gets a pension from the government he never would have had. Of course he lied to get it, but he has one. Maybe one day when my mother is no longer able to work, she'll get a pension, too. I don't know."

We turned on Avenida las Americas and slowly drove up the hill toward home. Humberto told me how he and Betty were the only Chavistas in the neighborhood. "People tell us we should leave. But we've been here forty years. We built this place ourselves," he said.

We sat out front of Colibrí, a towering white castle in the night. The gate opened and we pulled into the patio. We went inside. Humberto told me as we walked into the house how someone came from Caracas, no doubt a Chavista party hack, to try to convince him to take charge of a proposed school for toymakers. "How many students would there be?" Humberto asked the man. "Ninety," the man replied. Humberto shook his head. "No. No more than ten." "Ten?" cried the man in disbelief. "Yes," Humberto told him. "Because art can't be mass-produced. You can't teach ninety people how to be artists. With ten you can dedicate the time to cultivate the people and when you cultivate the people, they can go inside themselves and find their capacity to create art. Otherwise, you're just forming people for the factory." The man called Humberto "counter-revolutionary" and left.

"But it was he who was the counter-revolutionary," Humberto said, shaking his finger at me for emphasis.

We went in and said good night, and I went in my room, closed the door and got into bed with Damian Prat's book.

CHAPTER SIXTEEN

THE REVERSED MIRACLE OF VIRTUAL VENEZUELA

The images were startling: concrete blocks and brick walls collapsing; huge holes in tin roofs; bathrooms with urinals missing, or urinals without flush handles or simply a single semi-functional urinal fed with a hose of constantly running water coming out of the wall; huge paralyzed factories and rusting, broken-down machines; piles of industrial waste, garbage; and not a worker in sight.

This wasn't Detroit, but rather the facilities of Carbonorca, one of the nationalized industries of Guayana under the "Plan Socialista de Guayana" (Guayana Socialist Plan). Guayana is a region in the state of Bolívar and home of the once great Venezuelan Corporation of Guayana (CVG), otherwise known as the Basic Industries of Guayana. Guayana City, at the confluence of the rivers Caroní and the Orinoco, just over the state line from Monagas in the state of Bolívar, was once the city of the future. You can still see signs of that glorious past all over the city, even if the monuments are now chipped and faded.

Bordering the nation of Guyana, the Guayana region is the largest of the country, and an area rich in bauxite, iron, gold, and other minerals. The regional wealth led the dictator Marcos Pérez Jiménez to begin the construction of a steel mill at the site of present-day Guayana City, and the plant was 20% complete when Romulo Betancourt came to power in 1960. Betancourt had a vision for the development of regional wealth, to provide all the nation's manufactured goods consistent with the import-substitution industrialization policies that were popular at the time, so he made sure that the steel plant was operational by 1961. By 1962 the steel plant was not only providing the nation's needs, but also exporting 80,000 metric tons of steel and cast iron.

Through partnerships with international corporations, Betancourt was able to industrialize Guayana and provide highly-paid work for Venezuelans who flocked to the new, modern city looking for work in the industries. Through such partnerships and loans from international lending agencies like the International Bank for Reconstruction and Development, Betancourt was responsible for initiating the hydroelectric project at Guri with its "installed capacity of 4 million kilowatts, more than Egypt's Aswan Dam project."[1] Partnering with Reynolds Aluminum, Betancourt oversaw the founding of the aluminum industry with the company Venalum, which would soon be providing the nation's aluminum needs as well as exporting. To this, more industries like industrial coke, lumber, gold and the mining and refining of other exotic minerals would be gradually added.

While the CVG and its associated projects had ups and downs, they weren't in too bad shape when Chávez began nationalizing them in 2008. The year before nationalization, in 2007, steel producer Sidor had pumped out 4.3 million tons of their product, and other industries were also reaching their peak just as they were nationalized. But control by Chávez was the kiss of death, even though he later paraded out his "Guayana Socialist Plan," which promised to "reactivate" the industries. In fact, the decline was precipitous and immediate and by 2012 Sidor was down to producing 1.7 million tons of steel, and to less than half of that just two years later.[2]

While the drop in production and internal decay was occurring in all the nationalized industries, the collapse of CVG and the Basic Industries was emblematic of the failure of the Bolivarian dream to reintroduce import-substitution industrialization policies under the rubric of "endogenous development." They indicated, in fact, that the Bolivarian Revolution had not only been a catastrophic failure, but a lie. Nothing except stage sets for Chávez's television show, *Alo Presidente*, had been designed and created in Guayana during the years of Bolivarian rule, and even these had been left to collapse once the cameras were packed and taken back with their crews to Caracas.

I arrived at the guesthouse run by a German expat we'll call Carl, and his Venezuelan wife, Mireya. Carl was with the opposition and Mireya was an ardent Chavista so Carl had warned me to stay away from politics when the three of us were in the car together. Carl and Mireya met me at the modern bus station just as rain began to fall and drove me back to the guesthouse.

I had a room with a small refrigerator and an overhead fan, no television, but fairly consistent Internet access. As it turned out, the fan was the most important equipment in the room because without it I wouldn't have been able to sleep. Even the rain didn't cool the air down to a comfortable level—at least not for this gringo, accustomed to the climate of the San Francisco Bay Area.

The morning after I arrived, I decided to explore and try to find a newspaper or two. I took a bus into the center and after I bought papers and a few grocery items, I went out to look for a cab to bring me back to the posada. The taxi picked me up outside of a mall offered me a few minutes air-conditioned relief from the hot, Guayana sun. The driver listened with apparent interest to my tale of conversion from a convinced, but critical, Bolivarian, to a critical spectator. He laughed. "You were in virtual Venezuela for those years you were with the Chavistas. It's what the government projects out to the world, the 'Socialism of the Twenty-First Century' while behind that virtual world is a bankrupt society, a society of consumers who don't produce anything, but just live day to day. And a very corrupt government." He then passionately expressed the conviction, shared by a growing majority of Venezuelans, that the presidential elections two weeks before had been stolen.

Carl took me out the next day to visit the Basic Industries.

The industries were on the outskirts of the city, and it seemed to me that none of the factories appeared to be open as we drove through the area. Carl said they were still in production, although only for a few days per month. While that might have been true, there was no smoke coming out of the smokestacks of Venalum, Carbonorca, Ferrominera, or the other industrial plants; the parking lots were empty; immobile conveyor belts were rusted and so were the railroad tracks and railroad cars. The area looked, to say the least, underutilized and deteriorated.

Before I left Mérida I'd contacted Clavel Rangel at the *Correo del Caroní* to see if she knew how to get in touch with Damian Prat. He hadn't answered my emails asking for an interview nor returned my phone calls or messages. When Carl and I got back to the guesthouse I got an email from Clavel saying that Damian Prat would see me when he came into the office at four. I grabbed my camera and headed out to the street to find a cab to the *Correo del Caroní*.

I arrived a few minutes before Damian. When he arrived we went into a large reception area near to do our interview.

Damian began by addressing himself to the North American and European intellectuals who have been supporting the Bolivarian process for the past fourteen years. "Some of you in the critical, intellectual circles of Europe and the United States seem to think it's fine that in the countries of our Latin America there are arbitrary governments and processes full of abuses that in your countries you wouldn't consider allowing for a minute. No, in your own country you'd militantly reject the same things you seem to feel are perfectly fine to take place down here, so far way, where it's exotic and interesting."

I was taken aback. Damian knew I'd been supporting the Bolivarians up until just over a month before when I'd written a sincere paean to the late President Chávez.[3] And now he was right on the mark as he called me on it, and I felt it, deeply.

He said he was a political leftist and had been since his adolescence, but he'd never believed in this government of Chávez that was run by the military. Militaries don't make revolutions. "But of course you must know that this is no 'revolution,'" he said. It was, in fact, a throwback to an "antiquated left, one that had been debunked long ago." This Bolivarian process was based on what he called the "reactionary, retrograde model of Fidel Castro's 'revolution.'"

He and others in the democratic Venezuelan Left had been appalled by Castro's treatment of Heberto Padilla, what Damian called the "opportunistic" silence of Fidel before the killing of Mexican students in the Plaza of Tlatelolco in 1968. "And now, forty years later, they bring these outdated ideas to me and say this is the 'Socialism of the Twenty-First Century'? Give me a break!" he said.

Prat argued that the Bolivarian process was not only non-revolutionary, but retrograde, taking the country backward. He pointed to the government negligence that had resulted in the destruction of the Basic Industries of Guayana, the industries he'd followed very closely for thirty years. "If this were a revolution it would have increased production so we wouldn't need so many imports," he said, but the contrary has been the case. Venezuela before Chávez, he said, was "self-sufficient in aluminum; self-sufficient in iron—and, in fact, we exported both of those things. Well, now we import aluminum and iron just to cover our own needs and we're clearly no longer exporters. That is, we've gone backward."

Venezuela, he said, is more dependent on the "empire" than ever. "For the first time in decades we now depend on the United States for our consumption of gas. How is it that a petro-state now imports more than 100,000 barrels of gasoline daily from the United States?" He said that, as Venezuelans, "we've never been so dependent on the United States as we are now."

Prat mentioned the colonial relationship of Venezuela to the US and England under the Juan Vicente Gómez dictatorship, but that now the relations were changing again, to a colonial relationship with China. Chinese engineers were mapping the country's wealth and, according to Prat, the Bolivarian government was in the process of granting enormous mineral concessions to CITIC Corporation of China.[4] In addition to mapping the mineral wealth of the country, CITIC was given blocks of the Orinoco Oil belt. He asked why a so-called anti-imperialist government would "give a foreign power control over [its] mineral wealth?"

Damian was anxious to get to work, so I thanked him for his time and left to return to the guesthouse by cab.

The next day Carl dropped me off at SutraCarbonorca where I had arranged an interview with Emilio Campos. Emilio Campos was Secretary General of the SutraCarbonorca union, the autonomous union of Carbonorca, the nationalized plant for refining the coke used in steel and aluminum production. Of campesino origins, Campos grew up near Yaguaraparo in the state of Sucre where he went to school. After attending the university for a time, he dropped out, like many, to take a union job in the basic industries of Guayana. There he became part of Causa R (Radical Cause), a non-doctrinaire Marxist party formed in 1971 by MAS (Movement Toward Socialism) dissenters and ex-Communist guerrillas like Alfredo Maneiro, its brilliant founder. Maneiro argued that the sterile theoretical debates of the left should be abandoned in favor of a return to the grassroots, and that meant a return to the universities to organize among students, and to the factories, which, in the case of Venezuela, meant the industrial belt of Guayana and the Basic Industries. Radical Cause didn't do as well in the universities as it did in the factories, where its power grew among workers like Emilio.

Emilio claims that it was largely the fight he and his compañeros engaged in against the attempted privatization of the Basic Industries under the Rafael Caldera administration, and their subsequent backing of Hugo Chávez during that struggle that brought the latter to power in 1998. Eventually Emilio's passion, sense of justice, and commitment won him the recognition among his fellow workers that pushed him to the leadership of his union. He had just been re-elected six months before the interview, winning 80% of the vote from his fellow workers. Under Emilio the union had grown more combative, conducting numerous strikes for the long-denied contract and against a deteriorating wage that was eaten away by the nation's growing inflation. One of the strikes lasted fifty-eight days.

Like many union workers in the industrial belt of Guayana who had initially supported the changes Hugo Chávez brought to the country in 1998, Emilio had gone over to the opposition when he felt the Bolivarian process was "taking the country backwards."

"This is all a media show; that is, Venezuela is itself a big fantasy world. How can we call this socialism? Here we have capitalism disguised as socialism because they've stolen the socialist discourse to make it into capitalism." But Emilio considered himself a socialist and "more a revolutionary than those running the country." His socialism was in line with that of many others I would be interviewing over the coming days, akin to the Italian liberal socialist tradition of people like Carlo Rosselli, Norberto Bobbio, and others. "I'm a revolutionary in search of an alternative, a revolutionary for a plurality of ideas where a country seeks balance, not just for a party, or one sector of society. I believe in freedom of thought, in a diversity of ideas. But the hegemony of power makes you narrow-minded."

I asked Emilio about worker control and co-gestion or co-management in the Basic Industries. He thought it would be a great idea—if the proposal came from the workers. The problem was that, like everything else under Chávez, it was a top-down directive and had control as its objective. "I wouldn't call that 'worker control' but 'control of workers.' It's inverted." Another problem with the so-called "worker control" was that it was set up as a way to undercut the power of independent unions. Emilio said "they set [worker-control] against unions, as a parallel element to unions. There was a clash of interests. The unions directed the interests of the workers, and the interests of the state directed worker control. And not only worker control. Co-management and 'self-management' were done in parallel, in competition with the unions." Emilio said that the independent unions had been won through a great struggle and "you can't put out that flame." All these state-sponsored initiatives were attempts to "sabotage the workers."

It was lunchtime and workers were coming in to eat meals the union was providing, and among them was an unemployed man. Emilio got up from his seat and put his arm around him. "This guy is unemployed," he said to me, pointing at the man.

"Ask him if he's going to eat today. This man eats with us here and often we gather food for him to take home." Emilio said the community kitchens and "communal houses" give food out to "those who toe the political line" of the Chavistas. And despite the "Missions," poverty in Venezuela was still a problem. "I'd like you to visit the barrios around here and see how the people live; how they go around in the markets picking up garbage to survive; how our indigenous people live, begging for change at the stop lights so they can buy what they need because there's no flour, there's no rice, there's no spaghetti, there's nothing. Why? [Because the Chavistas] have progressively destroyed the entire productive apparatus of the country, all the productive initiatives for the development of the country. And why is that? To control everything. To tell you 'this is the piece of meat you're going to eat today, this is your portion of rice for today.' Cuban style," Emilio said.

The last comments rankled me. I no longer held Cuba as a model of anything but resistance to US impositions, but I came from a culture of the left that, even so, refused to criticize the island, primarily because many of us still considered the embargo and other US policies toward Cuba to be criminal, petty and mean-spirited. Only when I considered the problem from a Venezuelan oppositionist's point of view, could I begin to understand the perspective underlying the rancor. It's worth considering that here to put Emilio's comments in context.

Many Venezuelans feel that from the day he took power Fidel had attempted to gain influence over, and access to, Venezuela's oil wealth. Within days of his victory over Batista, Fidel had gone off to visit Venezuela's newly elected President, Romulo Betancourt, who had come to power after Venezuela's Democratic Revolution of 1958. Despite the fact that there was only a year separating the Cuban and the Venezuelan revolutions, there was an enormous political gulf between the two leaders from the beginning.

Betancourt was a committed social democrat. Indeed, he became best known for his "Betancourt Doctrine" that guided Venezuela's foreign policy of not recognizing any government of either the Right or the Left that had not come to power democratically. Betancourt had been a communist in his youth, and later co-founder of the Acción Democrática (Democratic Action, AD) party. AD was "a leftist-revolutionary, nationalist, populist, multiclass, anti-imperialist party" in its early incarnation, and Betancourt had moved it toward an ever-deepening commitment to democratic ideas in the struggle to overthrow the dictator, General Marcos Pérez Jimenez.[5] After the dictator fled in January 1958, several political parties, spanning the political spectrum, met at Punto Fijo, not the city, but rather the house of Rafael Caldera (of the COPEI) in Caracas.[6] There they signed the Pact of Punto Fijo, which committed the three parties in attendance to democratic procedures in government. The elections in 1958 drew out over 92% of the population to elect Betancourt with 49.2% of the vote.[7] Most notably, the far left Communist Party won 3.23% of the vote, the center left to the far right won 16.20% of the vote and the constitutional left won an amazing 80.55% of the vote.[8] Betancourt served his one complete term as president and left office, consistent with his commitment to democracy and to its corollary of alternation in power.

By contrast with Betancourt, Fidel had no commitment to liberal democracy or alternation in power, as he made clear over his nearly fifty years in power. It seems likely that Betancourt already knew what Carlos Franqui eventually discovered, that Fidel believed "all criticism is opposition. All opposition is counterrevolutionary" and that he "always thought of himself as the revolution."[9] Although little is known of the five hour meeting between the Cuban and Venezuelan presidents on January 25, 1959 in which Fidel hoped to gain preferential access to Venezuelan oil, it's likely that Betancourt recognized that Fidel intended to rule the country as a caudillo, much in the tradition of Batista who he'd overthrown—and he wasn't mistaken.[10] In any case, it quickly became clear to the two leaders that they were on different trajectories. We know that Fidel revealed his plans to nationalize US and Cuban industries, and it's also likely that Betancourt saw this as taking the heat of the US off of Venezuela (and himself, given his past leadership role in the Costa Rican Communist Party), allowing him to chart a relatively independent course in the hemisphere under the hegemony of the US while Cuba would be forced to ally more closely with the Soviet Union. [11]

Betancourt nearly paid for his commitment to democracy with his life. The right-wing Dominican dictator Rafael Trujillo was behind one assassination attempt, but the right wing wasn't the only political sector antagonized by Betancourt's AD, that "sought to carry out the programs of social democracy."[12] But Betancourt's coalition didn't include the Venezuelan Communist Party, and that caused deep resentments on the far left and would have powerful ramifications for the country in the future. Also feeling snubbed by the Betancourt government, by 1963 Fidel Castro began training and leading communist guerrillas to undertake a military campaign against the young Venezuelan democracy.[13] And so the first democratically-elected president of Venezuela who was allowed to serve a full term was a target of dictators of both the Right and the Left.

The communist insurgency was defeated and Fidel was isolated and had to wait forty years for another chance to get his hands on Venezuelan oil. But when his opportunity finally arrived, Hugo Chávez made sure Fidel got as much of the black gold as he felt he needed. At first the trade was fairly simple: oil for doctors who were sent to attend to poor people in the slums of the country. Few objected to that, although many right wing Venezuelans did find it objectionable. But after the coup attempt in 2002 Fidel convinced Chávez to turn over the direction of Venezuelan intelligence to Cubans, which his younger protégé did. At every point Venezuela paid more oil, and this didn't happen without Venezuelans taking note.

Venezuelans are a very patriotic people: you'll find a Plaza Bolívar in every village, town and city of the country and a bust or statue of the "Liberator." The fact that Cuban intelligence began pulling the strings in the country,[14] and that Chávez increasingly was moving toward a more authoritarian, and less democratic, model of socialism was very disturbing to many Venezuelans. Gradually, Cubans began to be seen in other branches of government, including the military, and in advisory roles everywhere. As the economy went south, many people blamed the Cuban influence, and with some justification: the long lines for scarce consumer goods in Venezuela had never been seen before, but they looked an awful lot like Cuba, with its failed socialist model. Before every crisis Chávez began meeting with his "grey eminence," and Maduro has carried on that tradition, flying to Cuba soon after his election to consult with what many view as his "superiors." All this added up to what many viewed as the complete subordination of Venezuela to a revolution without even democratic pretensions that clashed with the democratic and nationalist sensibilities of many Venezuelans, like Emilio. As Rory Carroll wrote of a Venezuelan named Andres who had been displaced in his job in the intelligence services by Cubans, "Like many Venezuelan leftists, [Andres] considered Fidel an anachronism, a cautionary tale of revolutionary idealism warping into totalitarian control and central-planning fiasco."[15] This view could would no doubt have gotten an "amen" from Emilio.

"I respected the greatness of Cuba, but more the greatness of the Cuban people, for their resistance, not those who rule over them and have brought them where they are today," Emilio told me. "That's not the socialism I believe in, that authoritarian model imposed on the people."

Emilio was first and foremost a worker, and that meant that he believed in work, and the dignity it brought people. The struggle to maintain that dignity of workers, despite a government that had refused for years to even discuss a collective contract in the Basic Industries, was what kept Emilio going. What he said next was prophetic, considering what happened to the country a year or so later.

"The idea that people don't need to work to eat, is dangerous. If the oil runs out or the prices of oil drop, how are you going to sustain the people who don't produce, if they don't go out into the fields and work? This could be a boomerang and come back on you and you'll have no response when the people who won't work keep coming back to ask for their money."

The government policy of "giveaways" was bizarre. At a time when the industries across the board were functioning at a quarter or a third of their capacity, the industries were increasing their workforce.

"When I came here, there were 450 workers [at Carbonorca]. Today we have 800," Emilio said. I knew that Carbonorca was at the time producing at about one quarter of its capacity. "Yes," he said, noting the shock on my face, "the state keeps adding more employees, without producing anything, and this is how they inflate the employment figures." He went through the different industries: Sidor had 10,000, now increased to 18,000, working at less than half of its capacity; Bauxilum had 1,500, but today it has 4,000, and so on, down the line. It was, as Emilio said, "an upside-down world." And now in the region where Chávez had enjoyed 80% support from the workers for fourteen years, there was a seismic shift as the workers came out massively to vote for Capriles.

So this would be another element explaining the shortages and scarcity of items in Venezuela: the expropriations and nationalizations. This would become an "anti-business" plan in which the company or the farm would be expropriated, the expropriated unit would double its workforce, and proceed to produce at half, or a quarter of its previous levels. The product of the nationalized economic unit, be it steel rods, aluminum bars, coffee, sugar, concrete, etc. would be affixed a "just price" that, in an economy approaching hyperinflation due to bad monetary policy, would immediately

be lower than the cost of production, and voilà, the only remaining impulse would be to hoard, due to inflation and
scarcity, to traffick, due to lower-than-market prices in the
country, and to speculate, since the government was effectively providing a risk-free environment to do so, given that
the value of commodities would be as certain to increase as
the value of national money would be to decrease. So this
was "socialismo Venezolano," the "petrosocialism" in which
bloated, non-productive state industries would be IV'd oil
money so they could be showcased in re-election campaigns
for the President.

Emilio was sitting near the air conditioner but sweat still
beaded on his forehead. I could tell he needed to go so I
thanked him for his time and said goodbye and he strolled out
of the office with a group of men who had been patiently waiting for the interview to end so they could attend to business.

I was trying to keep a low profile because Timothy Tracy,
another North American, had just been arrested for doing
what I was doing: video-recording interviews with people in
the opposition.[16] For that reason I decided not to go to the
May Day demonstrations, but I did head out to the mass rally the day before, on April 30 when Henrique Capriles came
to Guayana to address the workers. It was a combination of
a celebration of May Day, and a protest against the electoral
fraud. Earlier in the day I did interviews with a number of
union leaders, including Hernan Pacheco, from Bauxilum.
I'd asked him who in the opposition would represent their interests, given that Capriles has often been associated with big
capital. He responded, "Capriles himself! Look, he came to
Guayana and sat down with us and listened to us as we talked
about the problems of the country. Chávez never did that. He
never bothered to ask us, the workers, what we needed and
what the problems were!"

They were all there at the rally, the union people I'd interviewed, including Emilio Campos, and thousands more. The
officials at the airport had delayed Capriles in landing. After
landing, there were more delays with Bolivarian officials so he
was two or three hours late arriving, but the crowd waited for
him. I took up a place near the stage and at one point a union
official announced, "A North American writer, Clif Ross, is
here with us," and pointed me out to the crowd. I wanted to
hide. It was just the kind of publicity I didn't need if I hoped
to avoid Tim Tracy's fate.

Capriles finally arrived and the crowd went wild. He gave
an impassioned speech and I found myself involuntarily
moved by his passion and the response of the crowd. Just as
he was ending his speech, I made my way through the crowd,
hoping to get ahead of everyone else so I could get a cab back
to my posada before dark, and perhaps avoid being snatched
up by the SEBIN (Bolivarian secret police) or mugged by a
malandro (criminal). As I was walking toward a line of taxis
an old man came up to me and said, "Hey, you're that North
American they were talking about, right?"

I hesitated and then quickened my pace. He walked faster
to keep up with me. We were both going the same direction,
it appeared.

"Yes," I said at last. "But I really wished they hadn't said
anything. I'm here as a foreigner and have no protection from
the government."

He shrugged and shook his head. "Well, neither do we."

CHAPTER SEVENTEEN

AN ANARCHIST IN CARACAS

A few days later I left for Caracas where I hoped to get a few interviews. I took a room at the Hotel Odeon just to have something familiar to hold onto in a world that seemed to be changing so quickly that I couldn't keep up with it. I looked out my window to see an enormous billboard of Nicolas Maduro glaring at me. Most of the small posters of Capriles scattered around the country had already been torn down, but the government-funded billboards of Maduro remained everywhere, as did the Chavista graffiti.

I'd arranged to meet Rafael Uzcátegui in the morning and as I walked along the Avenida las Acacias toward Plaza Venezuela, everything looked the same: the newspaper kiosks, the man shining shoes in the shade of the pharmacy doorway, the woman frying empanadas in a big vat on the sidewalk. Nothing had changed but the world inside me, which was why I was suddenly seeing the world outside so differently.

I met Rafael outside of the Gran Café and we went upstairs to do our interview. As we sat down I took a good look at him: long dreadlocks trailing down his back from under his cap. He appeared to be in his early thirties and I could imagine meeting someone like him anywhere in Berkeley or San Francisco at the Latin rock shows I frequented in the '90s. Rafael seemed to be a person capable of traveling between many worlds: a "rockero," human rights activist, writer, anarchist. As he began talking I regretted not having contacted him and the other anarchists of Caracas on earlier trips. They seemed to be my kind of people, an extension of my tribe in Berkeley.

What was most striking for me, as Rafael talked, was his equanimity. In Venezuela I had gotten used to the manic energy common to Manichaean contexts where the polarization between Good and Evil generates sparks and even rods of lightning. Rafael had none of that, and he seemed somehow to be untouched by the phenomenon of polarization that Chávez had introduced into Venezuelan politics. Rafael was clearly more interested in honestly assessing the present problematic than he was to affixing blame, much less to assigning roles of Good or Evil to one or another side in a conflict. He seemed as comfortable criticizing the opposition as he was criticizing the Chavistas.

Since 1995 Rafael has been involved in the Venezuelan anarchist scene and worked on the magazine, *El Libertario*. He made his living as a researcher for PROVEA, although at the time of this writing his title is that of "General Coordinator" of the organization. Rafael has written and published two books, the first titled *Corazón de Tinta* (*Heart of Ink*), which is a compilation of articles on culture and politics from ten years of writing. Rafael's second book is *Venezuela: Revolution as Spectacle*, which has been translated and published in

French and English.[1] This latter book, Rafael described as "a synthesis of what we anarchists have thought and our critique of the Bolivarian process. He said "it includes the vision of other independent social actors of the left who, at present, due to the polarization in the country, have no place to express themselves." This included many groups and organizations I'd never heard of, mostly because all left forces that hadn't been included in, or joined, the Bolivarian project had been invisiblized by the government and its supporters—like Rafael and the anarchists in Caracas.

Rafael talked about a large, diverse sector of the "revolutionary left" that hadn't joined the Bolivarian project of Chávez. Tercer Camino (Third Way) and Rupture, which included the well-known guerrilla commander, Douglas Bravo; the union current CCURA (Corriente Clasista Unida Revolucionaria Autónoma, Autonomous United Revolutionary Class Current) organized with Orlando Chirino; Guevarist revolutionary groups; Christian base communities; pre-Chávez co-operativists like the well-known Cecosesola of Barquisimeto; militants working in the public health sector; the Committee of Victims against Police Abuse; indigenous people struggling against the mega-mining projects in the country, and many others. "These are the voices I wanted to include in the book [*Venezuela: Revolution as Spectacle*] as a whole group of people who aren't being properly recognized in their criticism of the government," he said.

I asked Rafael to talk about the polarization of the country, an intense polarization that many fear could slip into a civil war at any moment. He said that as a result of the polarization, the central political argument in the country was far too simplistic to accurately describe the complex process going on under the Bolivarians. "One side says that a Revolution is underway in Venezuela, while the other side says it's a Castro-communist dictatorship," he said. Rafael described the project of Chávez as a "nationalist project of a populist character with a left discourse and some authoritarian characteristics." Recognizing that this same polarization of opinions about the Bolivarian process was a global phenomenon, Rafael suggested that people interested in Venezuela should try to get their news from a variety of conflicting sources to be able to understand the complex reality of the country and that "if people really want to know more, they could visit and see what's happening on the street and what daily life is like for Venezuelans."

At first I thought I understood what Rafael meant when he went on to say that "the government of President Chávez has revitalized Venezuelan political culture." I thought he might be talking about the community radio stations, the plethora of free and subsidized literature, the "circus" that now seemed only to be lacking in "bread." But Rafael was referring to "the preponderance of the military; the figure of the strong personality, the personality of the caudillo; the use of the oil resources to give assets to people with few resources and capitalize on that through the electoral system; the attempt to create State 'social organizations,' for example the Chavista union movement which they tried to create by state decree, and different other 'social' organizations."

Ultimately, according to Rafael, this was no "revolution" because a revolutionary project would have implied a "rupture" with all that. "Nor has the government of President Chávez meant a rupture with economic globalization, but rather a continuation of the role of Venezuela within the international oil economy," Rafael said, and "you can't understand Venezuela without understanding the oil economy and the culture that it has generated in the country."

I asked Rafael what he thought about the Missions, the much-touted social programs that advocates of the Bolivarian process point to as indicators of the "Socialism of the Twenty-First Century." Rafael began to talk about the significance of Chávez's emergence in the crisis of governability that the *Caracazo* of February 1989 represented. There had been a crisis with the system of elites and the democratic system was seen as needing a complete overhaul. "So it's not a coincidence that a strong personality with a populist discourse of including the majority would be the person who would help to bring back this lost governability. Nor is it a coincidence that in other countries of Latin America where there have been large mass and social movements, as in Bolivia, Ecuador and Argentina, that you'd find similar figures: strong charismatic personalities with a discourse that would allow for the institutionalization of the demands of social movements."

The Missions that were conceived in conversations with Fidel Castro were Chávez's response to a crisis in his popularity in 2004, and they had what Rafael called an "undeniably positive impact" on the poor of the country who had been hardest hit by the drop in oil prices in the 1980s.

Nevertheless, Rafael points to three serious problems with the Missions. First, Rafael agreed with Zibechi that these policies problematize poverty and not wealth. So while there may have been improvements in the quality of life for the poor of the country, the Missions "didn't address the structural causes" of poverty. A second contradiction was that the programs were of greatest benefit to the urban poor, but Chávez's greatest popularity was among the rural poor. This had the effect of generating expectations of universal benefits, which were unrealistic given the economic reality of the country. Finally, there was the devastating impact of these policies on the social movements since "all these policies have incorporated under what in Venezuela is called 'Popular Power' all the different popular and community organizations to make them agencies for the State social programs. In that sense [the State] has broken, blocked, or dispersed independent grass-roots social organizations by getting people in the communities to implement these policies of social assistance in the poorest sectors of society."

I found the latter point particularly interesting as it fit perfectly with Zibechi's critique and with what Marcy and I had drawn from all the interviews with Latin American social movements in our book. I also found it very interesting that Chávez had succeeded in implementing, under the name of "Socialism," the neoliberal program of transferring the social responsibilities of the State to civil society.

In the US this neoliberal agenda of "privatizing" or devolving to the local communities the provision of social services had taken place under the Bush presidencies: first under George H. W. Bush's program described as "A Thousand Points of Light" then under his son George W. Bush's "Faith-Based and Community Initiatives." In the US the program had simply been directed at churches and business interests and NGOs to take on the responsibilities of anti-poverty programs. In Venezuela, Chávez had used social movement actors, first sidelining their organizations, and then recruiting their best and brightest to administer state welfare programs. As I thought of it, in Mérida all the old social movement and guerrilla left cadre were now in charge of one or another Mission, and their organizations were long gone. If there was a conscious plan for disarti-culating social movements, it appeared to be one of the very few the Bolivarians had carried out with any success.

This all raised questions about the paternalism in Venezuelan culture. Yes, Rafael said, agreeing with what Emilio Campos told me a few days before, the handouts from what Venezuelans called "Papa State" were "nearly as old as the beginnings of oil exploitation in Venezuela." The conception around the world that social programs in Venezuela began with Chávez is completely inaccurate. The programs rise and fall with the price of petroleum, and even the conservative Christian Democrats like Rafael Caldera had come into office in good times throwing money down to the poor.

"Already in the Constitution of 1960 education was declared free: it was the obligation of the state to give education to everyone," Rafael said, and that included college educations. This was all possible due to the mineral wealth, which from the Democratic Revolution of 1958 generated a culture and "a very paternalistic state that takes care of the material necessities of the people and in return asks for political loyalty and payback for the different favors."

Both parties, COPEI and Democratic Action, worked with "stipends and developed clientelistic networks from the State to all their militants who worked for them, and offered them social benefits," a culture and policy that Chávez only continued and deepened. But this had not only social costs in an impoverished culture of dependency and "rent chasing." Under all these governments, but particularly under Chávez, Rafael said, "the social and environmental consequences of a policy based in mega-mining have been ignored; all the environmental and indigenous networks in particular have been coopted and institutionalized by the government of President Chávez. All those movements that we see in other countries of the continent like Ecuador and Bolivia, of communities of indigenous peasants mobilized against the projects of mega-mining, are absent in Venezuela because the state has been particularly intelligent in institutionalizing and coopting all the indigenous and campesino movements of the country."

I asked Rafael about the unions since I knew very little about the union movement of Guayana. I knew he'd worked with Orlando Chirino and Rubén Gonzalez, two major union leaders who had suffered various kinds of persecution under the Bolivarians because they wouldn't "submit" to the government. Rafael said that Chávez had come to power criticizing the old institutions of the country, and that included the Venezuelan Workers' Confederation (CTV) that was the main union of the country, allied with Democratic Action. Chávez set to work to take over the union by introducing his candidate, Aristóbulo Istúriz, into the internal elections, but he lost that bid. Then Chávez took another common course of action, introducing and funding a rival union, the National Workers' Union (Unión Nacional de Trabajadores, UNT) to draw members away from, and thus weaken, the CTV. The UNT was instrumental in reactivating the oil industry after the Oil Strike (or Lockout) of late 2002. But when Chavez founded the PSUV and required union groups and unions to join, Rafael said that some, like Orlando Chirino, who was one of the national directors of the UNT, "rejected that measure because they thought that unions have to be an autonomous instrument of the working class and shouldn't be enlisted in the service of any particular political party." Orlando Chirino felt that unions needed "to have an independent and autonomous line" because "if the State and the President were the main bosses of the country it wasn't possible for the unions to be under the control of the principle boss."

After this, Chávez initiated his attacks with what Rafael called "the criminalization of worker and union protests." He pointed to the case of Rubén González, Secretary General of the union Sintraferrominera and also a member of the PSUV. Rubén was sentenced to seven years in prison for participating in a workers' strike called to demand a collective contract.

He spent seventeen months in prison but this situation gave way to an extraordinary display of working-class unity when both Opposition and Chavista workers and workers' organizations met in the streets to defend Rubén. The growing unity posed such a serious threat that Chávez had the sentence rescinded. But then Rubén was retried, now in Caracas where he was forced to regularly make the trip from Guayana to present himself before the court.[2] Nevertheless, it said a lot about the unpopularity of the government's tactics and a lot about Rubén himself that in the middle of all this he won reelection as Secretary General.

Rafael said that "this policy of criminalization of protest is important given that workers and unionists are in a state of permanent mobilization for the renewal of collective contracts, since [collective contracts] are one of the main problems here." In the Basic Industries of Guayana there's been what Rafael called "a situation of near paralysis of the collective contracts" for years and that has severely worsened living conditions of workers there and around the country.[3] In addition to wages eaten up in devaluations and inflation Rafael mentioned the problems of industrial pollution, and reduced health and other benefits as part of the "grave deterioration of working conditions." On top of this was the increased political pressure on people "who haven't shown adherence to, or appear to have not voted for the official [PSUV] party" and are therefore threatened with firings. Evidence of this was the incident just a week or so before of Popular Power Minister for Housing and Habitat, Ricardo Molina, being recorded as saying that opposition workers would be fired, regardless of labor law, for their views and activism.[4] Naturally, Rafael found it disturbing that a minister of the government would put out "a publicly stated intention to ignore labor norms that protect labor rights in the country."

Rafael mentioned the inspiring work of Marcela Masperó who is a member of the UNT and the PSUV but who is also part of what he hopes might be "a new articulation of grassroots union organization to defend workers' rights." Nevertheless, the government was continuing a policy of creating parallel institutions to undermine independent union activity. There was, for instance, "the Bolivarian Socialist Workers' Force (Fuerza Bolivariana Socialista de Trabajadores, FBST) and then the Socialist Workers' Union (Central Socialista de Trabajadores, CST) and others, created in an artificial manner by decree of the State" but none have been successful in realizing the government's objectives of subjecting the workers to its rule. All these parallel unions, as they clearly represent the government, and not the workers', interests, have been "overwhelmingly rejected by the mass of the workers."

At the same time, this government policy of creating parallel unions that compete with existing independent unions has created violent confrontations between workers, especially in the construction and petroleum labor sectors. Nearly 300 workers had been killed since 2005 in the country in a struggle over jobs. "So we have a unionism that is being perverted and degraded and slowly being turned into just a job generator, a job generator for workers," Rafael said.

Still, it was a difficult time for workers and those in the union movement, as the high cost of living and wage increases decreed by the government didn't make up for what was eaten away from salaries by inflation. To this Rafael added the problem of the increasing scarcity of basic necessities and high cost of food, problems which have only sharpened and grown more urgent since this interview. The social security of workers hasn't been guaranteed, and if "workers or their families get sick they have to resort to private clinics because the hospital system is in terrible condition," Rafael said. And Venezuela had also become more insecure in other ways: even the government recognized that at least 16,000 people per year, about 43 people per day, are murdered. This, Rafael said, has "the effect of ripping up social relations and the social fabric of the country."

And finally, this is related to the political polarization that "has created a situation of growing intolerance of people with different political opinions that has endorsed an attitude of extermination, either symbolically or actually, of those who don't think like you." He described it as "a sort of political Manichaeism, this dehumanizing and demonizing of adversaries, and there is no longer an attempt to recognize the democratic right of different political actors to express themselves and struggle for their objectives."

Rafael said that PROVEA promotes dialogue between the Bolivarians and the opposition but the situation is difficult, "for the social movements to reclaim their autonomy and for us to build a revolutionary left alternative. It's an uphill battle but many of us feel this is the struggle: to build autonomous, independent and belligerent grassroots social movements with their own agendas and demands, separate from the agendas of political parties struggling for power." This struggle has also been complicated by anti-terrorist legislation, particularly laws passed in January 2012 and applied against social movement activists who weren't part of the official and state sponsored "social movements." Rafael said that he's concerned that the laws "will be applied against union activists, campesino, and indigenous movements who'll demonstrate for their rights." The qualification of "terrorist" or "narco-terrorist" is vague and the description of crimes includes "all the historical arms of struggle for the popular movements in Venezuela. They're all being typified as 'terrorist:' closing a road, protesting at a government institution, painting graffiti on the walls of a public building." He says these laws have "to be rejected, regardless of one's political persuasion because, as we know, this entire mentality of needing to pass anti-terrorist laws, is a measure or policy implemented by the United States after the September 11 attacks on the Twin Towers."

In assessing the Bolivarian process initiated by the late President Hugo Chávez, Rafael felt there were some positive aspects that needed to be recognized, such as the emphasis on overcoming poverty, which Chávez had put "at the center of the discussion on public or state policy." But social movement activists internationally could learn a lesson about "the need to build autonomous spaces" and never allow themselves to be blackmailed or forced to "abandon their critical spirit, their own demands and agendas" in favor of those of an elite in power, as has happened in Venezuela. "We've been blackmailed for a long time to quiet our criticisms so as 'not to give ammunition to the enemy,' or 'ammunition to the right wing' or to 'imperialism,'" Rafael said. "And as a result of our silence the capitalist mentality, the mentality of economic polarization that has happened here, has resurfaced with new faces and new facets."

This has led, in Rafael's view, to "one of the most lamentable aspects of this whole Bolivarian process" which was that "critical thinking has been infantilized" under the Bolivarian government. He believed that "if there were a group of intellectuals or thinking people criticizing so as to advance and improve [government policies] we wouldn't be in the situation we're currently in, of open and flagrant contradictions, with a government that says one thing and yet has a contrary practice."

Rafael's critique rang true for me: even critical Chavistas rarely, if ever, turned their criticism onto Chávez. But the problem, it seemed to me, was that those who did criticize, even "to advance and improve" the situation, were usually written off by other Chavistas as "escualidos" or counterrevolutionaries and relegated to the opposition. In fact, as I was beginning to discover, there were many revolutionaries who criticized Chávez and his policies over the years—and they were all in the opposition.

CHAPTER EIGHTEEN

THE HAZARDS OF PETRO-SOCIALISM

My final interview in Caracas was with Margarita López Maya and it proved true my wife Marcy's long experience as a journalist. Even when she thinks she has the whole story, and is sometimes ready to ditch the final interview, that last meeting often proves to be the most powerful one. I went online and did some research on López Maya and I was impressed: She'd run for political office on the Patria Para Todos (PPT, Homeland for All, an offshoot of Alfredo Maneiro's *La Causa R*, Radical Cause) in the parliamentary elections of September 2010 and when she lost, she returned to her work as a writer, historian, and sociologist. Widely published in Spanish, Portuguese, and English, she matches her scholarly work with a regular column in *Ultimas Noticias,* a newspaper that at the time had a good reputation for objectivity and its independence (it's since been rumored to have been bought by Chavistas).

Margarita looked tired when I met her at her apartment. She said she had been working to finish an article for a Brazilian magazine on the recent elections.

We started there, since the elections, even now, more than two weeks later, were on everyone's mind. Margarita acknowledged that there was, indeed a crisis, and it had to do, more than anything, with how Maduro won the elections. She felt that Chávez had severely weakened the democratic institutions of the country, and this was another blow against them. She felt that Maduro had "competed in a very unequal manner in these elections. As president-in-charge he used all the resources of the state to win these elections," which, she said, is both "illegitimate and illegal." As examples of this she pointed to the *cadenas*, obligatorily broadcasted presidential transmissions on radio and television, as well as "openly using public resources for electoral propaganda to mobilize people; bringing them to meetings; giving them meals, using government transport, and transport from the city governments; using public buildings; and above all, using public media as campaign instruments of an electoral campaign for president."

Even with all those resources, and an election held on the anniversary of Chávez's victory over the coup of 2003, Maduro won, if he indeed won, by a 1.5% margin. Margarita called this "unconvincing" and "a technical draw."

In such a situation, Margarita felt it would be appropriate to open a national dialogue, but that didn't seem to be Maduro's approach. Worse still, the new president seemed to have no problem with violence perpetrated against the opposition, including the shocking incident in the National Assembly when PSUVistas, in the middle of a session, ganged up and beat six opposition parliamentarians, including María Corina Machado, William Dávila, and Américo

De Grazia and others. This appeared to be evidence that the Maduro government would increasingly rely on more authoritarian instruments to rule and continue the process begun under President Chávez's second government (2006–2012) of "destroying the institutions of the liberal representative," democratic state.

"The Venezuelan state of the Constitution of 1999 is a combination of liberal representative democracy with direct democracy and with institutions of participatory democracy," Margarita explained. "The Constitution set out these three forms of democracy. President Chávez in his second government set about to destroy the representative democratic part so as to leave nothing more than the mechanisms of direct democracy and the institutions of participatory democracy. This form of State, that is no longer the State of the Constitution, he called the Communal State. It is a non-liberal State, a State that doesn't follow the logic of Western democracies. It is a state that is more akin to the socialist states of the twentieth century, the Cuban model, the Soviet model, in which there is no universal, direct and secret voting, no independence and autonomy of public powers. The Communal State has no political pluralism. For one to be recognized by the Communal State, by the Communal Council or the Commune one has to profess the Socialism of the Twenty-First Century. That's what the law says."

And these laws themselves, Margarita reminded me, were passed by decree of Chávez, with no consultation of the people, despite the fact that the Bolivarian Constitution requires that "all laws be passed in consultation with the people." She said that the crisis arising over the elections had its roots in this authoritarian style of governing. But she felt we had to back up and look at the nature of the Venezuelan economy to understand its politics.

Venezuela, for the past century, has been a petro-state, which is a state *sui generis*. A petro-state doesn't live from taxing the people but, as Margarita said, "from the revenues it captures from the international world according to the price of the barrel of oil." The petro-state manages a huge amount of money when oil prices are high, but that can collapse in an instant when prices drop, making the petro-states very "volatile."

By contrast with normal states where government is expected to serve the needs of, and is accountable to, the taxpayers who pay to maintain it, in Venezuela and other petro-states the people expect to be paid, and be "maintained." This reminded me of what two Venezuelan journalists wrote, that many Venezuelans live under the illusion their country is "a utopia in which the state is the providential benefactor, all structure and rules are dispensable, effort is a distraction, and destiny is not a future to build, but a heaven that already exists, a treasure already won that needs only to be meted out properly."[1] Pondering this, I could almost see the little squares on the napkin that my poet friend Jose Gregorio drew for me to explain how land reform worked in Venezuela.

Fernando Coronil had described how, under previous governments, "the circulation of torrents of oil money not only undermined productive activity and stimulated the spread of financial speculation and corruption, but also facilitated the concentration of power at the highest levels of government,"[2] such as in a president ruling by the power of decree, granted him by the National Assembly under his command.

Margarita went on to say, "under the government of President Chávez we became even more dependent on the oil. Before we used to have industries, and we had more agriculture. But because the price of oil has been so high for so many years the country has quit producing." Despite massive investment in the countryside, nothing was being produced, and even coffee, rice, and white corn, all of which was once grown in Venezuela, was now being imported, and the list of imports was growing.

"The elites arrive to power when there are oil booms and they become intoxicated with the money and begin to have great fantasies, more delirious than you can imagine," Margarita said, and she added that she thought the "Socialism of the Twenty-First Century" was Chávez's delirious fantasy. "The elites arrive and see all this money that came out of nothing, not produced by any work, and society can't control them because they don't need their taxes to sustain them in public expenditures. So [the political elites] develop a sort of autonomy from society and they end up attempting to impose their dreams of grandeur on society."

Margarita compared Venezuela and Chávez to "Libya with Gaddafi, also a petro-state, also with a charismatic leader, who decided that Libya was going to have a unique, green Muslim socialism… and, well, these things can be done when you have all the money in the world."

The oil money funded military dictatorships that ruled, with the exception of the *Trienio Adeco*, all the way up to 1958.[3] The last dictator, Marcos Pérez Jiménez, began a modernizing project that continued under the early democratic governments. With good educational and development programs came good jobs, and this allowed for the growth of the upper, middle, and working classes. But then the price of oil dropped in the late seventies and the eighties and Margarita said "the elites didn't know what to do. They couldn't develop an alternative model and so they adopted the formulas of the International Monetary Fund (IMF) and moved toward neoliberalism." The poor suffered terribly under the new regime and "the breach between the rich and the poor delegitimized the political elite but it also delegitimized representative democracy. And into this breach came a caudillo."

With President Chávez, the military returned to power and Chávez expressed the polarization between the poor and the working, middle and upper classes, Margarita said, "with a very strong, and very aggressive, populist discourse: 'We are the good, they are the evil; we are the people, they are the oligarchy; they are the powerful, they're guilty for everything, we are the innocent, the good, those who never had power. And this discourse paid great political dividends for Chávez: he won the elections of 1998 and then seventeen of eighteen more elections thereafter."

Inflated by his great popularity, which coincided not incidentally with the beginnings of an unprecedented oil boom, Chávez decided to undertake the construction of a socialist project for Venezuela. After his election with 63% majority in 2006—an election that also had the lowest voter turnout from the Democratic Revolution in 1958 to the present—Chávez announced his new project of Twenty-First Century Socialism.[4] In order to begin, he had to modify the Bolivarian Constitution, which wasn't socialist. His referendum to do this failed in late 2007, the only election he ever lost, so he decided to impose the reforms by decreeing new laws and with "rules and other legal and administrative resources."

Margarita pointed out that "Chávez was able to do this because by that time he had managed to subordinate all public powers to his rule." He had packed the Supreme Court (Tribunal Supremo de Justicia, TSJ) and, indeed, the entire judiciary with his own people, 80% of whom, by 2013, were contracted or provisional judges.[5] He had increased the number of branches from three to five and had packed them all with loyal supporters so it wasn't likely that anyone would be able or willing to challenge what was an unconstitutional move.

As Margarita pointed out, the Bolivarian Constitutional Article 345 was "very restrictive and explicit in saying that a Constitutional reform could not be resubmitted."

I asked Margarita if she'd ever believed in the project of Chávez. She said she had indeed supported the first government (1999–2005), especially as he "promised to channel the discontentment of Venezuelans toward what were the old political elites and to push forward changes to the constitution." She explained that the reforms creating a decentralized state had been under discussion since the 1980s and had even led to street protests. In those days, like most petro-states, power in Venezuela was very centralized. Local and city governments wanted more power as well as "mayors elected by universal, direct, and secret suffrage" and Margarita said there was also "a demand for more direct citizen participation that would go around the political parties and avoid the discredited political leadership."

Chávez promised to carry forth the reforms demanded by the people themselves and he thus received the backing of a broad cross-section of the population, which led to his election in 1998. He promptly took steps that led to the new Constitution that included decentralization and greater participation, which he called "participatory and protagonistic" by which he meant "the participation and the protagonism of the people was going to be the most important feature, and that this would begin to weaken and lower the tone of the political parties." Margarita emphasized, "many of us supported this, not because it was a proposal of Chávez, but rather because it was a proposal of the Venezuelans."

It took many years for the opposition to accept the new Constitution and, in fact, they opposed it because it ended state subsidies to the church and other privileges of the old elite. One element of this opposition elite was the management of PDVSA, the state oil company, which had grown autonomous over the years since it had been nationalized on January 1, 1976. Much of the crisis leading up to the election of Chávez had been caused by the fact that PDVSA "no longer responded to the State, no longer paid dividends to the state" and "this had been a real factor in the impoverishment of the people in the eighties and nineties."

Then PDVSA management confronted the government with a "nearly deadly" oil strike or lockout in late 2002, after the earlier coup of April 11th the same year, but Chávez won both times.

The next year the opposition attempted to remove Chávez through a referendum process. But once again, good luck was on the president's side. The oil boom took off alongside the Referendum and with oil money filling the coffers of PDVSA, which he now controlled, he was advised by Fidel Castro to undertake the Missions so as to win the elections. So, in true populist fashion, Chávez began funding the Missions and distributing oil money as patronage down to his constituency.[6] As a result he won the referendum and the opposition was essentially demoralized and disarticulated as a result. That was about the time that I first arrived in Venezuela, in December 2004.

With all the money pouring in and under his control Chávez began to dream of building his "petro-socialism," beginning with reforms to the Constitution. "He tried to sell the idea to the people as if it were an extension of the Constitution of '99," Margarita said, "but in fact it was a very different project." It was significantly different in that it was a "recentralization of the State" because "the Communal State would essentially bring the governorships and mayoralties and elected officials to an end and create a structure of authorities that would depend on, and be chosen by, the president."

Of course Chavistas I knew believed that this "Communal State" would be a way of ending centralism, by bringing an end to representative democracy and implementing a more direct democracy through the communal councils. Margarita agreed that that was the message Chávez put out, but the projects of anti-liberal states, as she put it, have inevitably "ended in totalitarian or authoritarian projects. That's been true as much on the right with the cases of Italian or Spanish fascism and German National Socialism, as on the left as in the case of the Soviet Union, with Stalinism, and the Central European countries."

What was so interesting about the Constitution of 1999 for Margarita was "its proposal to maintain the liberal institutions but to put them into tension with direct democracy so the two would control each other. Because the tendency of Liberal representative democracy is toward elitism, toward what we could call 'privatization' through the political parties of the interests of the state. But the perverse tendencies of direct democracy are toward totalitarianism. Direct democracy of assemblies, and councils, up to now have ended in very authoritarian regimes that attempt to transform humanity... into the 'new man' and end up becoming totalitarian." The Constitution of 1999 was an attempt to "draw forth the virtues" and to complement each form of democracy since direct democracy allows the poor and marginalized majority a place to speak and be heard while the framework of liberal representative democracy would provide a set of institutional guarantees.

This was, for me, a turning point in the interview. I was recording Margarita and my attention up to the moment was on the sound levels, the poor lighting, which concerned me, keeping the subject properly framed, and all the other technical details of an interview when one person is the writer, camera operator, grip, director, interviewer, and errand boy. But now, suddenly, it occurred to me that I wasn't exactly sure what she meant by "liberal." Perhaps it was late and I was tired from traveling all over the country in very trying circumstances; perhaps also, I had my own idea of "liberal," defined by Phil Ochs, my Marxist friends, and my Berkeley culture, as a conformist wedded to the system, unwilling or afraid to take the necessary steps to "make the revolution," a reformist… In other words, a species that had presumably died out of the US political system, to the delight of conservatives and the revolutionary left alike. I'd done my part to disparage them.[7] But a tradition of its own? I asked her to explain to "North Americans" who "don't understand very well the liberal tradition." She was happy to oblige me.

"The Liberal tradition of the Western democracies held certain ideas that today are considered the great achievements of humanity," she said. "One idea would be the independence and autonomy of branches of government which make possible the counterweight between the different powers so they control each other and there would be no abuse of power." Chávez, as she'd mentioned earlier, had largely destroyed this autonomy. Then there was the liberal idea of political pluralism, severely damaged in Venezuela by the political polarization Chávez imposed to such a degree that now only Bolivarian views were heard on public media. If you disagree with the government, said Margarita, they bring "judicial proceedings against you, imprison you or persecute you; they criminalize you and stigmatize you in the public media. You aren't invited to the programs of public media in Venezuela because the public media has been confiscated by the PSUV and the President."

The limits on a diversity of viewpoints extends to collective political recognition as the "Communal Laws say that if you want to organize a Community Council in your neighborhood and be recognized by the State to be given resources to resolve community problems, one of the requirements of the Community Council is that it must build the Socialism of the Twenty-First Century. So if you decide in your assembly, that you don't agree with the 'Socialism of the Twenty-First Century,' well, then your Community Council won't be recognized by the State." Obviously, some vestige of pluralism still exists since the Opposition can still campaign and have a voice in private media, but that's dwarfed by the communicational hegemony of the petro-state with its vast pool of resources. She compared Venezuela under the PSUV to Mexico during the seventy years under the Institutional Revolutionary Party (PRI).

The secret ballot in the right to vote is often viewed as a crucial element in "free" elections: few voters feel "free" when the state camera is watching their ballot to see who they tick off. While secret ballot is guaranteed in Venezuela, in the community councils it is not so. There's no voting: everything is decided in assembly and as you know, assemblies can be interesting and important for some things, but also they have their defects. They're easily manipulated. All that's required are two or three leaders within an assembly to manipulate an assembly for or against a proposal." The direct democracy of the communal state is therefore extremely vulnerable to the "tyranny of the majority" where minorities can be deprived of their rights since there's no liberal framework to guarantee the rights of everyone.

I recalled that IWW convention in San Francisco when the proposal was on the floor to fund Darryl Cherney and Judi Bari, and how only Dave Karoly had the courage, knowledge, and independence of action to vote against it. It might have been quite different if there had been contrary opinions not only allowed, but encouraged; if Darryl and Judi had not been present for the vote; if the vote had been secret. But based on that, and the few community councils I'd attended, I knew what Margarita meant. That was, perhaps, a case of the worst of both forms of democracy: the convention inappropriately assumed the role of representative body on an issue that had needed to be voted on by the entire union, and had passed an initiative by means of the worst sort of "direct democracy."

It was getting late, and Margarita clearly wanted to end the interview, but I was curious about an interview with her I'd read in which she talked about the messianism of the Bolivarian movement. I asked her if she could talk a little bit about it, especially now that Chávez was gone.

Margarita said she'd been reading about the French Revolution and how the conception of popular sovereignty was rooted in the medieval world with the "Right of Kings" to govern, a right believed to be granted by God. "It's difficult to get rid of a king and try to legitimate a government that doesn't have that Divine Right, so there's a part of democratic theory that passes the Divine Right to Popular Sovereignty with the idea that, 'well, popular sovereignty is sort of divine. It can't be wrong, and what it decides is as if God were speaking. This idea that the People are wise and don't ever make mistakes is a religious idea, an idea of faith," and clearly as problematic as the right of Kings because people make mistakes, even as majorities. This "religious" conception of popular sovereignty is further complicated in a context such as Latin America, and Venezuela in particular, with the rule of populist caudillos who are believed to be leaders who "represent the popular sovereign, leaders that incarnate it and have, practically speaking, the 'divine right' to govern."

This, Margarita believed, was Chávez's view, that since "he was governing there was no need of unions to defend the interests of the workers" because he *was* the workers. Nor was there need for popular organizations, much less autonomous social movements because he *was* the State and the people. In other words, said Margarita, Chávez "had an image of himself that was quasi-religious."

When Chávez died, the government went into crisis. Clearly this divine right simply "couldn't be transferred to a mortal." The Bolivarian *nomenklatura* thus began to develop a "sort of civil religion in which Chávez delegated to his successors his 'Divine Right' to govern, in a manner of speaking." Thus Maduro, a follower of Sai Baba[8] who called himself the "Son of Chávez," said that Chávez had appeared to him as a little bird, like the Holy Spirit, to confer his blessing upon him.[9] This, Margarita argued, was invented to indicate that the "quasi-divine legitimacy has somehow been transferred to Maduro to govern."

It was an interesting theory, and it certainly was confirmed by the popular ethos, especially the mood among Chavistas who now referred to Chávez as the "Eternal Commander" (*el Comandante Eterno*). All the elements of a messianic and millenarian faith were in place, but the savior had only thus far resurrected in the form of a "little bird" that whispered its secret to his successor and then flew away, taking with it the plans for the Socialism of the Twenty-First Century.

CHAPTER NINETEEN

THE CURVES OF THE ROAD

THE PROUD SINNER'S PRAYER:

O God forgive me for having loved you more
than life itself and correct me in my ways;
make my way crooked
so I might delight in the curves of the road.
Give me more tasks and less success
that I may always be occupied with work
but never with fame.
And this daily bread
may I gain with the work of my own hands.
Withhold from me the love you bestow on prophets
and lead me not in the way of saviors
that I might have a long life,
unblessed by your rewards for the just.
May I never again fall into belief,

nor tarry long in the way of doctrine,
but rather live by my own experience,
guided only by the light of my soul.
Deliver me not from evil,
for in evil
have I found the good;
and lead me not,
for I have found my own way, straying
from the narrow path to the open field,
a realm that is your infinite loving heart,
where there is neither power, nor glory, nor kingdom,
forever and ever.
Amen.[1]

Even before I left Venezuela to return home, I'd organized
an event at the Public School, a community-based project that
came out of the Occupy uprising in late 2011. In my presentation I wanted to complement my experience with factual
information. So I began reading, studying, and researching,
starting with all the sources I'd ignored for years, like academics, mainstream journalist's reports, human rights reports, left
oppositionists, the economics/business sections of magazines
and newspapers and then reading the online opposition press
in Venezuela. I found and read *Dragon in the Tropics* by Javier
Corrales and Michael Penfold, and if one book put it all together, that was the book. After the interviews with Margarita
López Maya and Rafael Uzcátegui, I decided I needed to learn
more about populism, so I got a copy of *The Macroeconomics of
Populism in Latin America* by Sebastian Edwards and Rudiger
Dornbusch who, I was warned by a professor I met when we
went on tour with *Until the Rulers Obey*, were "right wingers."

He suggested that I complement their works with readings from the work of Kenneth Roberts and Carlos de la Torre on the same subject, which I happily did. Still, I found all of these writers, left and right, informative, and I practiced critical analysis and the guiding idea, suggested in the Anonymous programs, to "take what you like and leave the rest."

In the academic literature there was a whole range of opinions to read, but I also complemented academic analysis of Venezuela with news and analysis from the evanescent opposition press. I began to make a practice of daily reading the opposition newspapers online, until they were bought up or driven out of business by the Bolivarian government as has happened to so many newspapers in recent years, deprived of newsprint by the government.[2] Nevertheless, *El Nacional, Pro Davinci*, the right-wing news aggregator *Dolar Today*, so reviled by Maduro, *Run Run.es* by the excellent investigative reporter Nelson Bocaranda, Teodoro Petkoff's *Tal Cual*, all in Spanish, and sites like *Caracas Chronicles* (in English) all became my daily haunts. I still stopped in at the Chavista sites like *Aporrea* and *Venezuelanalysis*, but I ceased to rely on them for information as I once did. From the latter two sites I gained little else than the increasingly narrow and thin Bolivarian "government line."

Some twenty or so people showed up for my presentation at the Public School and I began by offering Kenneth Robert's list of the features of populism that Rafael Uzcátegui quotes in his book, which seemed to me to perfectly describe the Bolivarian process under Chávez:

1. A personalist and paternalistic model based on charismatic leadership
2. A multiclass political coalition targeting primarily the lower social sectors

3. A process of political mobilization directed from above to below that skips the institutional mechanisms of mediation or subjects them to more direct ties of the leader with the people.

4. An amorphous or eclectic ideology expressed in a discourse that exalts the subalterns or is anti-elite.

5. An economic project that uses redistributive or clientelist methods on a massive scale so as to build a material base so as to gain the backing of the popular sector.[3]

I talked about the destruction of the nationalized industries; the increasing reliance on imports (a policy in direct contradiction with "endogenous development") and an oil industry that was declining in production, at a rate of 3–4% per year, due to lack of maintenance and investment, and despite historically high oil prices; the growing authoritarianism; shortages of basic necessities and increasing rates of inflation that were pulverizing workers' salaries; the government's refusal to discuss collective contracts; the severe problem of corruption and impunity among PSUVistas and use of the judicial system apparently only to persecute political opponents.

I published an article at dissidentvoice.org entitled, "The Venezuelan Elections—Again" that drew criticism from Gregory Wilpert, directed at me, and also at the editors of Dissident Voice for having published my piece. About this time I did another talk in Berkeley for a Trotskyist group, Speak Out!, along the same lines as my earlier talk, only now with footage of the wrecked factories of the nationalized basic industries and charts showing production of those industries dropping dramatically after nationalization. Another of my articles came out a few days later posted, significantly, on July 19th, the anniversary of the Sandinista Revolution, at Counterpunch.org, under the title of "Building a Critical Left Solidarity Movement."[4] Within days of the publication of that article the attacks began, and continued through the summer, fall, winter, and into the following spring. I was informed by a few people who now qualified as "ex" friends, that they didn't any longer wish to be seen in public with me; they wanted no more contact with me; that they could no longer publish me and I should keep that to myself; that I was a "traitor" and, much later (2016), an "apostate."[5] The scatological comments came from academics, one saying in a message to a mutual acquaintance that Clif Ross had "lost his shit." Michael Lebowitz called my article "idiotic crap" and ended his "critique" saying "Anyone who has read Cliff Ross before will not be surprised by the shallowness of his work. The surprise, though, is that Counterpunch has valorised it. Are there no fact-checkers or editors there anymore?"[6]

In fact, no one bothered to "check the facts" because they would have found them to be accurate. Nor did anyone bother to address the issues I'd raised. And of all the people I knew, and of the many places I've published, still no one has addressed the issues I raised in that article. But evidently Lebowitz's comment was enough to end my relationship with Counterpunch.org as they quit responding to my submissions and queries from that time on.

There was one very touching moment in all this. Roger Burbach called me one day to see if he could "talk me back" to supporting the Bolivarian cause. Our review of his final book, *Latin America's Turbulent Transitions*, had just come out in the Summer issue of NACLA's *Report on the Americas* and he thanked me for the review. I was surprised because we hadn't been too enthusiastic about the book and I was now even more convinced than ever that "Twenty-First Century Socialism" was the same naked emperor of the twentieth century dressed up in a new set of visible clothes.

Roger and I spent nearly an hour on the phone in an intense discussion and neither of us could convince the other of his point of view. But what I did find moving was that the discussion was principled and avoided personal attacks, and it was one of few respectful conversations I've managed to have with my old solidarity comrades since I withdrew my support from that cause. Roger Burbach was an honest and courageous writer who had been one of the first North American solidarity activists to break with the corrupt Sandinistas under Daniel Ortega. At the time of our last conversation he was already in failing health, and he died less than two years later.

By the fall Marcy and I had finished most of the work on our book so when Arturo got in touch and suggested he and I do a movie on the Yukpa people in the Sierra de Perijá I jumped at the chance.[7] I knew that eventually my change of heart regarding the Bolivarian "revolution" would get around and it would be increasingly difficult for me to get in and move around Venezuela.

Sabino Romero, the Yukpa cacique (native chief) had been murdered around the same time Chávez had died, and the native people were all under attack. I thought that while I was in the country it might also be a good time to return to Guayana City and try to interview Rubén González, the Chavista and Secretary-General of the iron-worker's union who had been imprisoned for leading a strike.

By now Arturo had also come to believe that the process was at a dead end and that it had been an "*estafa*" (swindle, fake). We planned to meet in Cúcuta and then return to Mérida by taxis and buses.

Everything went according to plan this time. Arturo and I met up at a hotel and then the next morning went to the bus terminal to change dollars on the black market. I stuffed the bills into two compartments of my pack and into a folder in the main compartment and we caught a cab to the border. After passing through immigration we caught another collective cab from San Antonio to San Cristóbal. Midway to San Cristóbal we saw a checkpoint on the other side of the road, and then we knew we were in for trouble. Arturo had warned me about this when we were in Cúcuta.

"The National Guard has checkpoints around the country. We've got to be careful when we change the money to hide it well because they're stopping people and robbing them as they come over into Venezuela."

I thought of that now as we approached the checkpoint, and I said a little prayer. At this point in my life I no longer pray except when there's nothing else I can possibly do. I figure that Whatever It Is knows all, and my trying to tell it anything would be presumptuous. So I pray as an anxiety response, an involuntary spasm in response to conditions over which I have no control.

The prayer, I thought, had failed me because when the guardsman checked our identification, Arturo and I, sitting in the back seat, became the object of suspicion. When he searched Arturo's wallet and found another person's I.D. card, the soldier became convinced that we were traffickers. Arturo tried to convince the guardsman that it was the I.D. card of a friend who had left it at his house and he was holding it until the friend returned to reclaim it (which was the truth), but it didn't work. The guardsman went through his pack with a thoroughness that made my blood run cold. He found nothing but our hard drives and he asked about them. They were hard drives, Arturo explained, because we were documentary filmmakers. The guardsman looked at me with an expression meant to break me, but I showed nothing.

After he finished with Arturo, he began to go through my pack. He went through one side of pockets, but neglected the other side where he would have found a third of my money. Then he went through my pack, pulling out my socks, underwear and t-shirts; pulling out my camera bag and looking inside, but ignoring the one pocket where I had another third of my money; he searched through the book I'd just bought in Cúcuta, and he pulled out the folder, but didn't look inside where he would have found the other third of my money. Then he stood up and nodded at me to repack my things. By now I was trembling, but I carefully repacked my pack and suitcase. When Arturo and I were both packed up, he motioned for us to return to the car, which we did.

The taxi had patiently waited the forty-five minutes or so we were being searched, and now that we were inside, the guardsman stepped in front of the car and looked the driver in the eye. He stood there a moment, hesitating, then stepped aside and waved us on.

I stayed at Arturo's house in Ejido, just a few miles from the city of Mérida. We bought our bus tickets to Maracaibo, Zulia, on the Coromoto Line for seven in the evening. We arrived in plenty of time and went in to eat a couple of empanadas in the bus station before boarding our bus.

As he ate his empanada, Arturo smiled broadly. "This is the beginning of a big adventure," he promised. I looked back at him without saying anything. I'm sixty, I thought. At my age I don't need, I don't *want*, any more adventures. I smiled back.

We boarded the bus, and looked for our "buscama" or "bus bed" but the "bed" turned out to be dirty blue seats with dirty white seatcovers on the heads that were embroidered in English, "Elegance on Wheels."

We put on all our clothes to get ready for the night ride in the freezing conditions of the air-conditioned bus. I had on three t-shirts and a special light polyester jacket perfect for such conditions. Only my nose would get cold in the night as I could put my hands in my jacket pockets. Arturo wasn't as fortunate, but with a couple of towels and a washcloth and other clothing he managed to get comfortable.

We arrived at sunrise, groggily gathered our bags, and hailed a cab to take us to the place where we were to meet Lusbi. We waited at the appointed spot, in front of the offices of *Panorama Newspaper*, for nearly an hour, and by nine o'clock the heat was unbearable, even in the shade. Even Arturo was sweating. Finally, Lusbi arrived and we went to a café to have a juice before heading over to his friend's house for the interview.

Lusbi Portillo came up through the Socialist League of Venezuela but found the vanguard approach not to his liking. After graduating from the university, he moved across the north side of Lake Maracaibo to Cabimas. He found his experience in the League of great value since he'd learned there that though he wasn't a great orator, he excelled in organizing, and he put his skills to work with the Indigenous movement in Zulia, working with the Barí, the Yukpa, and the Wayuu as part of his work teaching at the University of Zulia. His non-profit NGO, Homo et Natura (Humans and Nature), has been working on land and mining issues as they relate to the indigenous people of the region. For the past fifteen years or so Lusbi has been targeted by ranchers as a communist guerrilla. At the same time the Chavistas accuse him of being CIA because he defends indigenous people from the Bolivarian government. Lusbi sees himself as a left social movement activist in a struggle for indigenous rights.

The protests of indigenous people of Zulia and the work of Homo et Natura Society forced President Chávez to back down on mining concessions he'd planned to hand out in 2009, but President Maduro has since been negotiating with Chinese and Russian corporations to exploit the rich coal reserves, Lusbi told us.

Lusbi wondered aloud, with a wind energy park in the extreme northern region of Zulia, the Goajira, why would they want to exploit the coal? And there were the plans for the natural gas line that would begin in Anzoátegui in the east, cross all of Venezuela, continue through Colombia, and pass Panama into Costa Rica, through Central America and Mexico, to arrive in the United States. Surely, Lusbi said in disbelief, "they're not planning to send the lowest polluting fuel to the United States and burn the worst polluting here?"

"Zulia also has incredible potential for solar energy, so let's use the clean energy of the sun and wind and the cleanest fossil energy, natural gas; all this is there to be used so there's no reason at all to open coal-generated electrical plants with all these other options."

But the governor of Zulia, Arias Cárdenas, other military officials, and transnational capitalists, are colluding to make a deal on the Sierra's coal. There's also another coal-fired plant they want to build, planned for Venezuela by the Initiative for the Integration of the Regional Infrastructure of South America (IIRSA). The IIRSA began in 2000, under the Brazilian presidency of Fernando Cardoso and funded by the Interamerican Development Bank, with strong private business input. Cardoso, as Lusbi put it, "tricked" all the presidents of South America, including Chávez, into the plan that is designed according to the needs of the transnationals and Europe.

"The transnationals, with Colombian, Venezuelan, and US capital, want to use the coal they plan to mine for their own purposes. And at whose cost? At the cost of more CO_2 that will worsen climate change, at the cost of the mountains, the rivers, the forests, and the lands of the indigenous people because the Sierra de Perijá is the ancestral territory of the Wayuu, the Yukpa, the Japrería and the Barí…" he said, listing them off.

Lusbi said that the environmental impact study had already been completed and all that was left was to grant the mining permits. The Wayuu opposed the mining because it would be done on their territory, and those living nearby would be negatively impacted by the coal dust and pollution. Two great reservoirs, the Manuelote and the Tulé provide water to Maracaibo and the region and he said, "if the coal is mined, the days of life of these two reservoirs are numbered." The mines would be located between the rivers Guasare and Maché and in a zone of various water flumes. In the end, a choice will have to be made, Lusbi said: "What do they want: water or coal?"

I'd remember seeing programs on government television in which people talked about all the legal and constitutional protections native people enjoyed and I asked Lusbi about that. Oh yes, indeed, there were all sorts of protections for native people, but they weren't enforced, he said, "laws about language and the obligatory use of indigenous languages in their territories, and requiring translators when they go to the cities, or when they are involved in legal processes" were all good, but they hadn't been put into effect.

As for the return of land to the native people, in Venezuela the "state doesn't just turn over a space to the indigenous people as part of their original territory. No, rather it's done as it's done with campesinos in land reform, that is, they're given title of land but on the condition that the use of energy and mineral resources remains the option of the state. These lands that are turned back over there are tertiary rights, under a civil code that is a copy of the Napoleonic code. So the indigenous people who are given [back] their land have to respect the rights of tertiary parties, and the tertiaries are the transnationals, the national and international mining companies, the lumber companies, the cattle ranchers, the campesinos, those with farming parcels." This, said Lusbi, "is an ongoing massacre of the indigenous people."

Lusbi said a railway was also planned as part of the IIRSA program. It would run along the foothills of the Sierra de Perijá, carrying phosphate from Táchira, coal from the mines in the foothills and, intersecting with railways from Colombia and eventually terminating in the Puerto America or what is now called Puerto Bolívar. Lusbi said that the planners at IIRSA and big business needed to break "bottlenecks" in transport of raw materials. The Andes and the Amazon presented obstacles to transport between the Atlantic and Pacific.

What was to be done with the large meandering rivers? Well, of course they would have to be straightened out and made into water highways. The great forests would be penetrated with highways and the mountains… would be blasted away. And so "all this becomes the struggle of the Indigenous people. They are the real 'vanguard' of the struggles of the world; they're the real ecologists and environmentalists; the real anti-imperialists because they oppose the presence of the transnationals, the imperial businesses, in their territories."

The IIRSA has a "focus on integration and development hubs (EIDs), new geo-economic referents for South American territorial planning" with the "end of improving competitiveness and promoting sustainable growth in the region" by integrating regional transport, energy, and tele-communications. In this scheme Puerto America will become one such "multimodal port where the oil, the coal, all the coal production from northern Colombia and Santander will leave from," said Lusbi. But the IIRSA is a regional initia-tive, and it isn't discussed inside the countries, but rather at a transnational level.

"Venezuela," Lusbi said, "is like a trampoline in this config-uration. Not only a trampoline for the drugs that come from Colombia, but it's a trampoline for all the merchandise that comes out of Colombia through the Free Trade Agreement with the US. Venezuela is a thoroughfare of the IIRSA, an outlet to the Atlantic Ocean, to the US, and Europe. That's how they'll carry away the lands of the indigenous people. The great losers will be the rivers, the forests, the indigenous people, the peasants, the people, the fishermen … Because the two most important fishing zones in Venezuela are Sucre and Zulia, the Gulf of Venezuela. And the fishermen will die out, and move to another trade."

Post-Panamax ships, which are too large to traverse the Panama canal, according to Lusbi, "will be coming and go-ing, interrupting the spawning of shrimp, the movement of dolphins and big fish, the blue crab. So this fishing zone of great importance for Venezuela will disappear. And what does Venezuela have to sell on these railways and through these ports? Nothing. All Venezuela has to sell is oil, and that goes out by boat, and if it's gas, it'll be a pipeline."

Who makes all these decisions? It's not the people, not the Wayuu, the Añu, the Yukpa whose land is being destroyed by all this extractive industry. Rather, it's the technicians, the World Bank, the Interamerican Development Bank, the US, European, and now Chinese and Iranian capitalists. "So now we're substituting the US empire with the Chinese empire."

Lusbi said that Tarek el Aissami, in his role of Minister of the Interior and Justice of Venezuela began recruiting the *caciques mayores* (great caciques, or leaders), and began to undermine indigenous authority and traditional forms of organization by imposing community councils on them and selecting the caciques who would go along with their project as mediators.[8] "The community councils have nothing to do with the traditions of the indigenous peoples," Lusbi said. "And then the money came, the community councils were funded with 400, 800 million bolívares and those community councils did what they wanted with it. The caciques bought trucks and houses in Machiques, and some handed out money to their people, an amount that wasn't enough to do anything with."

"The Yukpa, before contact with the Capuchin missionaries and others didn't have caciques: they were communal people with power residing in families. They'd been struggling since the dictatorship of Juan Vicente Gómez for their land. But now Tarek El Aissami was able to gain control of indigenous communities through the caciques who essentially became government employees." Only Sabino, and a small group were left to carry on the fight, Lusbi said.

"[In Ecuador with President Rafael] Correa you have the same thing; he has the same model. He doesn't respect the [indigenous] movements or CONAIE or the campesino movements, "Lusbi said, adding that Correa also thinks he is The State, and the Citizen Revolution is based on individualism with no conception whatever of people's organizations or social rights. It's an "entrepreneurial state" that sees citizens as employees. Unions aren't allowed, and "CONAIE means nothing." "Everything is seen in its function as raw material for the transnationals, who are the real imperialists, all the oil and minerals of Venezuela and Ecuador," Lubsi said, "It's the same colonial policy. If it weren't for these so-called "revolutionary governments" the transnationals couldn't have moved forward. AD and COPEI couldn't have managed to get the oil and ironworkers and indigenous people on board with the development proposal, called "*Plan de la Patria*" (Plan for the Homeland*)*. There had to be a Chávez with a pseudo-left, so-called "revolutionary" proposal, the same with Correa and Kirshner and Lula.

This "revolutionary" model is what allows the imposition of the IIRSA, which represents the recolonization of America. "All the virgin areas, all the spaces that neither the Spaniards nor Portuguese could destroy will be handed over by the 'revolutionary' governments, by these so-called 'revolutionaries.' For all this you need a [Rafael] Correa to destroy CONAIE... and a [Hugo] Chávez, since no one else could have the worker's movement, the ironworkers, oil workers and indigenous people in his pocket."

I asked Lusbi if there had really been a revolution in Venezuela. It was the question that had been rumbling around in my mind at that point for nine years.

"A revolution?" he echoed. "Yes, there was a revolution here. A capitalist revolution, a revolution that Capital needs, that the rich, the entrepreneurs, and modernity all need. It's the logic of modernity, of positivism. It's the logic of North American welfare that it wants to impose on the world, on China, the Arab [world], the Wayuu, the Yukpa, the Barí. Whether it be Chávez, Carlos Andrés Pérez, or [Colombian President Juan Manuel] Santos or [former Colombian President Alvaro] Uribe, it's the same logic of progress of Auguste Comte, of Capital."

I asked Lusbi about alternatives. Where would we find the alternatives to all this?

"The alternative," he said, "the alternative is community groups. Social groups. What did Chavismo do? It destroyed social organizations by making a formula, a single formula. The micropower, Foucault called it, and micropower is controlled by the community councils. So the campesinos, the indigenous, the neighborhoods all have one formula: community councils. There's a Law of Community Councils, a ministry that controls it and there's a Minister of Community Councils, a minister for something more that is the union of community councils with others, which is called communes, so everything is regimented. So life will be as the government says, not according the will of community groups."

In Maracaibo, as elsewhere, Lusbi estimated "some 99.9%" of the social movement and community organizations went to work for the Bolivarian government. Camera people, sound people, he said, "went to work at the 'community radios' which are the government's, financed by the government, under permission of the government, with the propaganda of the government." Others went to work in the Bolivarian Universities of Venezuela (UBVs), others with the Universities of the Police, the UNERS, and still others went to the villages… So the whole social movement was defeated; the Left was defeated. Chavismo came along and mounted all this; Chávez took over this social irreverence, he crucified it, cut it up, gave it all a name, put it all under a single law and brought the social movements to an end."

Homo Et Natura, Lusbi said, didn't go along with it, and so the Chavistas said he and those around Homo Et Natura "are 'imperialist agents,' 'escualidos,' 'counterrevolutionaries.' They kicked us out of projects that we were in like Funda Ayacucho where we had a social and cultural project of growing chickens. They kicked us out of all that and they persecuted us, and they still are persecuting us. They built alliances with miners against us, alliances with cattle ranchers, and even *sicarios* [paid killers] against us, saying we were counterrevolutionaries. They called us paramilitaries because we didn't form community councils and put ourselves under their formula."

"But we defeated the government on the issue of coal mining. We defeated the racist policy of the government in the surveying and about the jurisdiction of indigenous lands. So we're an example of how a few 'nobodies' [can win], of how the real power isn't in the community councils, or in the city governments or in the ministries. It's the organized people, the social organizations. These are what [Ecuadoran President Rafael] Correa wants to destroy, and [Colombian President Juan Manuel] Santos wants to destroy, and what they want to destroy in Brazil and here in Venezuela, it's the social movement organizations: the organizations that aren't government or state. We aren't the state. Nor are we enemies of the state. We're not enemies of the government because if it develops the policies with the people, we accept it and can get along with it."

He said there needed to be that "revolution in the revolution: a popular revolution." And the people needed to have real political power, which meant "the ability to design society, determine the design of a country, the life of a people. That's power, people deciding for themselves. Chávez should have used all that power to empower the people, not for an office, and a salary, and to fulfill one orientation, but so many schools would develop, many different ideas. Not taking away the microphone from anyone, but having more microphones, making it more complex. But they say 'no, we can't do that because then the escualidos would defeat us.' No. If there's no diversity of thought, no eternal, ongoing discussion, there's no revolution."

These last words reminded me of Emilio Campos, and his call for more and different points of view to break the

Bolivarian plan of "Communicational hegemony." It also made me think of Margarita López Maya's defense of liberalism and the need to build a society with plural perspectives, based on respect for differences. Wasn't that the left I was part of in Berkeley? I thought of Damian Prat. Perhaps he was right that this Bolivarian project was the farcical repetition of the socialism of the twentieth century, the Leninist project of an elite to impose its utopia on people and movements who had their own ideas of what world they wanted to live in.

It was late morning and Arturo and I had to get to Machiques by the late afternoon so we brought the interview to an end and got on our way. We were to meet Ana María Fernández, a Yukpa woman who had lost two brothers, and would soon lose a third, in a struggle to reclaim their land.

We spent the next few days in the Sierra de Perijá with Ana María and the Yukpas, recording interviews with them about their struggle to wrest control of their land from the mining interests and cattle ranchers. They hoped the Maduro government would deliver justice, but I wasn't optimistic, given that elements of the government colluded in the crimes against the Yukpa. In fact, just months after we met, June 24, 2014, two more of Ana María's brothers were so brutally beaten by National Guardsmen that one, Cristóbal, died.

It was, indeed, the adventure Arturo had promised it would be, but I was glad to get back to Mérida. We spent a few days in Ejido recuperating at Arturo's house and, while there, Arturo introduced me to a neighbor of his, Miguel, a former teacher who described himself as "neither of the left nor the right, but a free thinker."

We'd gone over to Miguel's house so I could get online to check and send emails since Arturo didn't have Internet at home. Miguel welcomed us into his home and served us coffee and we started talking.

Miguel had clearly been much more allied with the Chavista project at some point in time, especially when he worked with a number of educators at a national level redesigning curriculum for the Bolivarian project. That project fell apart, Miguel noted mysteriously, "as a result of a rumor" and that was the end of his time working with the government.

"This process is failing," he said somberly. "It's reached a ceiling beyond which it cannot go. There has to be a big crisis that blows everything apart so something new can arise from below. I hope we'll see youth take a leadership role."

Miguel mentioned having known Kleber Ramírez Rojas, an important revolutionary thinker from Mérida whose ideas had been a significant influence on Chávez. Miguel talked enthusiastically about Kleber and gave me some electronic documents from his USB drive about which he spoke passionately. After finishing the coffee Arturo and I went home and I left with a strong feeling that this "free thinker" who was neither of the right or left was, nevertheless, of the left, even if he was no longer a believer.

Arturo's wife, Mayi, was home for the weekend. She worked for the government in Child Protective Services in El Vigía during the week, barely making enough money to pay her transportation back and forth in collective taxis, but she wouldn't quit work because, she said, there would be no one to look after the children if she weren't there. Things had gotten bad for her because she challenged some policies in the office. She was thereafter labeled escualida and no longer was given office supplies and found everything she did blocked or hindered by the Chavistas.

We flew to Guayana and Carl met us at the airport and brought us back to his posada. The next day he drove Arturo and me around Guayana so we could record images of the city. He dropped us off at *Correo de Caroní* where we did interviews with Clavel and a Sidor ironworker who happened to be in the office to do another interview. The worker told us we might find Rubén at the Sidor plant since there was an action planned for the afternoon, so we took a bus to the plant.

We'd been here at the Sidor plant a day or two before and tried to record a gathering in front of the plant, but people had surrounded us and told us to stop recording. A few were quite hostile and wouldn't listen to us as we explained what we were trying to do. I immediately stopped filming, but Arturo got into an argument with a few people and I had to intervene and tell Arturo to "back off." I hoped this time around we'd have better luck and Rubén would allow us to film.

And, indeed, we were in luck; Rubén was meeting with workers outside the plant and we arrived just as everyone was taking a break. Rubén and I recognized each other from a brief meeting in April before the rally with Capriles when I tried unsuccessfully to arrange an interview with him. Neither of us wanted to miss this opportunity so he agreed to do an interview on the spot.

Rubén said that Venezuela was rich in resources and could sell raw materials to China, but it would, in the process, lose the added value of refining the materials itself. "Refined, hot-briquetted iron can sell for up to $300 per ton. But raw iron sells for $70–100 a ton. We're losing two hundred percent by selling raw iron. But what's happening here is the absence of investment. This government, and for that matter, previous governments have had no investment policy. And that's another way of saying that we're 'underdeveloped.' We have all the capacity to be developed, all the natural wealth to be developed, wealth unlike any other country in Latin America, but we haven't had a government with that vision; we haven't had a government that understood this wealth isn't for them to enrich themselves from but rather to use it to build the wealth of the people."

Rubén said that the union had been undertaking protests and actions for a collective bargaining agreement and against the criminalization of protest. "We want the government to obey the Constitution and the labor laws and deal with collective contracts. We want an end to blackmail, attacks and persecution, because this is what we've been subject to. Our struggle has been, simply put, for respect. We'd love to see some reforms, but more importantly, we just want [the Venezuelan state] to fulfill its obligations under the law."

Rubén also insisted that the wages needed to be tied to inflation so there wouldn't be a constant deterioration of acquisitive power that has "unfortunately left workers in the state of misery that they're in today."

Arturo asked about the attempts of the government to impose its own union on the workers of Sintraferrominera (the independent union that Rubén leads) and Rubén said that, yes, some people from the government union movement had come around, but the workers had ignored them. "The workers here are clear that they didn't represent their interests, but rather the interests of the government." He took this further when he said that "the FBST (Fuerza Bolivariana Socialista de Trabajadores, Bolivarian Socialist Worker's Force) and Movimiento 21 are part of the government and they're traitors to the workers' movement. The government locates them in all the industries to divide workers."

I asked Rubén about the previous encounter Arturo and I had had with workers in front of the entrance and Rubén was apologetic. "You have to understand that you've come into a situation where workers have suffered from great disrespect and many injustices, such as being subjected to judicial proceedings by the political authorities and so the workers are predisposed to be suspicious, especially since the government has also been recording events and using those recordings to bring people to the tribunals."

I asked Rubén about his support for Chavismo and he said that, like many in Venezuela, he'd initially supported a project that broke with the hegemony of the AD and COPEI as the two ruling parties. But then the new government under Chávez mismanaged the economy and wasted the windfall from the historic oil boom. And then in the midst of all this, Chávez had him jailed for seventeen months "just for doing my job in the union and defending the rights of workers." Those experiences have made him a more critical activist as now, "we don't defend any process, or any person blindly. Here we work with a clear and conscious grasp of the reality that we're living. And the reality is that here there is a generalized deterioration and if we defend this government, we're defending the generalized deterioration of this company. So what do we want? Let me be frank. This government isn't going to change its policies because they're not the losers in this. They've all become multimillionaires while the poor are poorer by the day and the only thing that concerns them is 'governability.' Meanwhile we live in a situation here that is 'asphyxiating.' In this adversity God has given us the creativity to meet it, so we're going to take one step up on the ladder to victory. We can't be afraid because dignity is priceless."

Arturo asked him about the so-called "economic sabotage" and the narrative of the "economic war" against Venezuela and Rubén responded with a wry smile. This narrative of sabotage and economic war is a "generalized misconception across the country, and it reflects very bad politics. Remember, politics is the art of governing, but governing with efficiency, transparency, and quality. The politics [of the present government] is expressed in the art of lying. In other words, all the industries of the government, including those they 'rescued,' are all in deterioration and approaching bankruptcy. That's the situation of PDVSA, Sidor, Bauxilum, Alcasa, Ferrominera, Carbonorca, etc. In other words, we have the same thing across the entire country and it's not the fault of the workers or the 'right wing' but rather those in government, who never thought of governing, but rather of enriching their little group in power. They never invested in these businesses, but totally bled them dry. They themselves are the saboteurs." He noted that, "of course if you say this they accuse you of being in the opposition. But I'm not with the opposition nor the government. I'm a social [movement] worker who sees things clearly and if it were the bad policies of the opposition, I'd also denounce them the same way. And I'm not saying I'm always right: I make my mistakes. But the important thing is when we make mistakes to recognize them because that's the only way we can correct our ways."

At this point Rubén said he had to end the interview and get on with his work so we thanked him and left. I had completed my work in Guayana; now I could go home.

We had Carl take us to the bus station and Arturo got his ticket back to Ejido and I managed to get the last seat on a night bus headed to Cúcuta. I said goodbye to Arturo and settled into my seat just as the rain began pouring down.

We rode all night and the next day through a succession of intense rainstorms. A few miles from the border our bus was stopped at a military checkpoint so the soldiers could check IDs. When they came to me, the soldier handed me my passport back and sent me into the station. There were a couple of other people in front of me, but when the officer saw me he sent them back to the bus. He asked me the usual set of questions and I remained calm, and alternated between acting bored and indignant that I'd been pulled from the bus. In fact, I was really worried about the interviews I had on my camera. I'd downloaded a number of them, nearly all of them, in fact, onto a hard drive which I had well-hidden in my suitcase in the luggage hold of the bus, but if they found the footage on the camera in my pack, they'd certainly be motivated to go through my suitcase. But after some ten or so minutes of questions, they let me go and I ran back through the rain to re-board the bus.

I arrived in San Cristóbal in the late afternoon and caught the bus to San Antonio and crossed over into Colombia where a taxi driver waved at me and asked me if I wanted a ride into Cúcuta. We agreed on a price and I put my bags in his trunk and got in the car. The cool breeze was a relief from the late afternoon heat. I heaved a huge sigh of relief.

"They say Colombia is a country you have to worry about, but I feel so much relief when I leave Venezuela behind, and come back to Colombia," I said to the driver.

He laughed. "Colombia is safe, man. But Venezuela…" he just shook his head.

Then I noticed a wad of bills in his window visor.

"You just leave your money there?" I asked incredulously.

The driver smiled and shrugged. "Why not? It's easier to get at there."

"You wouldn't do that in Venezuela," I said.

He looked at me as if to say, "are you crazy?"

"Ni modo! No way!" he laughed. "I wouldn't carry money there." Then he told me about a friend of his, also a taxi driver, who was robbed twice in one day in Venezuela. At gunpoint. He was lucky both times. They didn't kill him.

CHAPTER TWENTY

PUTTING THE PUZZLE TOGETHER

Cúcuta again, and what a welcomed sight! Here I was able to wander around carefree for a day or so before my flight out, and it was a perfect place to assimilate all the contradictions of the country I'd just left behind and compare them with the paradoxes of the country I'd just entered. After all, the border between Venezuela and Colombia is the fault line where a rising capitalist Colombia and Venezuela in the throes of a failing utopian project collide like two tectonic plates. In this collision, Colombia definitely comes out the winner, and how this dramatic encounter plays out also reveals a very different view of the world than the one the Bolivarian government tries to pass off as the reason for the collapse of Chávez's vision of "Twenty-First Century Socialism."

The narrative the Bolivarian government and its supporters offer about why the economy of Venezuela is becoming one of the world's great disasters is very simple and unoriginal, but its very simplicity and familiarity make it appear credible. This view was captured in a statement one solidarity activist, who had been in Chile during the coup that overthrew Salvador Allende in 1973, made to me, "what's happening in Venezuela is a repeat of what happened in Chile." He was, of course, referring to the CIA destabilization activities that eroded Allende's popularity, from black propaganda in newspapers to planning, logistics, and material support to the military in the coup. This, and other anti-democratic, illegal and, in some cases genocidal, covert operations for which the CIA came to be known, give credence to the claim that the same thing has been going on in Venezuela under the Bolivarians.

Nevertheless, Venezuela is not Chile, nor are Maduro or Chávez Salvador Allende, and even the United States government is not the same government that helped overthrow Allende. While it seems probable that the Bush administration encouraged and supported the coup against Chávez in April 2002, no one has offered credible evidence of CIA plots against the Bolivarian government since that time, nor even that the Bush administration was a *major* player in that coup attempt.[1] Moreover, given the very different international context (the absence of a Communist bloc, and the end of the Cold War), a very different executive branch under Obama, with a focus quite different from that of Richard Nixon's, the narrative seems distinctly outdated. This is not by any means to say that imperialism is no longer a factor in international politics, but that in the post-Cold War world it uses other (mostly international) mechanisms, strategies, and tactics.

What Bolivarians can point to, with compelling evidence, are programs that fit with the post-Cold War US government policy of "democracy promotion" in Latin America or what is in fact polyarchy, "a system in which a small group actually rules, and participation in decision making by the majority is confined to choosing among competing elites in tightly controlled electoral processes."[2] Bolivarian supporters point to the $15 million-dollar-a-year program the US government has for training Venezuelan opposition activists in the use of social media or the $5 million per year to "help civil society to promote institutional transparency, engage diverse constituencies in the democratic process, and defend human rights."[3] As threatened as some activists might feel by money the US spends on promoting "transparency" and engaging "diverse constituencies in the democratic process" or defending human rights in Venezuela, it's not out of proportion to what the US spends in other countries of Latin America.[4] Indeed, as Corrales and Penfold write, "aid provided by the United States to non-state actors in Venezuela seems puny in comparison to aid allocated to other nations, and to the level of funds the Venezuelan government itself has spent abroad."[5]

As an example of the latter we could cite the Bolivarian funding of the internal opposition—in the US. Perhaps the most egregious incident of Bolivarian lobbying went through CITGO as it sought to hinder provisions in the Clean Air Act perceived to negatively affect its interests. In that particular case the amount came to well over US $100,000 paid out to the Dukto Group, subsidiary of DCS, according to Casto Ocando.[6] Compare that to the $53,400 the National Endowment for Democracy (NED) funneled to the Venezuelan opposition during the Referendum against Chavez in 2004.[7] While there is always the possibility the US has a "black budget" for destabilizing the Bolivarian government, what it spends publicly to fund "democracy promotion" projects in Venezuela is chump change compared to what Chávez was tossing around in the US during the oil boom: In 2004 alone he spent over ten times that, precisely US$553,699.43, funding the Washington-based Venezuelan Information Office for salaries and expenses in order to improve his image in the US.[8] And then there's the case of Democratic Senator Mary Landrieu who seems to have been key to the vetoing of a US Senate bill to sanction Venezuelan human rights violators after she was lobbied by Patton and Boggs, a firm representing CITGO in the US.[9] In all, Casto Ocando's research on the Bolivarian "interventions" in the US total over 500 pages and he estimates from the information he compiled that the Bolivarian government has spent over US $300 million, lobbying, influencing, propagandizing, and otherwise "interfering in the internal affairs" of the United States.[10] At current rates of US funding to "democracy" programs in Venezuela, it would take sixty years to catch up to what Chávez spent on influence in the US.

Bolivarian oil money appears to have paid off in the US left's media reporting on Venezuela. In an email *Z Magazine* sent out as a fundraising plea, editor Michael Albert acknowledged that, starting in mid 2014, when student demonstrations and protests were still ubiquitous in Venezuela, *Z Magazine* began receiving up to $10,000 per month from TeleSur, an amount that Albert openly admitted had sustained the magazine through that time.[11] TeleSur is a television channel started by Hugo Chávez and supposedly funded by various governments in South America, although 70% of its start-up money and, more importantly, its direction and its political "line," come from the Bolivarian government.[12] Whether or not, or to what degree these Bolivarian petrodollars shaped *Z Magazine*'s political line is an open question, but it's noteworthy that its communications site, Znet, only published its first article critical of

Venezuela after the money was cut off.[13] In any case, money that came into the coffers of left media has served to shore up a solid pro-Bolivarian consensus on the international left that only began to crack with Chávez's death.

Evidence is fairly strong that United States policy under Obama has been much less ideological and far more pragmatic toward Bolivarian Venezuela. In fact, US anti-Venezuelan pronouncements had already declined dramatically as early as 2006 as a result of US policy even as "some of the most antagonistic policies adopted by Venezuela occurred after 2006."[14] Less than two months after the April 2013 presidential elections in Venezuela, US Secretary of State John Kerry met with Venezuelan counterpart Elías Jaua in Guatemala to discuss closer relations between the two countries.[15] Notably, no high-level US government official met either before or after those elections with Venezuelan opposition presidential candidate Henrique Capriles.

The US continues to be Venezuela's number one trading partner with $41.4 billion in annual trade that drops some US$30 billion petro-dollars into the Bolivarian government's bank account. The fact that democratic institutions are being undermined by the Bolivarian government, and that Venezuela is rapidly morphing from a petro-state into a narco-state and that its economic policies are so destructive of the country that it now faces a humanitarian crisis apparently are concerns of the US government, as all that could destabilize the region and put a great burden on neighboring governments.[16] But these are also issues that should worry humanitarians and solidarity activists.

There are many indications that the nature of US imperial interest in Latin America has changed since the days of the Cold War when the US government saw "red" whenever anyone in its "sphere of influence" raised a hand in protest to capitalism. Communism is no longer a credible threat in the Americas, especially as even Cuba is returning to the fold of those operating with capitalist market economies. The US government under Obama, as it has shown in normalizing relations with Cuba, is far more interested in economic globalization under the transnational treaties and agreements than in engaging in ideological wars that pay no interest or dividends.

Indeed, the "left" governments of Latin America, as Raúl Zibechi told us when we visited him in Montevideo, and has amply detailed his writings, have been a perfect tool for the transnational corporations to manage populations while they continue extraction of resources. Left and environmental activists will think twice, and very carefully, before attacking a "left" or "progressive" president over concessions given to transnational corporations to extract public resources and damage the environment in the process: consider the delicate, cautious, and sympathetic approach of US environmentalists to Obama's fracking (even if Obama is arguably neither "left" nor "progressive"). The same concerns social movements in Venezuela have, as Rafael Uzcátegui so clearly pointed out, that left criticism will play into the hands of the right wing, are also at work in the minds of US activists.

No doubt the US has several contingency plans for Venezuela as the Bolivarian project unwinds due to incompetence, corruption, mismanagement, and plummeting oil prices, and among those, no doubt, would include the search for an alternative elite to replace the Boligarchy. But I see no convincing evidence of US interest over the past decade in destabilizing the Bolivarians—to the contrary, at least in the short term, US farmers, business, and corporate interests have benefited greatly as Venezuela increased imports from the US under the Bolivarians which now include even oil[17] and gasoline (in 2013 it imported double the amount of gas that it exported[18]). If the US threw in $5 million per year to fund "democracy" programs in Venezuela perceived to benefit the opposition, it poured $30 *billion* into Venezuelan government coffers buying its oil.

Considering all this, blaming the economic and political disaster on US interference just doesn't wash. But that has been the core of the Bolivarian and left solidarity argument to explain the failure of the Bolivarian project, and essentially the only argument most left media has been willing to entertain. James Petras went so far as to assert "Washington… encouraged hoarding and price gouging by commercial capitalists (supermarket owners). It encouraged smugglers to purchase thousands of tons of subsidized consumer goods and sell them across the border in Colombia."[19] According to the Bolivarian narrative that Petras and other solidarity activists like him also promote, the problems facing Venezuela today are almost entirely the result of imperialist policies and a malicious capitalist class.

Petras's argument may be patronizing in its portrayal of the Venezuelan opposition as passively awaiting orders from Washington, but it also dovetails perfectly with the Bolivarian argument of a presumed "economic war" in which the Venezuelan money (bolívar) is being "attacked" in undefined ways by speculators, and the scarcity of products is the result of "sabotage" by manufacturers and those who traffic goods into neighboring countries to sell at higher prices, or those who "hoard" products.

No doubt there are Venezuelans who profit from activities that damage the country's economy, but there is strong evidence that the government and its supporters have the greatest share of the responsibility, and this is in keeping with the views of a majority of Venezuela's best economists, including

Chavistas like Nicmer Evans and Felipe Pérez Martí.[20] They would all agree that this narrative is a complete reversal of logic, making effects responsible for causes. They argue that the real cause of Venezuela's economic woes are government and ruling-party corruption, impunity, incompetence, cronyism; bad economic policies, especially price and currency controls; lack of investment in nationalized industries; bad management and administration and a complete lack of accountability; the absence of "rule of law" and protection of property rights; and other misguided government policies. It would require another book to do justice to these issues but we could at least consider a few of them here.[21]

Price and currency controls are part of an economic program implemented in Venezuela in 2003. Currency controls were put in place ostensibly to prevent capital flight and to protect national industries after the PDVSA "oil strike" (or "lockout"), and price controls were imposed to protect the poor from the impact of inflation in basic necessities that could result from currency controls.

In such a situation, unless all the controls are very stringently enforced, the economy can become extremely distorted as the money becomes overvalued, giving rise to inflation, and the "decreed" prices of commodities become unrealistically low. This situation gives rise to two black markets: one in currency that is artificially overvalued, and another in the marketplace where products are artificially undervalued.

In the currency market the difference between the official value of the bolívar, set by the government, and the market rate, that is, what people in the real world of buying and selling with that very currency determine its value to be, began to diverge early on. But with increased state expenditures, especially on social and development programs so crucial to keeping Chávez and his people in power, the government financed its overspending ("monetized debt"), by essentially taking over Venezuela's Central Bank and running the money-printing presses 24–7 to cover those internal obligations. The Venezuelan Central Bank, for instance, increased money supply by 70% in the year from November 2012 to November 2013 and has since then continued a similar policy,[22] essentially guaranteeing inflation and inducing hyperinflation.[23] By early 2016 the government would effectively double the money supply with an order of 10 billion bolívar notes (adding to a late 2015 order of 5 billion notes). By then not even those bills would be produced in the country: They would be printed outside, and flown into Venezuela on some three dozen 727 cargo planes. This mountain of money would surely "stoke inflation," which, in 2016, economists agree would be at least 720%.[24] Such monetary policies have resulted in a dramatic loss of wealth to inflation for Venezuelans: since 1999 when Chávez came to power, combined inflation has been an estimated 34,258%.[25]

At the same time the government relied heavily on price controls to keep inflation down, but in a context of constantly increasing money supply, with decreasing success. In other words, Chávez and Maduro both seemed to believe that by decree they could win a war against the "law of supply and demand." They didn't need an economist to tell them that if you increase the money supply, and decrease the supply of commodities (by restricting your imports to save your foreign currency, for instance) you'll have both inflation and scarcity.

Scarcity was further exacerbated when those price-controlled items increasingly became attractive as contraband to be sold at market prices across porous borders. But of course there were also ways to make those same commodities magically reappear in disguised form as commodities without price controls. Rice, for instance, was a price-controlled item, but *flavored* rice wasn't.

But price controls also led to scarcity by destroying national production. As inflation hit the prices of non-controlled items related to production like insecticides, fertilizers, tractor, or factory parts, inputs for manufacturing, etc. it increased the costs of production beyond the controlled price of the commodity. Gradually, farmers, manufacturers, industrialists, small craftsmen, and all other productive members of the economy found they couldn't afford to produce rice, corn, milk, cheese, or just about anything that was under price controls. As a result, Venezuela began to rely even more heavily on imported products. When it costs twice as much to raise chickens as you can [legally] sell them for in the market, due to price controls, it becomes more profitable to traffic them. As one Venezuelan complained to me, "they import chicken from Brazil and subsidize it so that the price is lower in Venezuela than it is in Brazil. So it's no surprise, then, that this food then becomes contraband, sometimes returning to its country of origin to compete as a lower-priced 'import.'" You could find it all in Cúcuta, for instance, feeding the thriving black, gray, and legal markets with corn, coffee, rice, and anything else you might want.

There was another element to the growing scarcity, besides trafficking goods out of the country, "disguising" price controlled items, and overpriced inputs that destroyed national production. Currency control effectively centralized control of imports and put it all in the hands of the government. Let's say, a manufacturer needs screws to make widgets, and those screws are no longer being made in Venezuela because the screw manufacturer can't compete with cheaper screws imported from Colombia. So the widget maker also needs to import screws. But he can't pay the Colombian manufacturer in bolívares (bs.) since international transactions have to be made in the reserve currency of the world (US dollars) or, in this case, Colombian pesos. But with currency controls, he has only two options: either he can change his bs. on the black market, where the screws would cost him an arm and a leg, buying dollars at well over 1000 bs.; or he can try to get dollars through the government at 10 bs. to the dollar (or the SIMADI, another official rate, at 400 bs. to the dollar). Either way, he now stands before the gates to two parallel hells. The process of getting dollars from the government has a distinctly Kafkaesque quality, and it's far from guaranteed that, after submitting all the forms with dotted "i"s and crossed "t"s, that the government will approve your request.[26] And even with the approval, it might take a very long time to receive the money. Meanwhile, production could come to a full stop, making it necessary for the country to look elsewhere for widgets. They could, after all, be imported… and probably at a lower price! But to import them, the widget importer would need foreign exchange to pay for the widgets.

If you have a direct line to the government or if, for instance, you happen to be in the PSUV, or know someone in government, or you're an important person, this whole process suddenly can become very simple, and very easy. In that case, the approval, and timely delivery of your dollars are suddenly streamlined and practically guaranteed.

And so while price controls, especially when managed by a corrupt and incompetent government, became a convoluted way of "solving problems" that resulted in exacerbating them, currency controls became the "seedbed for corruption in the country" which has been used as "an assault mechanism on the public treasury for the benefit of a few."[27] That is to say, the corrupt officials who had surrounded Chávez all those years, were invested in keeping the currency controls so as to make their huge fortunes with shell companies, or by one of many "import-export" schemes.[28] As the discrepancy between the black market and the official rate grew, so did currency arbitrage, that is, the buying of money at one rate (as of February 2016, 10 bs to $1), and selling it at another (over 1000 bs. to $1).[29]

It's common knowledge in Venezuela that this is a problem rampant among the Chavista hierarchy, the military and Bolivarian-connected ("enchufados") business people privileged to get cheap dollars. Fitting that profile to a "T" was long-time "Number Two" in the government, Diosdado Cabello—a military man of the Chavista hierarchy with many businesses. Diosdado was fingered by none other than *rojo rojito* (redder than red) Chavista talk-show host Mario Silva in a private conversation Silva had with a Cuban intelligence agent, later obtained and released by the opposition.[30] Among Cabello's many lucrative activities, is alleged to be drug trafficking, which is increasingly taking up the slack for the government's need for foreign exchange as oil prices drop.[31]

Although the possibility of a family dynasty in Venezuela was complicated by the early death of Hugo Chávez, his family and associates have their fingerprints on all the goods of the country—including suitcases full of cocaine shipped through the country.[32] Drug traffickers connected to the present First Family gain access to hangars reserved for government officials; their pilots are active duty military, and they're given diplomatic passports to carry out their work.[33] In Chávez's place is his handpicked successor, Nicolás Maduro and his wife, Cilia Flores (both of whom have moved their family members into positions of power), while former Vice President Jorge Arreaza, is Chávez's (ex) son-in-law, formerly married to Rosa Virginia Chávez. But it's really her younger sister who was closest to daddy President, María Gabriela Chávez, and reputed to be the wealthiest person in Venezuela with a net value of US $4.2 billion.[34] María Gabriela, who filled in as ersatz First Lady until her father's death, is known in Venezuela as "the Rice Queen," since she has been "accused of pocketing illicit income by over-pricing Argentine rice imports at a time when food shortages are rampant in Venezuela.[35] There is speculation that this was the reason she was made Venezuela's deputy permanent representative to the UN, to give her immunity from prosecution in the case. Brothers, cousins, and a coterie of friends of the "Comandante Eterno" still occupy other posts and no doubt the case of María Gabriela offer them encouragement to follow in her footsteps to success, given that the risks to those associated with the Chávez family name are few, and the currency controls can be worked any number of ways to almost guarantee jackpot winnings.

Honest Chavistas, including Felipe Pérez Martí, former Minister of Chávez who actually helped design the currency controls, now argue against them. Martí says that the "controls are designed for the corrupt" politicians. Nicmer Evans, one of Chavismo's most astute and serious intellectuals and member of the left opposition, Marea Socialista, claims some $259 billion has been taken out of the country through the controls themselves, facilitated by the Bolivarian bureaucracy (Boligarchs) and their favored (Bolivarian) capitalists.[36] Chávez's former economic minister Jorge Giordani and former minister Héctor Navarro quibble with Evans on the number: they put the money gone "missing" at $300 billion dollars, or roughly a third of all the money Venezuela took in over the course of the decade-long oil boom.[37] If any explanation is needed for the troubles Venezuela faces today, and will surely face for many more years, one need look no further than the currency controls and the way it has enabled the Boligarchy to strip the nation of its wealth.

In this dysfunctional economy where the elite has decreed a system of robbery for itself, those without access to dollars have been forced to make their living working the price controls in contraband and smuggling of goods, or by becoming "rent chasers," getting scholarships or grants from studying or otherwise engaging in government social programs.

As if all this were not enough, in addition to the many minor factors contributing to the destruction of Venezuela under the Bolivarians there were two major factors which we might mention here: Nationalization of industries and massive borrowing—and the two issues are often intimately connected.

Nationalization isn't necessarily a bad move, depending on the enterprise, how it's carried out, and administered, and other factors. However, in Venezuela, with a government so rife with corruption, riddled with cronyism, and basically inept, the nationalizations of industry have been an unqualified catastrophe. One could select *any* example to demonstrate the case, but PDVSA stands out both for its importance to the country in obtaining dollars and for its symbolic status as representing Venezuela to the world.

That Venezuela now is forced to import oil and gas and that PDVSA's output has dropped at a rate of 3 to 4% per year *during the years of the oil boom* only hint at the gravity of the problems the nation's most important company faces. The debt the company has accrued *precisely during the oil boom itself* is a slightly better indicator of the depths of decay to which this once stellar international actor has fallen. The company now teeters on the edge of bankruptcy due to enormous debts that Chávez and Maduro took out to fund social programs they knew would win them reelection.[38] In 2014, when the government was still releasing economic information, debts then totaled some $43.8 billion.[39] Summing up the situation of PDVSA, Venezuelan economist José Toro

Hardy said "we're not producing the gasoline that we need. Crude oil drilling plants are not operating, and we're importing crude oil to be able to meet international deals … PDVSA is the example of a true disaster."[40]

While other oil-producing countries like Norway, Saudi Arabia, and even Trinidad and Tobago were putting money in the bank for the rainy day when oil prices would tank, Chávez was spending wildly on clients at home and abroad, shoring up his loyalty with petro-dollars. And when oil prices dropped, Venezuela's bank accounts were not only empty, but in deep red: rojo-rojito red.[41]

PDVSA's biggest debt is to bondholders, but Chevron (at $2 billion) and Chinese loans ($7 billion) are also outstanding. And to simply service the debt in 2016 and make the $5.2 billion debt payments[42] with oil prices around $30/barrel is going to require around 90% of what the country takes in from oil sales,[43] leaving only 10% of the petro-dollars to run the country and buy the needed imports. Since oil exports now account for somewhere between 95–98% of all export earnings (up from 70% when Chávez came to power), the government is increasingly relying on taxes to maintain its domestic obligations, including the feeding of its citizens.

And that brings us back to the problem of scarcity, which is directly tied to the massive debt obligations of the government and its prioritization of debt payments over the welfare of its people. The Bolivarian government by 2013 began saving its dwindling foreign currency reserves to pay Wall Street bond-holders rather than making that money available for necessary imports, and in the process, worsened the scarcity of basic necessities in Venezuela, especially medicines.[44] As Venezuelan economist Ricardo Hausmann put it, the fact that Maduro's "administration has chosen to default on 30 million Venezuelans, rather than on Wall Street, is not a sign of its moral rectitude. It is a signal of its moral bankruptcy."[45] It's ironic and even comic that an elite economist would find it incumbent on himself to make such a statement to a "worker" president like Nicolas Maduro. Maduro's response, in turn, would be reminiscent of that of the Queen of Hearts in *Alice in Wonderland*.[46]

February 17, 2016 Maduro took five hours airtime to announce a few minor economic changes that amounted to a devaluation, wage and price adjustments, but nothing that would seriously address the nation's economic problems. Rather than taking responsibility and much-needed steps toward a functional economy, such as removing currency and price controls, he used his air time to continue pushing the narrative that Venezuela was fighting an "economic war:" he blamed a news aggregator website, *Dolar Today*, for the country's "induced" inflation, national capitalists, smugglers, and hoarders for the scarcity of food, and the United States for the low price of oil. Meanwhile, earlier the same day, Alfonso Riera, vice president of the National Council of Commerce and Services (Consecomercio) had called for an end to the currency and price controls, saying that in some regions of Venezuela 20–40% of businesses had permanently closed this year—that is, in the first six weeks of 2016. Riera went on to point out that six of ten jobs in the country are in commerce.[47]

CHAPTER TWENTY-ONE

CHRONICLE OF A SUICIDE FORETOLD

In the years just before his death, Chávez had already begun to lose his electoral edge, which was the major reason for throwing the country into debt as he tried to continue and expand his policies of patronage and maintain an advantage in the elections.[1] This spending reached "extreme levels," according to Chávez's own Minister of Planning, Jorge Giordani, in the lead-up to the elections of October 2012.[2] When the electoral competitiveness of the Bolivarian/Chavista movement was further damaged as it lost the physical presence of its symbol and leader, there was nothing left for Chávez's handpicked successor to lean on but the use of force.[3]

Nevertheless, Nicolás Maduro still had one electoral card to play in the pending December 8, 2013 mayoral elections, and that was his ability to pillage a still relatively intact private sector. In these crucial elections, economic problems and a limited budget to entice Chavistas to vote, polls signaled potentially big losses for the Bolivarians. Nevertheless, despite bad poll numbers just a month before, the PSUV pulled forward in the end with a six-point lead over the opposition. The victory, according to the *Economist*, could be attributed to "the efficiency of the government's electoral machine and to its lack of scruples in employing all the resources of the state for partisan advantage." The *Economist* article went on to say that "Vicente Díaz, the only opposition-leaning member of the five-strong board of the National Electoral Council (CNE), said this was the most unfair election in modern Venezuelan history. With the government's grip on radio and TV now almost complete, the opposition was rendered virtually invisible in media terms."[4]

But there was another reason for the victory of the Bolivarians, and it appears to have been far more significant. Exactly one month before the mayoral elections, Maduro went on the offensive and called on electronics retailers, specifically the Daka chain, to lower their prices and sell at "just prices." He ordered the Daka stores to be occupied and that everything be sold, "nothing should be left on the shelves." Within no time looting occurred all around the country at the Daka chains where, indeed, soon nothing remained on the shelves.

The people lined up around the country at stores that were forced by decree to sell out their stock at "just prices," in some cases amounting to 77% discounts. It was a brilliant way for a bankrupt populist government to continue its patronage, by privatizing it and making its enemies pay the bill. The fact that, as I wrote at the time, "Maduro was throwing chunks of the business sector to the mobs to tear apart" gave the Bolivarians a leg up on the elections, so they won most of the rural areas, and a majority of the mayoral races, even though the opposition nevertheless consolidated its hold on the major urban centers of the country.[5] The "Dakazo," as it came to be known, had a lasting impact on suppliers and manufacturers of electronics and home appliances: Two years later there was a 95% scarcity in this economic sector.[6]

But the discontent was building, especially after the January 6, 2014 murder of beauty queen (Miss Venezuela 2004) actress and model, Monica Spear, and her ex-husband, by a band of *malandros* (gang-bangers). Maduro's response to the murders was viewed as inadequate (he blamed telenovelas for their deaths) and it left many outraged. The murders touched a nerve in Venezuela because, in addition to the economic disaster, Venezuelans are extremely disturbed by the escalation of violent crime in the country. In this fifth most violent country in the world (and second only to Honduras in the Americas), the government has been seen as doing nothing to stop the violence that has increased dramatically since the Bolivarians came to power.[7] To cover up the gravity of the problem, the government quit keeping statistics on the murder rate in 2003, but the number ranges between the official (as of February 2016) number of 18,000 per year (or 58 per 100,000) and nearly 28,000 (or 91 per 100,000).[8] Either way, Venezuelans put "insecurity" as their top concern, and Gallup ranked Venezuela the most insecure country in the world in 2013.[9]

A little less than a month after the murder of Spear, students gathered to protest insecurity in San Cristóbal, Táchira after an attempted rape on the university campus. Police response was violent, and hundreds of students were arrested. Outrage increased after national, intelligence, and military police, in a joint operation with paramilitaries, killed three people on February 12.[10] In a bizarre twist, two days later the government issued orders for the arrest of opposition leader Leopoldo López, holding him responsible for the violence.[11]

What had been a student rebellion soon drew in other sectors of society, like journalists whose newspapers were being forced to close as they were deprived of newsprint by the government agency in charge of distribution (this was a tactic the government used to effectively destroy the opposition press); workers whose wages were no longer adequate to put food on the family table; the middle-class, which had seen its prospects disappear, along with its democratic rights. The poor, government workers, and others dependent for their lives on subsidies or patronage, for the most part preferred to sit this one out rather than be identified as "*escualidos*" (opposition) and lose every possibility of survival in an increasingly grim situation.

Censorship, even of social media like Twitter, became more strict as the government began censoring the Internet, and imprisoning people on charges of "cyber terrorism for tweeting."[12] The "head of the National Telecommunications Commission (Conatel) warned journalists that any coverage of violent events was banned, and that anyone contravening the prohibition would be punished"[13] under the very strict 2004 Law on Social Responsibility in Radio, Television, and Electronic Media (*Resorte* Law).[14]

Police and military response was brutal from the first moments of the outbreak. From testimony, human rights reports put out by PROVEA and others, and from what could be seen from videos online, police and national guard rampages all over the country were common, and, like in April 2013 in the aftermath of the Presidential elections, the "*colectivos*" emerged, now clearly acting as a paramilitary force of the government.[15] Those demonstrators arrested faced torture and mistreatment and other human rights abuses at the hands of the police and National Guard, according to Amnesty International.[16]

There were two responses to the government repression. First, was an extension and broadening of the peaceful protest movement. According to the Venezuelan Social Conflict Observatory some 2,248 protests occurred in the country throughout February, with a total of 9,286 for the year, the largest number of protests in Venezuelan history.[17]

Secondly, some in the opposition undertook more violent tactics at the *guarimbas* (or barricades), arming themselves with guns and other deadly weapons, and stringing wires across the road to protect themselves from the *colectivos*, known for their use of motorcycles in their actions. This violence upped the ante, took more lives, and it also caused division in the opposition.

I was surprised to see the socialist and solidarity left in the United States and much of the world backing the Bolivarian government as it carried out the repression against the demonstrators. Amy Goodman highlighted the Bolivarian perspective on her show, *Democracy Now,* and the demonstrators were written off in other left media as "middle-class" and "fascist" and "ultra-rightists" (these latter two being President Nicolás Maduro's qualifications). The usual pro-government propaganda, and nothing else, poured out of all the places where I'd previously published, but now most didn't want to hear any other perspective, much less the perspective of social movement activists under the club. In keeping with the Leninist heritage of much of the socialist left media, only the views of the "vanguard" in power in "socialist" Venezuela mattered and only those social forces that backed the "vanguard in power" were to be recognized.

I managed to post a few things at the Latin American Solidarity listserve, which were attacked, but I considered the discussion, even if most of it coming at me was *ad hominem*, to be positive, since at least there was *some* discussion.

Then I posted my translation of a piece that Rafael Uzcátegui wrote about censorship in Venezuela and, ironically, that was when I received an email from the moderator of the listserve, Stansfield Smith, dated 2/24/14, saying, "Because of the right-wing disinformation you post on the LASC list, those on the LASC Coordinating Committee voted to unsubscribe you. You can still send things in to be posted, but we will read them first and decide it if merits being posted. Bye, Stan Smith LASC list moderator for LASC-CC."[18] It was evidently pointless to make any further submissions there.

It's part of the official narrative to blame the current economic woes of Venezuela on the late-2014 drop in oil prices, but that doesn't account for the decline in living standards that were already well underway several years before. Indeed, as I noted earlier, there were significant shortages even after the April 2013 elections, and poverty had been increasing even before that. This was made evident by a joint study of the University of Simón Bolívar, Central University of Venezuela and Andrés Bello Catholic University, on living conditions in Venezuela, conducted between August and September 2014, when the price of oil was still over $100/barrel. The study was based on information from the government's own National Statistics Institute (Instituto Nacional de Estadística) and it concluded that the poverty rate, including the extremely poor and the poor, was then 3.4% higher than it was in 1998, the year Chávez won the presidency. According to the "Poll on the Conditions of Life in Venezuela 2014" (Encovi, for its name in Spanish) 48.4% of households were poor or extremely poor, compared to 45% in 1998. Most significantly, extreme poverty rose from the pre-Chávez figure of 18.7% to 23.6%.

The later 2015 study by Encovi showed that the drop in oil prices had, indeed, taken its toll with 73% of Venezuelan households now in poverty and of that number, 49% were in extreme poverty. Notably, in 1989, the year of the "Caracazo" when the country exploded after the price of oil dropped and Venezuela was under a neoliberal structural adjustment program (SAP) the number of households in poverty was "only" 58.9%.[19] In other words, seventeen years of the "socialist" project of the Bolivarians, many of those years with historically high oil prices, ultimately brought greater poverty to the country than a Neoliberal SAP.[20]

In 2015 the lines outside of supermarkets grew exponentially for scarce items, but the regular demonstrations never grew to the size they had in February of the previous year. Everyone appeared to be waiting patiently to make their anger known at the polls in the December elections.

The judicial persecutions also continued, with the most egregious example being the conviction of opposition politician Leopoldo López on charges that he "incited Venezuelans to violence through subliminal messages."[21] "The 13 years and nine months prison sentence against a Venezuelan opposition leader without any credible evidence against him shows an utter lack of judicial independence and impartiality in the country," Amnesty International's Americas Director Erika Guevara-Rosas wrote on the organization's website. "The charges against Leopoldo López were never adequately substantiated and the prison sentence against him is clearly politically motivated. His only 'crime' was being leader of an opposition party in Venezuela," Guevara-Rosas said.[22] As Lopez supporters awaited the verdict outside the courtroom on September 10th, mobs of Chavistas armed with sticks and called in by Chavista Parliamentarian Jacqueline Faría, attacked the peaceful crowd, injuring many, and killing one person.[23]

All this led inexorably up to the December 6, 2015 elections for the National Assembly, on which the country pinned its hopes for change. They came at a time when nine of ten Venezuelans saw the country as being on a bad course, and Maduro's popularity was hitting rock bottom. This election would become the turning point of the Bolivarian process, when even the clientelistic networks cultivated over the years failed to bring out voters for the PSUV. Many reacted like Ezequiel Montero, a Chavista who abstained from voting because, as he wrote in the popular Chavista website, Aporrea, "I consider the present PSUV directorate, along with the great bureaucratic band that goes from the ministers to the directors in ministries and institutes and, to my great pain, a good part of regular chavistas organized in the community councils and other forms of social organization, to be infested, rotten with corruption. With exceptions, but the rot has advanced to such a form over the years that soon there won't be a single healthy person. I don't say this pointing fingers, but with a deep sadness, and even more, with great concern."[24]

On the other side, however, the opposition led an inspired, and well-organized campaign that drew in a new generation of committed activists. Some of these activists took great risks as poll-watchers. They refused to allow the government to perpetrate a fraud by illegally keeping the polls open after hours so it could bring in its people for a "second round of voting."[25]

With a 74.25% turnout (the largest turnout for a parliamentary election since 1983 when voting was still compulsory), the opposition Democratic Unity Roundtable (MUD) won a qualified majority and a mandate to take the country on a new course. The reconstruction of the country after fifteen years of populist economics is guaranteed to be long and rocky but Venezuela's resource gift—or "curse," depending on your perspective—would make it possible for the country to make an economic recovery with less pain than most other countries that have undergone the national delirium that populism represents.[26]

The opposition in Venezuela has changed considerably from what it was in the first years of the century, and at present one could only qualify it as "right wing" out of ignorance or pure demagoguery. While there are right wing parties in the coalition of parties grouped together under the Democratic Unity Roundtable (MUD), there are also centrist and left parties like Movement Toward Socialism (MAS), Radical Cause (LCR) and the far left Red Flag (BR). The bulk of the opposition, at the time of this writing, could be characterized as social democratic and would include parties like Popular Will (VP), Democratic Action (AD), A New Era (UNT) and others. Indeed, the coalition is so diverse—including in its ranks, for instance, the first transgender member of a national assembly in Latin America— that maintaining unity in the medium or long-term will likely be an issue. The only unifying objective appeared to be the restoration of democratic processes after many years of increasingly autocratic rule under the hybrid populist regime of a caudillo.

The December 2015 elections represented another battle in the ongoing struggle in Venezuela between advocates for liberal democracy and its associated institutions, including checks and balances, separation of powers, accountability, rule of law, etc. on one hand and, on the other, populist corporatism under a caudillo with a strong role for the military in governance, centralized power, organized in clientelistic networks.

While liberal democracy was first established in Venezuela in 1958, the corporatist rule by caudillo goes back to the time when Venezuela was a colony of Spain and it was reinforced by Simón Bolívar.[27] As Hal Draper noted, quoting Bolívar, "the people are in the army" and "as for others 'Their only right is to remain passive citizens.'"[28] Former Lt. Colonel Hugo Chávez represented a reintroduction of this model of military rule by caudillo after forty years of liberal democracy. As president he brought 1614 military officers into the government, even as the rest of Latin America was removing the military and military juntas from power.[29]

The new National Assembly met toward the end of the first week to hash out a work plan for their first meetings in January. Contrary to fears they would impose a "neoliberal" package on the people (which some still consider to be worse than the economic chaos generated by the Bolivarian government), Jesus Torrealba, the former Communist and Secretary General of the MUD "gave priority to the recovery of an agenda of social priorities." In doing so, he emphasized "universalizing" the Missions and removing the clientelist elements from them; giving titles and services to those who received housing from the Housing Mission; ensuring that salaries and pensions be paid; reactivating national industry and production; passing a law of amnesty (and the release of Leopoldo López) and focusing on "reconciliation."[30]

The PSUVistas apparently had no interest in "reconciliation" or governing with the new opposition National Assembly. In the final weeks of December 2015 they forced judges out of their Supreme Court (Tribunal Supremo de Justicia) and, with their lame duck parliament, illegally packed that branch of government with their people.[31] The TSJ, if the ploy were to succeed (and it apparently did), would be able to annul any or all laws passed by the National Assembly. And so, among the first acts of the TSJ was a refusal to recognize three National Assembly representatives from the state of Amazonas, an act aimed at weakening the two-thirds majority of the opposition.[32] The new TSJ would soon become a major weapon in a battle to destroy the power of the National Assembly.[33] After all, in a 2014 study of the court, in over 45,000 cases, it had yet to go against the Bolivarian government in a single ruling.[34]

Even as the MUD became more conciliatory (for instance, accepting the TSJ ruling on the representatives from Amazonas), Maduro and the hardline Chavistas took an increasingly more uncompromising stance. PSUVista Ministers called before the National Assembly refused to appear; initial laws passed were struck down by the PSUVista-packed TSJ; and President Maduro was able to use the TSJ to uphold Economic Emergency Decree 2184 over the veto of the National Assembly and to impose a State of Exception in Decree 2323 in May of 2016. Confrontations between the two political elites appeared likely to increase, despite calls from the opposition MUD for unity to resolve the country's severe problems.

Most Venezuelans, weary from the long lines for scarce products at supermarkets, inflation, a general deterioration in the standard of living, crime and insecurity, seemed only to want some form of normalcy restored. But after seventeen years of the Bolivarian project, it was anyone's guess what "normalcy" could possibly mean in Venezuela. Meanwhile, despite the Economic Emergency Decree, Maduro made nothing but small and superficial economic changes (such as raising the price of gas, further devaluing the Bolívar to 10 to the dollar and allowing one exchange system to "float" and then changing the names of the new exchange rates to DIPRO and DICOM, respectively). And few expected anything to come of the State of Exception, and military maneuvers that cost the country an estimated $20 million, but more repression as the calls for a referendum on Maduro's government increased.[35]

In February 2016, Felipe Pérez Martí said "Maduro won't last another five months." Martí believed that Maduro was at the center of a "hard core" of six people but that other factions and a majority in the PSUV are more rational and willing to work with the opposition to try to correct the problems the country faces. He felt that the moderate sectors of Chavismo could and should be included in a new government, and that some institutions, such as the community councils and communes could play a positive role in rebuilding Venezuela, neighborhood by neighborhood, after the hegemony of the Bolivarians comes to an end. He was optimistic that with its extraordinary resources Venezuela could rebuild from the ruins of this populist project some were convinced represented "Twenty-First Century Socialism."[36]

It's never a good idea to make predictions in politics, and even less so when political systems appear to be descending into chaos, as is presently happening in Venezuela. The ruling Bolivarian elite is desperate to maintain its impunity and continue to maintain and increase its power and wealth; the Bolivarian base has mostly fallen away, but a hard-core continues to advocate for "deepening the process." On the other hand, the overwhelming majority just wants the new start the National Assembly they voted in had promised them.

But opportunities to correct the situation and avoid the disaster scenarios of civil war, an outright military dictatorship or a failed state are vanishing. By spring of 2016 Venezuela appeared to be entering a death spiral. Lootings and spontaneous food riots became pandemic as desperate Venezuelans found government market shelves empty, the normal markets crumbling, and both being replaced with black markets that sold products illegally at many times their legal market price. Plunder began to replace shopping as a means of sustenance, especially as food prices rose so high that by May 2016 a family of five required more than eighteen minimum wages simply to feed itself.[37]

Rolling blackouts, due to government neglect of the national electrical system, pulverized what was left of the productive economy.[38] Scarce food resources that required refrigeration spoiled during prolonged blackouts and the darkness offered cover for more looting, which, in turn, became a process for acquiring products for sale on the growing black market. The opposition hoped to be able to stave off a violent finale to the crescendo of misery, violence, disintegration and lawlessness and resolve the issues politically with a referendum on the President later in the year, Maduro and his packed court permitting. But the problems all fed into each other in an increasingly tense social context that seemed destined to explode. By mid-year, the only question seemed to be: Who would remain standing after the conflagration?

The issue of how to respond to the Venezuelan crisis has become even more urgent, given this dramatic turn of events. The complex, contradictory and unpleasant reality of what's going on in the country needs to be faced honestly, fearlessly, and without ideological agendas. The conflict, for one thing, is not between the "left" and the "ultra right" but rather between an elite that is equal parts a holdover of Leninist socialism and a decaying populist movement united by a dead caudillo (the Bolivarians) and a very mixed opposition united tenuously by a desire to restore liberal democratic processes and governance (and, no doubt, in many cases, to regain power).

But in fact, the entire situation of left governments in Latin America is also extremely complicated in this age of globalized capitalism when the U.S. continues to be a major imperial "enforcer" but is now joined by other imperial actors, some of them traditionally "left." Chinese corporations are building the mega-canal through Nicaragua, destroying the land and displacing tens of thousands of Nicaraguans and quietly taking over land and resources all over the developing world.[39] In the long run, China's competition with Latin American exports pose a particular threat to Latin America's economic development, arguably a greater threat than any the U.S. might offer at this historical juncture.[40] Meanwhile, in Venezuela, the Cuban government directs intelligence operations for the unpopular Bolivarian elite.[41]

The solidarity left that has traditionally seen its role as supporting vanguard revolutionary organizations (often uncritically) taking state power in national liberation struggles needs to rethink its presuppositions. Should anti-imperialists support the "left-wing" governments like those of Daniel Ortega and Nicolás Maduro or rather the thousands of environmentalists, indigenous people, and campesinos opposing their destructive extractivist or developmentalist policies?[42] What is the proper stance to take toward left governments that collude with Chinese communist imperialists (or corporations like Chevron) and cede huge territories to be "sacrifice zones" for the extraction of resources?[43] When we ally ourselves with those left governments, are we not collaborating with imperialism and the destruction of the earth? Is covering up this ugly reality and the complicated conflicts the role of a "solidarity activist"? But even these governments' apparently positive social programs raise questions about clientelism, the inculcation of dependency in the population, and, when funded by the extraction of resources, questions about environmental costs and sustainability.

All these contradictions and, the corruption that characterized many of the left governments of Latin America during the commodities boom in the first decade of this century—corruption "uncovered" just as the boom went bust—have apparently brought an end to the "Pink Tide."[44] In its moment the left turn in Latin America could have represented a positive break from poverty, underdevelopment and other ills associated with neoliberalism. But as Noam Chomsky said of the Pink Tide, "a lot of great opportunities, to a great degree, have been wasted in very disagreeable ways." In Venezuela, he specified that "there were significant proposals, efforts, and initiatives … little related to popular initiatives, and with some participation, but they came principally from above." And he also noted that "the tremendous corruption and incompetence of the country never allowed them to free themselves from near-total dependence on its sole export, oil." He said that "Latin America has been plagued by a type of Bonapartism," and so "the model of Chávez has been destructive. South America needs massive popular movements that would take the initiative to bring about extensive social change. And to a certain degree this has happened." He offered as a prime example of the latter, the indigenous movement.[45]

Chomsky confirmed what I heard from so many thoughtful activists in the social movements throughout Latin America about the nature and limitations of the Pink Tide governments. In the globalized world economy of the twenty-first century, governments of the right and left alike are less free than ever to set social agendas and national policies. Such agendas and policies are increasingly set by an emerging, globalized, transnational capitalist state to which Lusbi Portillo referred when he said that there had indeed been a revolution in Venezuela, but that it was a "capitalist revolution." And the only force that could stand in its way, as Lusbi noted, were social movements.

JOURNEY TO THE EARTH

Since my childhood Sundays in Air Force base chapels I've lived in the apocalyptic-utopian-millenarian matrix (AUMM), rarely giving much thought to what that meant. Then in April 2013, when I unexpectedly found myself in the dark side of utopia, I realized I needed to take a deeper look into what turned out to be a very complex phenomenon.

The positive side of the AUMM is, I think, fairly obvious. As we live in an imperfect world—some might go so far as to call it "degenerate" and the religious fundamentalist might even see it as irredeemably evil—visions of utopia provide relief, hope, and possibilities the present world fails to offer, dreams toward which we might strive. Utopia, especially since Thomas More, has been a transcendent vision by which we often judge our world and the shortcomings of all our human institutions. Utopia inspires us to push against the limits of the "reality" our society wishes to impose upon us. It was the pursuit of utopia, the glittering chimera of the "Sixties," that motivated my entire generation to set out on the road on a great search, and I believe much good came from that process.

But when we try to realize that "nowhere" somewhere, or, more accurately, when we attempt to *impose* it in our imperfect world, its shadow inevitably emerges. There's an enormous difference between the freely chosen, "limited" worker or living cooperative, and the "unlimited" project often undertaken in a revolution. While in the former case, utopia is an opening path to liberation, in the latter it is the closing door of a jail cell or a gulag. Yet while the utopian path to liberation can sometimes end up leading into a jail cell or a gulag, never has a jail cell or a gulag opened a path to liberation.

Nicholas Berdyaev, who was a participant in the Revolution of 1905 and a witness (and prisoner) of the Revolution of 1917, saw the "forces of revolution…opposed to the value of personality, of freedom, of creativeness and, indeed, to all spiritual values." A revolution, for him, was a "rationalistic madness, a rationalized irrationality" in which "the irrational submits to the tyranny of the rational, and the rational, in imposing the tyranny, becomes irrational."[1] Karl Popper echoed this idea when he said that the utopianism revolutions proposed was "the wrong kind of rationalism." As an "all too attractive theory" he considered it therefore "dangerous and pernicious" and inevitably leading to violence.[2]

Those processes of a revolutionary utopian sort often require the fanatical adherence of its activists. Here the communist and fascist revolutions of the twentieth century come to mind, but one could also look back to the Jesus of the *Book of Revelation* who says of the vacillators, the critical, the uncertain, the hesitant, the doubting—in the end, the normal, everyday moderates—that he would prefer them to be "hot or cold" but "since ye are lukewarm I will spew thee out of my mouth."[3] This fanaticism was present from the beginnings of Christianity and, indeed, it could already be seen in the original Zealots of the Maccabean revolts nearly two centuries before the birth of Christianity. But with Christianity came the assault on pagans and "heathens," leading to crusades against infidels and heretics, inquisitions, witch-hunts, and pogroms against Jews, a genocidal conquest of the Americas, all culminating in the bloody internecine religious wars that wracked Europe until the middle of the seventeenth century. Even as the Christian West secularized, but within the same AUMM, the slaughters continued: European colonization that brought "light" (and death) to Africa, Asia, and the Americas; the genocide of Native Americans in the US to build the "American Dream"; and finally, the class extermination and gulags of Communism.

Certainly nothing I witnessed in Nicaragua or in Bolivarian Venezuela (up to the time of this writing) has come close to the brutality of earlier attempts to realize "the Kingdom of God" or some version of utopia. But the brutality was still there, in the militant Manichaean conception of the world that saw no middle ground between the armies of the Good and the forces of Evil.[4]

But the middle ground is what most of the world calls "home." And this home turf where the majority attempt to engage in civil politics is increasingly encroached on from every side by fanatics who not only refuse to listen to those viewed as "enemies," but also believe that those enemies shouldn't be granted the right to speak. The middle ground is the world of skeptics, doubters, agnostics, critics, and those with questions, uncertainties, and hesitations, that is, the terrain guarded by philosophers, scientists, artists, poets, mystics, and ordinary people attempting to understand a very complex world, guided only by their own inner light. To disregard the voices of thoughtful, cautious people is to disrespect, if not a majority, at least a significant, and crucial, part of humanity: that part of humanity grounded not in the utopia, but in the "real world."

On the other hand, as my old friend William Everson impressed upon me, expressing a basic Jungian truth, everything has its shadow. And so the "middle," too, has its shadow, and we know it as "mediocrity." The flat, plain, ordinary, "middle," the tepid, temperate, moderate, and lukewarm: Most of us, and certainly I, can understand why the Jesus of the Apocalypse, living with such passionate intensity, would spew this sector of society out of his mouth. My generation fled the middle ground, middle-America with its middle class, to find a way into burning deserts or freezing altitudes where we could experience life on the edge and in the margins. It is, I suppose, my own enantiodromia now to seek balance, temperance, moderation, and sobriety after a lifetime of extremes.

Anyone who has witnessed or participated in a revolution or other similar utopian project knows how intoxicating the experience can be. Everything seems possible, and that's part of the problem. Those of us who are in recovery from intoxicants of various types can recall a parallel experience: We feel "heady" and capable of anything in that state of mind, like driving cars, shooting guns, and so on. The problem, as both Berdyaev and Popper point out, is that people in these irrational states of revolutionary intoxication usually end up making and guiding the construction of utopia. And they'll stop at nothing to ensure its realization.

I'm not saying that we don't need deep and radical change in our world. Quite the contrary: We really do need to change everything about how we live on our planet. But I'm convinced that some sort of sober spiritual practice needs to guide our political activism, and I'm not the first one to come to this conclusion: The American Indian Movement (AIM), especially as it has evolved from a "strictly political force, now defends itself as a religious movement and strongly advocates abstinence from all intoxicants for its members."[5] At its website, AIM describes itself as "first, a spiritual movement, a religious re-birth, and then the re-birth of dignity and pride in a people…"[6] The Six Nations, Iroquois Confederacy or *Haudenosaunee* people, in their historic document, *A Basic Call to Consciousness*, write that "In our ways, spiritual consciousness is the highest form of politics" and "the destruction of the natural world and its peoples is the clearest indicator of mankind's spiritual poverty."[7]

From the Six Nations people emerged one known as "the Peacemaker" and under his influence the nations gathered in a council to draft the Great Law of Peace. At the core of this law, the first principle was the recognition that "vertical hierarchy creates conflicts" so "they dedicated the superbly complex organization of their society to function to prevent the rise internally of hierarchy." The document, drafted in 1977, was a "call to a basic consciousness which has ancient roots and ultra-modern, even futuristic, manifestations."[8]

These are the ones Lusbi calls the "vanguard in the current phase of struggle." Many of the original people have managed to maintain a non-apocalyptic view of the world and keep the idea of "progress" at bay through rituals that affirm cycles, unchanging processes, and ways of life. I find the same deep spiritual non-apocalyptic clarity in the *Tao Te Ching* and other ancient masterpieces of world spiritual literature. This view of life, as Wade Davis has pointed out, was precisely what so offended the English settlers arriving in Australia and finding that the Aboriginals "had no sense of progress."[9] Bruce

Chatwin also remarked on the difference between the white settlers and the Aboriginals, saying, "The Whites were forever changing the world to fit their doubtful vision of the future. The Aboriginals put all their mental energies into keeping the world the way it was. In what way was that inferior?"[10]

For obvious reasons, we can't return to an original or Aboriginal past: after all, most readers, I suspect, aren't original or Aboriginal people. But neither is the world the world in which the Aboriginal people lived. Whether we like it or not, we already live in "the future." But we can learn from the wisdom of original peoples and grapple with how we might apply that understanding in a late modern context where "degrowth" is a necessity and we find it necessary abandon "progress" for survival. In the light of their wisdom we can consider not only what we need to change, but also what we need to preserve.

The project of socialism in the twentieth and twenty-first centuries was, in theory, and in some sense, an attempt to retrieve a sense of human values and provide an alternative to "savage capitalism." Many, if not the majority, of those who fought and gave their lives for this project were no doubt sincere, convinced that the new [utopian] order would be adequate to restore what they considered endangered human values. But those leading this struggle, the "vanguards" of those revolutions, were guided by the same messianic spirit that guided apocalyptic and totalitarian movements of Christianity before them.[11]

The moral foundation of the modern vanguards turned out to be made of purely utilitarian sand, since "good" and "evil," "right" and "wrong" were defined exclusively in terms of what advanced the revolutionary cause as defined by the "vanguard." As Leszek Kolakowski wrote of Lenin, "if law, for instance, is 'nothing but' a weapon in the class struggle, it naturally follows that there is no essential difference between the rule of law and an arbitrary dictatorship. If political freedoms are 'nothing but' an instrument used by the bourgeoisie in its own class-interest, it is perfectly fair to argue that communists need not feel obliged to uphold these values when they come to power."[12]

What Kolakowski wrote of Trotsky's interest, or more accurately, lack of interest, in "democracy as a form of government, or of civil liberties as a cultural value" has also proven true for the Bolivarians, especially as the support for their project erodes down to a "hard core" of perhaps a quarter of the population. As long as power was in the hands of the vanguard, Kolakowski wrote, "then by definition this was an authentic democracy, even if oppression and coercion in every form were otherwise the order of the day... but from the moment that power was taken over by a bureaucracy that did not represent the interests of the proletariat, the same forms of government automatically became reactionary and therefore 'anti-democratic.'"[13] In this logic of the double-standard, one had the "right to be indignant and to attack democratic states when they infringe the principles of democracy and freedom but one must not treat a Communist dictatorship in this way..."[14]

This is the heritage of the Marxism-Leninism of the twentieth century, and it guides the Bolivarian government today. It explains why independent, autonomous social movements never emerged under Left governments of this kind since all social bodies were coopted or in some way forced to submit to the will of the vanguard. Unquestionably, social movements haven't had an easy task organizing themselves under liberal democratic governments in capitalist countries, but they've at least done better there than, ironically, under the "peoples' democracies" of communism and socialism.

This is no minor problem. Social movements, in my thinking, are not ancillary to the work of social and political transformation: they are at the core of that process.[15] If the indigenous movement is "the real 'vanguard'—or "anti-vanguard"—of the struggles of the world" (Lusbi Portillo, p. 286), then the social movements in general are the "little green things that poke up after a fire through the blackened forest floor" (Staughton Lynd, p. 2). It's a fitting image, since the unregulated market seems destined to leave behind a scorched earth, but peoples' movements will only come back more forcefully in that Polanyian double-movement.

But social movements are also crucial to "monitoring" and correcting popular governments, which is why some argue that democracy should have greater priority over other social changes.[16] Partly for this reason, and also for my basic belief in the "Golden Rule," I decided in 2013 that I could no longer support the Bolivarians when I saw them treating people in the opposition in ways they themselves would refuse to be treated, and certainly in ways I would refuse to be treated. Damian Prat brought that lesson home to me with dramatic effect when he said we [North Americans, Europeans] support governments in Latin America that we'd never tolerate in our own countries.

As a result of my disillusionment with the Bolivarian process I've grown more cautious as I recognize the possibility for unintended consequences in all actions, and the need for constant vigilance and self-correction even when we act with the best of intentions. It may seem that such an approach is inappropriate for the present, given the really "apocalyptic" situation we find ourselves in as we face climate change. It's quite possible, at this point, that we don't have time to make the dramatic changes that will ensure our survival. But every drug addict has to face a similar problem when he or she hits bottom: At the bottom the damage may already be too great to be healed. Nevertheless, it is at "the bottom" that one also recognizes that, no matter how dark or impossible a situation may appear, while there's life, there is still the possibility for renewal and transformation. Yet this transformation runs counter to the ecstatic intoxication of a life immersed in the AUMM, and that's because genuine transformation comes from spiritual practice based on steady, balanced, and consistent discipline, one day at a time.

John Gray may be correct when he says, "Ditching the myths of historical teleology and ultimate harmony is highly desirable, but it is also extremely difficult. The western belief that salvation can only be found in history has renewed itself again and again. The migration of utopianism from Left to Right testifies to its vitality." He goes on to say that "an irrational faith in the future is encrypted into contemporary life, and a shift to realism may be a utopian ideal."[17] Berdyaev would agree when he said that utopias have been "brought about far more easily than we supposed, and we are actually faced by an agonizing problem of quite another kind: how can we prevent their final realization?"[18]

Bolivarian socialism on the Left and neoliberalism on the Right have both expressed their aim to remake humanity and the world and force us all into their respective gulags or jail cells they define as "utopia." As a "hybrid regime" Venezuela is part of a bloc of nations with governments of both the Left and the Right that lean toward authoritarianism, but with democratic forms.[19] While the US ranks in last place as a "full democracy,"[20] it increasingly has the characteristics of a national security state, or what David Unger calls the "emergency state."[21] Even though political scientists might be able to draw fine lines between a socialist hybrid regime tipping toward authoritarianism and a neoliberal democracy tipping toward a national security state, both seem to me to be headed the same direction and looking more and more alike. And while Venezuela, thanks to Chávez and Maduro, has a head start down that road to dystopia, the US isn't too very far behind. Both increasingly rely on militarizing the police who target low-income and immigrant communities in particular;[22] imposing strict "anti-terrorist" legislation and extending powers of surveillance; silencing whistle-blowers with threats and imprisonment; censoring the press to the greatest degree possible; and imposing restrictions on liberal rights to dissent, peaceful assembly and protest. All this, we're told, is necessary to create, and protect, the great project of remaking humanity and the world.

It appears that John Gray may be right, that some sort of revolutionary utopianism seems to "migrate"—or perhaps "careen" is a better word—from Left to Right, and back again. Under governments of the Left and the Right, we on the bottom live increasingly insecure and marginal lives, while the elites, who have stepped into power on our backs, enrich themselves with no apparent limit or consequence. Who now, we ask, will save us from our saviors? They keep us mesmerized with promises of utopia that will come from "socialism," or from a "self-regulating market," but while the spectacle of the imagined destination has frequently been spellbinding, we have to wake up to the dark side of this often beautiful lie. We have to come to our senses, enter our own lives and try to find our way home, back to earth. After all, as the story goes, that's where the real treasure awaits us.

ENDNOTES

Introduction

1　Manichaeanism is a third century A.D. "heresy" of Manichaios Manes with roots in the Zoroastrianism of Persia. It proposes a dualistic conception of the world in which Good and Evil are two forces in a war of equals. Zoroastrianism was the source of what became known as the "apocalypticism" of Judaism and Christianity. See Norman Cohn, *Cosmos Chaos and the World to Come* (New Haven: Yale University Press, 2001).

2　John Gray, *Black Mass: How Religion Led the World into Crisis* (New York: Farrar, Straus and Giroux, 2007), 6.

3　There's an enormous body of literature on the apocalyptic ideas of Jesus, including Bart Ehrman, *Jesus: Apocalyptic Prophet of the New Millennium* (Oxford: Oxford University Press, 1999).

4　See, for instance, Norman Cohn, *Cosmos Chaos and the World to Come*.

5　"The Book of Revelation" or "The Apocalypse of John," "apocalypse" from Greek *apocalypsis*, meaning "revelation."

6　For more on these Medieval apocalyptic and millenarian movements, see the classic work by Norman Cohn, *In Pursuit of the Millennium: Revolutionary Millenarians and Mystical Anarchists of the Middle Ages*, Revised ed. (Oxford: Oxford University Press, 1970).

7　Judith Shulevitz, "When Cosmologies Collide," http://www.

nytimes.com/2006/01/22/books/review/22shule.html?ref=design.

8 Ernest Lee Tuveson, *Millennium and Utopia: A Study in the Background of the Idea of Progress* (New York: Harper and Row, 1964), 133.

9 Nathan Hatch, *The Sacred Cause of Liberty* (New Haven, CT: Yale University Press 1977).

10 Ruth H. Bloch, *Visionary Republic: Millennial Themes in American Thought, 1756–1800* (Cambridge: Cambridge University Press, 1988).

11 Ernest Lee Tuveson, *Redeemer Nation* (Chicago, IL: University of Chicago Press Midway Reprint, 1980), 12.

12 Charles L. Sanford, *The Quest for Paradise* (Urbana, IL: University of Illinois Press, 1961).

13 See, for instance, Paul Boyer, *When Time Shall Be No More* (Cambridge, MA: Belknap Harvard, 1994).

14 See John Gray, *Black Mass.*

15 Friedrich Engels, *The Peasant War in Germany* (New York: International Publishers, 1976), 56.

16 See George Woodcock, *Anarchism: A History of Libertarian Ideas and Movements* (Cleveland, OH: World Publishing Company, 1969), 381–383. Woodcock compares the Spanish anarchists to the "radical sects of the Reformation."

17 Quoted in E.J. Hobsbawm, *Primitive Rebels: Studies in Archaic Forms of Social Movement in the 19th and 20th Centuries* (New York, NY: W.W. Norton & Company, 1965), 83.

18 William McCants, *The Isis Apocalypse: The History, Strategy, and Doomsday Vision of the Islamic State* (New York: St. Martins Press, 2015).

19 See Jean-Pierre Filiu, *Apocalypse in Islam* (Berkeley: University of California Press, 2011) and David Cook, *Contemporary Muslim Apocalyptic Literature* (Syracuse, NY: Syracuse University Press, 2005).

Chapter One

1 Some Evangelical Christians believe that history is divided into distinct periods during which God had distinct "covenants" or dispensations set by agreements with humanity. During early Judaism, for instance, God was seen as requiring animal sacrifice, which changed under later Judaism and Christianity.

Chapter Two

1 Many Evangelicals believe that Jesus will return to earth and take Christians, living and dead, to heaven. This has come to be known as the "Rapture."

2 The cult was led by the late "Moses" David Berg and continues under his wife Karen Zerby.

3 The album was comprised of devotional Hindu temple music, chants and religious songs to Krisna and other deities.

4 John Nelson Darby was the 19th century Plymouth Brethren theologian responsible for the development of dispensationalism, premillennialism (the belief that Jesus would return to earth before reigning for a millennium on earth) and a "futuristic" reading of the biblical *Book of Revelation*.

Chapter Three

1 I recognize that "the Movement" often refers to the Civil Rights Movement, but in the 1970s, as that movement converged with other movements, such as the Third World Liberation Movement, the Anti-War Movement, the Gay Liberation Movement, the Feminist Movement, etc. all of these collectively became known by many as "The Movement."

2 David R. Swartz, *Moral Minority: The Evangelical Left in an Age of Conservatism* (Philadelphia, PA: University of Pennsylvania Press, 2012).

3 While Quakers, emphatically, are not Christian, they emerged from that faith.

4 See Harlan Douglas Anthony Stelmach, unpublished thesis entitled "The Cult of Liberation: The Berkeley Free Church and the Radical Church Movement 1967–1972" online at https://archive.org/details/cultofliberation00stelrich.

5 Email sent from Anthony Nugent, August 4, 2015.

6 Stelmach, "The Cult of Liberation," 373.

7 See Max Elbaum, *Revolution in the Air* (New York: Verso, 2002).

8 Swartz, *Moral Minority*, 93.

9 "Anabaptist" simply means "baptized again" and it was used as a term to refer to a very diverse group of late Medieval radical Christians who split from the Catholic Church and believed in returning to the faith of Jesus, the right of believers to read the Bible for themselves, and a believer's baptism after conversion,

hence, "ana-baptist" since they had already been "christened" in the Catholic church.

10 John Howard Yoder was a Mennonite pacifist theologian and author of the book, *The Politics of Jesus* (Grand Rapids, MI: Eerdmans, 1994), among others.

11 Cohn, *In Pursuit of the Millenium*, 286.

12 Francis Schaeffer was an Evangelical intellectual and rationalist critic of modern secular culture. In his dozen or so books he analyzed, and introduced many Evangelicals to, secular arts, culture and philosophy, albeit through the distorted lens of Evangelicalism.

13 See William D. Miller, *A Harsh and Dreadful Love: Dorothy Day and the Catholic Worker Movement* (New York: Image Books, 1974).

14 Nicolas Berdyaev, *Towards a New Epoch* (London: Geoffrey Bles, 1949), 87.

15 Introduction, "Poems of the Third Epoch," A supplement to the May/June 1980 issue of *Radix Magazine*, (Berkeley, CA: Carmarthen Oak Press, 1980).

16 John Gray, *Black Mass*, 9; also in Albert Camus, *The Rebel: An Essay on Man in Revolt* (New York: Vintage, 1992), in "State Terror and Rational Terror" he demonstrates the common utopian roots in Christianity of the great revolutionary Karl Marx and the reactionary Joseph de Maistre.

17 See John Gray's, *Black Mass*.

Chapter Four

1 People's Temple, a cult organized around the Reverend Jim Jones, drew in many progressive and Left Christians with its ethnic and class diversity and Jones's radical politics. It came to a tragic end after the community moved headquarters to Guyana and later faced a US Congressional investigation that culminated in Jones ordering the suicide, or murder, of all members. Only a few escaped, but 918 died in "Jonestown" on November 18, 1978.

2 Rosa Luxemburg, *Rosa Luxemburg Speaks* (New York: Pathfinder Books, 1970), 132.

3 Camilo Torres, *Revolutionary Priest* (New York: Random House, 1971), 350–351.

4 Camilo Torres, *Camilo Torres, His Life and His Message* (Springfield, Il: Templegate, 1968), 74.

5 Jose P. Miranda, *Communism in the Bible* (Baltimore: Orbis Books, 1981).
6 Frederick Engels, *The Peasant War in Germany*, 61.
7 It should be said that the situation of Christians in East Germany under communism was relatively better than the situation of their fellow-believers in the USSR.
8 Dorothee Sölle, "Reflections on Christians for Socialism," *Radical Religion* Vol. IV #3–4.

Chapter Five

1 "Contra" meaning "Counter" as in "Contra-revolucionario" or "counterrevolutionary."
2 Claribel Alegría is a Nicaraguan poet, journalist, novelist and essayist who has published numerous books, including oral histories, written in collaboration with her late husband, Daniel Flakoll.

Chapter Seven

1 Clifton Ross, *The Light the Shadow Casts* (Devon, UK: Stride Publications, 1996).
2 Published in *The Americas Review*, Spring–Summer 1997, Vol. 24, Nos.1–2.

Chapter Eight

1 Ben Clarke and Clifton Ross, eds, *Voice of Fire: Communiqués and Interviews from the Zapatista National Liberation Army* (Berkeley: New Earth Press, 1994), 19.
2 Ibid, 43–44.
3 The Palmer Raids took place in the context of the "Red Scare" after World War One, under President Woodrow Wilson and carried out by Attorney General A. Mitchell Palmer from late 1919 to early 1920. Over five hundred labor, anarchist and communist activists were arrested and/or deported and many organizations were crushed, including the IWW, which never really recuperated its former strength or numbers.
4 Clifton Ross, *Venezuela: Revolution from the Inside Out* DVD (Oakland: PM Press, 2008).

5 Here I'm using the terms "worker cooperatives," "worker-controlled collectives," and "worker-run enterprises or businesses" interchangeably to designate a business that is owned and controlled by the workers themselves, as distinguished from Employee Stock Ownership Plans, ESOPs, in which workers own shares of the company, but do not technically own or control it.

6 Sharryn Kasmir, *The Myth of Mondragon: Cooperatives, Politics, and Working-Class Life in a Basque Town* (Albany, NY: State University of New York, 1996), 108–110.

7 Raúl Zibechi, *Territories in Resistance: A Cartography of Latin American Social Movements*, trans. Ramor Ryan (Oakland: AK Press, 2012), 253–257.

8 I find James Scott's perspective on the "petty bourgeoisie" so refreshing in this context, and it's also a great look at anarchism: James C. Scott, *Two Cheers for Anarchism: Six Easy Pieces on Autonomy, Dignity, and Meaningful Work and Play*, especially Chapter Four, "Two Cheers for the Petty Bourgeoisie" (Princeton, NJ: Princeton University Press, 2012).

9 See Henri Pirenne's fascinating, dated, but classic, work, *Economic and Social History of Medieval Europe* (New York: Harcourt, Brace and Company, 1937), available in reprinted editions; also his *Medieval Cities: Their Origin and the Revival of Trade* (Princeton, NJ: Princeton University Press, 1969). Both are a good starting point for an understanding of the origins of capitalism.

10 Scott, *Two Cheers for Anarchism: Six Easy Pieces on Autonomy, Dignity, and Meaningful Work and Play*, 84–100.

11 Hilary Abell, *Pathways to Scale* (Takoma Pk, MD: The Democracy Collaborative, 2014).

12 Georgeanne Artz and Younjun Kim, "Business Ownership by Workers: Are Worker Cooperatives a Viable Option?" http://institute.coop/sites/default/files/resources/businessownership.pdf, 9.

13 Peter Schnall and Erin Wigger, "The Mondragon Corporation: Criticisms—Part 3 of 3," http://unhealthyworkblog.blogspot.com/2013/01/the-mondragon-corporation-criticisms.html.

14 See Tobias Buck, "A fine balance between solidarity and survival," http://www.ft.com/intl/cms/s/0/26740e3e-2aee-11 e5-acfb-cbd2e1c81cca.html#axzz3xdcVyyaI. This figure is contested. According to Vincent Navarro, the wage differential is 6.5 to one. See http://www.counterpunch.org/2014/04/30/the-case-of-mondragon/.

15 Norwegian Business School *Business Review*,
    http://www.bi.edu/bizreview/articles/
    News-2011/A-culture-of-smaller-wage-differences-/.

16 Kasmir, *The Myth of Mondragon*, 110–118.

17 For a look at the difference between worker-owned and con-
    trolled workplaces and ESOPs, go to http://www.cdi.coop/
    coop-cathy-worker-coops-esops-difference/.

18 Kasmir, *The Myth of Mondragon*, 197.

19 Karl Polanyi, *The Great Transformation: The Political and Economic
    Origins of Our Time* (Boston: Beacon Press, 2001).

Chapter Nine

1 Plan Puebla Panama, now known as the Mesoamerica Project, is
   a controversial development and infrastructure improvement plan
   that will tie into the Initiative for the Integration of the Regional
   Infrastructure of South America (IIRSA). For more on IIRSA, see
   the section of the book with the interview with Lusbi Portillo of
   Zulia, Venezuela.

2 One of Cardenal's essays, perhaps the one I read, but certainly
   representative of his thinking at the time, is archived at http://www.
   casa.cult.cu/publicaciones/revistacasa/235/cardenal.htm.

3 See Brian A. Nelson, *The Silence and the Scorpion* (NY: Nation
   Books, 2009), 265 and the footnote on page 367 about how the
   crew of this film manipulated the facts around the killings carried
   out from the Llaguno Overpass on April 11, 2002, and colluded
   with the Chávez government in making, and distributing the
   film. See *X-Ray of a Lie* on Youtube at https://www.youtube.com/
   watch?v=DtDl7SuHRkM.

4 This seems to be a fairly straightforward, non-controversial
   statement. For the unconvinced, see http://nymag.com/
   daily/intelligencer/2012/06/yes-bush-v-gore-did-steal-the-
   election.html about Florida, and http://www.michaelparenti.
   org/stolenelections.html. http://whatreallyhappened.com/
   WRHARTICLES/2004votefraud.html or do your own research.

5 Barbara Koslowski, *Theory and Evidence: The Development of
   Scientific Reasoning* (Cambridge, MA: MIT Press, 1996), 57.

Chapter Ten

1 Most of my articles from this period are archived at www.dissi-dentvoice.org, and some, where they were published or reposted at www.counterpunch.org, www.venezuelanalysis.com and www.upsidedownworld.org.

2 I was attacked in 2007 by Dozthor Zurlent for using Venezuela as a "source of income" after I criticized Heinz Dieterich's version of "Twenty-First Century Socialism." I found the response nothing more than ad hominem but the reader may find it amusing: http://www.aporrea.org/ideologia/a38675.html.

3 This problem is explored in depth by the late Fernando Coronil in his classic work, *The Magical State: Nature, Money and Modernity in Venezuela* (Chicago, IL: University of Chicago Press, 1997).

4 Dorothy J. Kronick, "The Kingdom of Darkness," https://newrepublic.com/article/62656/the-kingdom-darkness.

5 Clifton Ross, *The Map or the Territory: Notes on Imperialism, Solidarity and Latin America in the New Millennium* (Berkeley, CA: New Earth Publications, 2014, revised 2015), 42.

6 Rafael Uzcátegui, *Venezuela: Revolution as Spectacle* (Tucson: See Sharp Press, 2010), 184

7 Ibid., 183

8 This interview was translated and almost in its entirety in the book I co-edited with Marcy Rein, *Until the Rulers Obey: Voices from Latin American Social Movements* (Oakland, CA: PM Press, 2014).

9 I wrote, directed, edited and produced *Venezuela: Revolution from the Inside Out*. I was a "protagonist" in Marc Villá's documentary, *Yo Soy El Otro* (2008, Villa del Cine).

10 Clifton Ross and Marcy Rein, eds, *Until the Rulers Obey*.

11 COPEI, Comité de Organización Política Electoral Independiente, "Independent Political Electoral Organization Committee," a social Christian party, one of the two parties ruling in Venezuela before the accession of Chávez.

Chapter Eleven

1 *The Telegraph*, "Honduras's Zelaya and coup leaders both broke law, says truth commission," http://www.telegraph.co.uk/news/worldnews/centralamericaandthecaribbean/honduras/8624691/Hondurass-Zelaya-and-coup-leaders-both-broke-law-says-truth-commission.html.

2 Roger Miranda and William Ratliff, *The Civil War in Nicaragua: Inside the Sandinistas* (New Brunswick, NJ: Transaction Publishers, 1993), 51.

3 Ibid, 87. Bayardo Arce was speaking in a "'secret speech' to the Nicaraguan Socialist Party, 1984.

4 Clifton Ross, "Sandinista Venezuela," http://caracaschronicles.com/2015/10/20/sandinista-venezuela/.

5 Roger Miranda and William Ratliff, *The Civil War in Nicaragua*, 231.

6 Ibid.

7 Timothy C. Brown, *The Real Contra War: Highlander Peasant Resistance in Nicaragua* (Norman, OK: University of Oklahoma Press, 2001), 7.

8 Miranda and Ratliff, *The Civil War in Nicaragua*, 232

9 Ibid., 233

10 Stephen F. Diamond, *Rights and Revolution: The Rise and Fall of Nicaragua's Sandinista Movement* (Lake Mary, FL: Vandeplas Publishing LLC, 2013), 51.

11 Ibid. p. 84. Diamond cites this number as representing the size of the FSLN one year before the final victory.

12 Ibid., 68.

13 Ibid., 72.

14 Ibid., 122.

15 Ibid., 84.

16 Ibid., 95.

17 Ibid., 97.

18 For more of the history of Daniel Ortega's political transformation see my introduction to the Nicaragua section in Ross and Rein, *Until the Rulers Obey*.

19 An excellent critique from a Left perspective of this Pact and Ortega's consolidation of rule as an autocrat was written by Mónica Baltodano, former Sandinista commander and co-founder of Movement for the Rescue of Sandismo can be found at http://isreview.org/issues/50/nicaragua.shtml.

20 See http://rhrealitycheck.org/article/2013/07/17/the-politics-of-abortion-in-latin-america/.

21 See http://nicaraguadispatch.com/2013/12/nicaraguas-new-pacto/.

22 See http://elpais.com/diario/2008/09/22/opinion/1222034405_850215.html.

23 Ross and Rein, *Until the Rulers Obey*, 133.

24 I focused on Daniel's story in this piece: http://upsidedownworld.org/main/nicaragua-archives-62/2330-a-nicaraguan-farce.

Chapter Twelve

1 See, for instance, the critique of the anarchists at *El Libertario*: https://www.nodo50.org/ellibertario/english/Memories%20of%20popular%20power.rtf. The failure of the cooperativist strategy for building "socialism" is implicitly acknowledged even by Bolivarian advocates like Burbach, Fox, and Fuentes in their book, *Latin America's Turbulent Transitions: The Future of Twenty-First-Century Socialism* (New York: Zed Books, 2013), 62—although they put the figure of actual surviving cooperatives at 15%.

2 Marcy Rein and Clifton Ross, "Workers Take over Mérida Newspapers, Appeal to Chávez for Support," http://venezuelanalysis.com/analysis/5954.

3 See our interview with her in Ross and Rein, *Until the Rulers Obey*.

4 Of course Marcano and Tyszka would have another explanation for the corruption in the Chávez administration: according to them, the caudillo knew all about it and used it as a means of controlling his underlings. He also refused to tolerate "insubordinate" underlings, and even close friends, who suggested he clean it up. See especially pages 135–137 of *Hugo Chávez: The Definitive Biography of Venezuela's Controversial President* (New York: Random House, 2007).

5 Leszek Kolakowski, *Is God Happy? Selected Essays* (NY: Basic Books, 2013), 9–10.

6 A "COPEista" is a member of the COPEI, see note 11, Chapter 10.

7 See Rafael Uzcátegui's article, "An Autonomist at the Service of State Hegemony," in which Uzcátegui accuses Zibechi of "fearing his own theoretical constructions" and avoiding discussion of Venezuela's dependence on resource extraction and the lack of independence from the state of Bolivarian "social movements." Uzcátegui concludes by asking why Zibechi's critique of the other "Pink Tide" governments doesn't seem to apply to Venezuela. The article is archived at http://periodicoellibertario.blogspot.com/2014/04/un-autonomista-al-servicio-de-la.html.

8 "The New Socialism," review of *Latin America's Turbulent Transitions* in NACLA Report on the Americas, Summer, 2013, archived at https://nacla.org/article/new-socialism.

9 Import-substitution industrialization was a twentieth century development model in which a nation would industrialize to make its own products and replace imports. The model collapsed with the Latin American debt crisis of the 1980s and the difficulties competing with transnationals in an era of globalization.

10 I find much to be said for the argument put forth by the Trotskyist Johnson-Forest Tendency that Stalinism and what came to be known as "Communism" was actually state capitalism. See CLR James, with Raya Dunayevskaya and Grace Lee Boggs, *State Capitalism and World Revolution*, (Oakland: PM Press, 2013). I distinguish here between monopoly or transnational capitalism and state capitalism.

Chapter Thirteen

1 Maria L. Pallais, "Venezuela's Vanishing Billions," https://100r.org/2011/10/venezuelas-vanishing-billions/.

2 Bryan Ellsworth and Eyanir Chinea, "Chavez's oil-fed fund obscures Venezuela money trail," http://www.reuters.com/article/2012/09/26/us-venezuela-chavez-fund-idUSBRE88P0N020120926#S6W81BZekUKWb6li.97.

3 Francisco Toro, "How exactly do you misplace $29,342,391,393.66?," http://caracaschronicles.com/2011/08/27/how-exactly-do-you-misplace-29342391393-66/.

4 Ellsworth and Chinea, "Chavez's oil-fed fund obscures Venezuela money trail," this report dates back to 2012 but in late 2015 when I checked on the status of the company, the official government page continues to describe the plant in the future tense: http://www.cenditel.gob.ve/node/671.

5 Brian Ellsworth, "Billions unaccounted for in Venezuela's communal giveaway program," http://www.reuters.com/article/2014/05/06/us-venezuela-communes-special-report-idUSBREA450CA20140506.

6 Marcano and Tyszka, *Hugo Chávez*.

7 Matt Kennard, "BB interviews…Noam Chomsky," http://blogs.ft.com/beyond-brics/2013/02/15/bb-interviews-noam-chomsky/.

8 See this other post by Francisco Toro, for example: http://caracaschronicles.com/2011/11/07/fondens-accounting-is-all-greek-to-me/.

9 "Hugo Chávez a Capriles: 'Eres un cochino, no te disfraces,'"

http://elcomercio.pe/mundo/actualidad/hugo-chavez-capriles-eres-cochino-no-te-disfraces-noticia-1375430.

10 https://www.youtube.com/watch?v=MjvS6qLf2mI.

11 On Sai Baba, Hannah Strange and Alasdair Baverstock, "Nicolas Maduro: 'All we see are poor Chavez imitations and stupid distractions,'" http://www.telegraph.co.uk/news/worldnews/southamerica/venezuela/10502766/Nicolas-Maduro-All-we-see-are-poor-Chavez-imitations-and-stupid-distractions.html. On Maduro and Marxist-Leninism, Cristina Gonzalez, "El mentor entre sombras de Nicolás Maduro," http://patriaurgente.com/?p=15583.

12 Agence France-Presse, "Venezuela closes borders ahead of election" http://www.globalpost.com/dispatch/news/afp/130409/venezuela-closes-borders-ahead-election.

13 Jonathan Watts, "Nicolás Maduro: post Chávez bluster disguises pragmatism of a deal-maker," http://www.theguardian.com/world/2013/mar/06/nicolas-maduro-post-chavez-bluster.

Chapter Fourteen

1 A guarimba is an opposition demonstration, usually involving road blocks.

2 "Cacerolazo," from cacerola (Spanish, "stew pot") is a form of protest in which demonstrators bang pots and pans.

Chapter Fifteen

1 These numbers were all gleaned from my reading of the daily press which I annotated at the time and I have no doubt they could be confirmed in the list of discrepancies filed by Henrique Capriles before the CNE.

2 "Carter Center Releases Final Report on Venezuela's April 2013 Presidential Elections," http://www.cartercenter.org/news/pr/venezuela-052214.html.

3 Misión de Estudio del Centro Carter Elecciones Presidenciales en Venezuela http://www.cartercenter.org/resources/pdfs/news/peace_publications/election_reports/venezuela-final-rpt-2013-elections-spanish.pdf.

4 Ibid. My translation.

5 For the complete story (in Spanish) see Chapter 3, "It's True,

we added False Votes" in Emili J. Blasco, *Bumerán Chávez: Los Fraudes que Llevaron al Colapso de Venezuela* (Washington, D.C.: Center for Investigative Journalism in the Americas and Inter-American Trends, Second Edition 2015), 96.

6 Juan Cristobal Nagel, "It which cannot be named," http://caracaschronicles.com/2015/04/22/.it-which-cannot-be-named/.

7 Juan Cristobal Nagel, "Leamsy vs. Puzkas …," http://caracas chronicles.com/2015/05/04/leamsy-vs-puzkas/.

Chapter Sixteen

1 Robert J. Alexander, *The Venezuelan Democratic Revolution: A Profile of the Regime of Rómulo Betancourt* (New Brunswick, NJ: Rutgers University Press, 1964), 210.

2 Nick Miroff, "A once-proud industrial city, now a monument to Venezuela's economic woes," https://www.washingtonpost.com/world/the_americas/a-once-proud-industrial-city-now-a-monument-to-venezuelas-economic-woes/2014/09/03/4b577663-8f18-4841-b958-eee3b8830ad9_story.html.

3 Clifton Ross, "Venezuela: Adiós Presidente," http://upsidedownworld.org/main/news-briefs-archives-68/4172-venezuela-adios-presidente.

4 Humberto Márquez, "China Maps Out Venezuela's Valuable Mining Resources," http://www.ipsnews.net/2013/02/china-maps-out-venezuelas-valuable-mining-resources/.

5 H. Micheal Tarver and Julia C. Frederick, *The History of Venezuela* (NY: Palgrave MacMillan, 2006), 102.

6 This is a constant source of confusion. For instance, see George Ciccariello-Maher, *We Created Chávez* (Durham, NC: Duke University Press, 2013), 10, certainly the most minor point of many much more serious problems in the book, Ciccariello-Maher writes of the "power-sharing pact signed at Punto Fijo (and therefore colloquially known as puntofijismo)…"

7 Institute for Democracy and Electoral Assistance, "Voter turn-out data for Venezuela," http://www.idea.int/vt/countryview.cfm?CountryCode=VE.

8 H. Micheal Tarver and Julia C. Frederick, *The History of Venezuela*, 99.

9 Carlos Franqui, *Family Portrait with Fidel* (New York: Random House, 1984), 162.

10 The elections in the Confederation of Cuban Workers (CTC)

November 18, 1959, according to Franqui, delegates were chosen "By direct, secret, and free ballot—in the first and last free elections held under Fidel Castro," 160. That is, not quite a year after Castro took power.

11 Edgardo González Medina, *Venezuela, Capitalismo de Estado, Reforma y Revolución*, 80, archived online at http://www.eumed. net/libros-gratis/2007a/244/1a.htm.

12 Tarver and Frederick, *The History of Venezuela*, 102.

13 Héctor Pérez Marcano and Antonio Sánchez Garcia, *La invasion de Cuba a Venezuela: De Machurucuto a la Revolución Bolivariana* (Caracas, VZ: Libros de El Nacional, 2007), XIX.

14 Rory Carroll, *Comandante: Hugo Chávez's Revolution* (New York: Penguin, 2014), 100.

15 Ibid., 99.

16 María Eugenia Díaz and William Neuman, U.S. Filmmaker Held in Venezuela Sought to Show Political Divide, Friends Say," http://www.nytimes.com/2013/04/27/world/americas/tim-tracy-sought-to-show-venezuelas-divide-friends-say.html?_r=0.

Chapter Seventeen

1 Rafael Uzcátegui, *Venezuela: Revolution as Spectacle* (Tucson: See Sharp Press, 2010).

2 Rubén González was finally declared innocent nearly five years later in April 2014.

3 A very good article on the situation of workers in Guayana and around the country can be found at http://www.wsj.com/articles/unions-confront-venezuelan-leader-1411600050.

4 Ultimas Noticias, "Ministro Ricardo Molina amenaza con despedir a empleados opositores," http://www.ultimasnoticias.com. ve/noticias/actualidad/politica/video--ministro-ricardo-molina -amenaza-con-despedi.aspx.

Chapter Eighteen

1 Cristina Marcano and Alberto Barrera Tyszka, *Hugo Chávez*.

2 Fernando Coronil, *The Magical State: Nature, Money and Modernity in Venezuela* (Chicago, IL: University of Chicago Press, 1997), 11.

3 Trienio Adeco was the Three Year rule of Democratic Action, 1945–1948, between military dictatorships.
4 Institute for Democracy and Electoral Assistance, "Voter turnout data for Venezuela."
5 See Carlos Tablante and Marcos Tarre, *Estado Delincuente: Como actúa la delinquencia organizada en Venezuela*, foreword by Baltasar Garzón (Caracas: Cyngular Asesoría, 2013), 210–211.
6 Marcano and Tyszka, *Hugo Chávez*, 270.
7 Clifton Ross, "Love the Pigs?" http://www.counterpunch.org/2011/10/07/love-the-pigs/.
8 Hannah Strange and Alasdair Baverstock, "Nicolas Maduro: 'All we see are poor Chavez imitations and stupid distractions.'"
9 Gustavo Heredia, "Nicolás Maduro Assures Hugo Chávez Appeared To Him As A 'Little Bird' To Bless Him," http://www.huffingtonpost.com/2013/04/03/nicolas-maduro-hugo-chavez-little-bird_n_3007965.html.

Chapter Nineteen

1 Clifton Ross, *Translations from Silence: Selected Poems* (San Francisco: Freedom Voices, 2009).
2 Gustavo Hernández A., "Newsprint wars, memetic wars," http://caracaschronicles.com/2015/05/11/newsprint-wars-memetic-wars/.
3 Rafael Uzcátegui, op. cit. in Spanish, my translation.
4 Archived online at http://www.counterpunch.org/2013/07/19/building-a-critical-left-solidarity-movement/.
5 Their article: http://dissidentvoice.org/2016/01/chavismo-and-its-discontents/ and my response: http://dissidentvoice.org/2016/01/the-two-lefts-and-venezuela/.
6 Archived at http://www.mitfamericas.org/Venezuela.htm.
7 Ross and Rein, editors, *Until the Rulers Obey*.
8 Tarek el Aissami was at the time of the interview Minister of Internal Relations, and, at the time of this writing, Governor of Aragua. El Aissami also has close relations with Iran and Hezbollah and was later accused, along with Number Two in the government at the time of the interview, Diosdado Cabello, of involvement in drug trafficking and money laundering. See http://www.wsj.com/articles/venezuelan-officials-suspected-of-turning-country-into-global-cocaine-hub-1431977784.

Chapter Twenty

1 Eva Gollinger attempted to portray the US as the "éminence grise" behind the coup of April 2002 in her book, *The Chávez Code*, but the research and substantiation for that claim is shaky, at best. See http://vcrisis.com/?content=letters/200506021909.

2 William I. Robinson, *A Theory of Global Capitalism: Production, Class, and State in a Transnational World* (Baltimore, MD: The Johns Hopkins University Press, 2004), 82.

3 Cyril Mychalejko, "Manufacturing Contempt for Venezuela," http://upsidedownworld.org/main/venezuela-archives-35/4728-manufacturing-contempt-for-venezuela.

4 See the US State Department Budget, available online at http://www.state.gov/documents/organization/238222.pdf.

5 Javier Corrales and Michael Penfold, *Dragon in the Tropics: Venezuela and the Legacy of Hugo Chávez*, Second Edition (Washington, D.C.: Brookings Institute Press, 2015), 112.

6 Casto Ocando, *Chavistas en el Imperio: Secretos, tácticas y escándalos de la Revolución Bolivariana en Estados Unidos* (Miami, FL: Factual Editores, 2014) excerpts available online at: http://kindleweb.s3.amazonaws.com/content/B00IZRZN98/gz_sample.html.

7 Ibid., Ocando, 64.

8 Ibid., Ocando, 54.

9 emiduarte, "Evil in the Bayou," http://caracaschronicles.com/2014/08/05/aholes-and-oil-1-human-rights-0/.

10 Ocando, *Chavistas en el Imperio,* 10.

11 From a fundraising appeal from *Z Magazine*, signed by Michael Albert and dated February 20, 2016.

12 http://archive.boston.com/news/world/latinamerica/articles/2005/07/27/channeling_his_energies/?page=1. As for current funding, one *Al Jazeera* piece posted in 2012 says that "here the story gets murky—which only goes to reinforce the notion that Telesur is TeleChavez in disguise." See http://www.aljazeera.com/programmes/listeningpost/2012/09/20129229131584380.html.

13 Lucas Koerner, "Venezuelan Social Movements Rally Against Open-Pit Mining in the Orinoco Arc," https://zcomm.org/znetarticle/venezuelan-social-movements-rally-against-open-pit-mining-in-the-orinoco-arc/

14 Ibid, Corrales and Penfold, 113. They make the argument that "Chávez was ideologically predisposed to lock horns with the United States and he did so from the start of his administration"

(p. 111) and that "one could even argue that Venezuela's initial anti-Americanism and uncooperative behavior explains U.S. criticisms 2002–2003, rather than the other way around," 112.

15 Carl Meacham, "The Kerry-Jaua Meeting: Resetting U.S.-Venezuela Relations?" https://csis.org/publication/kerry-jaua-meeting-resetting-us-venezuela-relations.

16 In this regard the report issued by the Strategic Studies Institute of the US Army War College written by Dr. R. Evan Ellis is quite interesting and illuminating. Among the conclusions Dr. Ellis draws are that the US should not interfere with Venezuela, but that it should also prepare to send humanitarian aid to its neighbors when the inevitable crisis hits. The report is worth reading in its entirety: http://www.strategicstudiesinstitute.army.mil/index.cfm/articles/the-approaching-implosion-of-venezuela/2015/07/10.

17 Patrick Gillespie, "Oil-rich Venezuela is now importing U.S. oil," http://money.cnn.com/2016/02/03/news/economy/venezuela-imports-american-oil/.

18 Reuters, "Oil-rich Venezuela became net gasoline importer in 2012," http://www.reuters.com/article/venezuela-gasoline-idUSL2N0DU2NT20130514.

19 James Petras, US and Venezuela: Decades of Defeats and Destabilization," http://www.globalresearch.ca/us-and-venezuela-decades-of-defeats-and-destabilization/5434884.

20 Spanish-readers would benefit from reading the many good opposition economists like Anabella Abadi, Jose Guerra, Enzo del Bufalo, Angel Alayon, Luis Vicente León, Asdrúbal Oliveros; others, like Ricardo Hausmann, Juan Nagel, and Francisco Toro regularly publish in English.

21 I go into much of this at length in my book *The Map or the Territory* (Berkeley: New Earth Publications, 2014), some passages of which are reproduced in part here.

22 Carlos Alberto Gómez Grajales, Why is Venezuela hiding its official statistics?," http://www.statisticsviews.com/details/news/8277681/Why-is-Venezuela-hiding-its-official-statistics.html. The government finally published a partial account of the economy in January 2016 for Nicolas Maduro's Memoria y Cuenta speech (equivalent of State of the Union speech) but they have been called "fantasy figures." See http://www.economist.com/blogs/graphicdetail/2016/01/graphics-political-and-economic-guide-venezuela.

23 MercoPress, "Venezuela joins the hyperinflation club: 54.3%

in last twelve months and climbing," http://en.mercopress.
com/2013/11/08/venezuela-joins-the-hyperinflation-club-54.3-
in-last-twelve-months-and-climbing. This policy has only worsened as the government increased money supply.

24 Kejal Vyas, "Inflation-Racked Venezuela Orders Bank Notes by the
Planeload," http://www.wsj.com/articles/inflation-wrought-
venezuela-orders-bank-notes-by-the-planeload-1454538101.

25 Xabier Coscojuela, "Elías Matta: 'Aquí había un relajo con el tema
de la corrupción,'" http://www.talcualdigital.com/Nota/122995/
elias-matta-aqui-habia-un-relajo-con-el-tema-de-la-corrupcion

26 See, for instance, http://caracaschronicles.com/2013/03/19/
sicad-birth-of-a-red-tape-behemoth/.

27 Carlos and Marcos Tarre, *Estado Delincuente*, 130.

28 Juan Cristobal Nagel, "Crazy Cadivi subsidizes Colombian
smugglers," http://caracaschronicles.com/2013/10/23/
crazy-cadivi-subsidizes-colombian-smugglers/.

29 The price of the Bolívar can be tracked in real time at https://
dolartoday.com/.

30 El Universal, "Transcript of Mario Silva's recording,"
http://www.eluniversal.com/nacional-y-politica/130524/
transcript-of-mario-silvas-recording.

31 Jackson Diehl, "A drug cartel's power in Venezuela," https://www.
washingtonpost.com/opinions/a-drug-cartels-power-in-venezu-
ela/2015/05/24/9bc0ff14-ffd6-11e4-8b6c-0dcce21e223d_story.
html.

32 Reuters, "Venezuelan president's relatives indicted in US for
cocaine smuggling," http://www.theguardian.com/world/2015/
nov/12/venezuela-president-relatives-indicted-drugs.

33 Caribbean 360, "Venezuela military pilots flew drugs to Haiti
for trafficking into US, reports say," http://www.caribbean360.
com/news/venezuela-military-pilots-flew-drugs-to-haiti-for-
trafficking-into-us.

34 Andrew F. Puglie "Maria Gabriela Chávez Net Worth: Hugo
Chávez's Daughter Richest Woman in Venezuela, Worth $4.2
Billion," http://www.latinpost.com/articles/71424/20150812/
maria-gabriela-ch%C3%A1vez-net-worth-hugo-ch%C3%A1vezs-
daughter-richest-woman-in-venezuela-worth-4-2-billion.htm.

35 Daniel Lansberg-Rodriguez, "How Do You Solve a Problem Like
Maria Gabriela?," http://www.theatlantic.com/international/
archive/2014/08/how-do-you-solve-a-problem-like-maria-gabrie-
la-venezuela/379167/.

36 Jolguer Rodríguez Costa, "Nicmer Evans: 'El madurismo es un error histórico,'" http://www.el-nacional.com/siete_dias/Nicmer-Evans-madurismo-error-historico_0_554344571.html.

37 Eyanir Chinea and Corina Pons, "Venezuela ex-ministers seek probe into $300 billion in lost oil revenue," http://www.reuters.com/article/us-venezuela-politics-idUSKCN0VB26F.

38 Francisco Toro, "PDVSA and the Abyss," http://caracaschronicles.com/2016/02/15/pdvsa/.

39 Pietro Pitts, "Venezuela's PDVSA Says Debt Fell by $2 Billion Last Year," http://www.bloomberg.com/news/articles/2016-01-22/venezuela-s-pdvsa-says-debt-fell-by-2-billion-last-year.

40 Sabrina Martín, "As Socialist Economy Implodes, Venezuela Creates Army-Run Oil Firm," https://panampost.com/sabrina-martin/2016/02/16/as-socialist-economy-implodes-venezuela-creates-army-run-oil-firm/#at_pco=smlwn-1.0&at_si=56c5f f4e0a768106&at_ab=per-13&at_pos=0&at_tot=1.

41 Ibid.

42 Alexandra Ulmer, "Venezuela's PDVSA still mulls debt refinance proposal," http://www.reuters.com/article/us-venezuela-pdvsa-idUSKCN0UQ2C720160112.

43 Kenneth Rapoza, "Venezuela Default Imminent, Chavez Legacy Rests In Pieces," http://www.forbes.com/sites/kenrapoza/2016/01/20/venezuela-default-imminent-chavez-legacy-rests-in-pieces/#47173d96208f.

44 Dolar Today, "PANORAMA 'SOMBRÍO': Luis Vicente León 'el país está rodando por el barranco,'" https://dolartoday.com/panorama-sombrio-luis-vicente-leon-el-pais-esta-rodando-por-el-barranco/.

45 Ricardo Hausmann and Miguel Angel Santos, "Should Venezuela Default?" https://www.project-syndicate.org/commentary/ricardo-hausmann-and-miguel-angel-santos-pillory-the-maduro-government-for-defaulting-on-30-million-citizens--but-not-on-wall-street?barrier=true. Hausmann has since been joined by other economists expressing shock that a "socialist" government would prefer to pay Wall Street rather than use its foreign exchange to provide necessities for its people. See http://www.forbes.com/sites/francescoppola/2016/02/22/venezuelas-collapse-one-year-on/#6b106fa0516e.

46 Jose Orozco and Sebastian Boyd, "Venezuela Threatens Harvard Professor for Default Comment," http://www.bloomberg.com/news/articles/2014-09-12/

venezuela-threatens-harvard-professor-for-default-comment.

47 Zayda Pereira, "Se anuncian cierres definitivos de comercios en varias regiones," http://www.elmundo.com.ve/noticias/economia /gremios/riera--hay-regiones-que-anuncian-cierres-definitiv. aspx#ixzz40WhVLU7f.

Chapter Twenty-One

1 See Javier Corrales and Michael Penfold, *Dragon in the Tropics*, 202.

2 Jorge Giordani, quoted in Corrales and Penfold, *Dragon in the Tropics*, 191.

3 Corrales and Penfold, *Dragon in the Tropics*, 190–203.

4 P.G., "A Country Divided," http://www.economist.com/blogs/ americasview/2013/12/venezuelas-local-elections.

5 Clifton Ross, "Elections in Venezuela: Did anyone notice?" http:// www.pmpress.org/content/article.php/20131213143334233.

6 Nicolle Yapur, "A dos años del 'Dakazo' la escasez de electro-domésticos es de 95%," http://elestimulo.com/elinteres/sec-tor-de-electrodomesticos-aun-siente-los-efectos-del-primer-dakazo/.

7 Elyssa Pachico, "Chavez's Legacy: An Explosion of Violence and Drug Trafficking," http://www.insightcrime.org/news-analysis/ chavezs-legacy-an-explosion-of-violence-and-drug-trafficking.

8 Jim Wyss, "Dueling data blur Venezuelan murder rate," http:// www.miamiherald.com/news/nation-world/world/americas/ venezuela/article59098558.html.

9 Jan Sonnenschein, "Latin America Scores Lowest on Security," http://www.gallup.com/poll/175082/latin-america-scores-lowest-security.aspx.

10 Over two years later, only one person has been held responsible in the three murders which were immediately covered up by the Bolivarian government: http://www.el-nacional.com/politica/ cabos-sueltos-impunidad_0_793120743.html.

11 Andrew Cawthorne and Daniel Wallis, "Venezuela seeks protest leader's arrest after unrest kills three," http://www.reuters.com/ article/us-venezuela-protests-idUSBREA1B1K220140214.

12 Patricia Laya, Sarah Frier and Anatoly Kurmanaev, "Venezuelans Blocked on Twitter as Opposition Protests Mount," http://www.bloomberg.com/news/articles/2014-02-14/ twitter-says-venezuela-blocks-its-images-amid-protest-crackdown.

13 Christopher Deloire, "Right to information more endangered than ever in national crisis," http://en.rsf.org/venezuela-right-to-information-more-26-02-2014,45933.html.

14 According to the Freedom House website, "The 2004 Law on Social Responsibility in Radio, Television, and Electronic Media (Resorte Law), amended in 2010, contains vaguely worded restrictions that can be used to severely limit freedom of expression. For example, the law bans content that could "incite or promote hatred," "foment citizens' anxiety or alter public order," "disrespect authorities," "encourage assassination," or "constitute war propaganda." It also restricts content that the government deems to be of an adult nature—including news stories that cover sexual or violent topics, in a country with one of the world's highest homicide rates—to the hours between 11 p.m. and 5 a.m. Consequently, many broadcasters are forced to present a watered-down version of national and international news during the hours when most viewers tune in. In addition, the law requires all broadcasters to air live government broadcasts (known as *cadenas*), which can come at random and supersede regular programming. The law empowers the Venezuelan National Telecommunications Commission (CONATEL) to oversee enforcement and permits it to impose heavy fines or disrupt service at its discretion. In 2011, CONATEL levied a $2.16 million fine against Globovisión, Venezuela's last remaining opposition television network, over what CONATEL deemed to be "excessive" coverage of a prison riot "that promoted hatred and intolerance for political reasons." The fine, which was ratified by the Supreme Court in June 2012, represented 7.5 percent of the company's gross 2010 income. Globovisión paid the fine after the Supreme Court ordered the company's assets seized. Separately, in March, after Chávez accused the press of "media terrorism" in reporting on possible water contamination in the center of the country, courts barred the media from covering the story unless they could base it on a "truthful technical report backed by a competent institution." Archived at https://freedomhouse.org/report/freedom-press/2013/venezuela#.U1Z_RdJDvl4.

15 "Venezuela 2014: Protesta j Derechos Humanos," http://www.derechos.org.ve/pw/wp-content/uploads/Informe-final-protestas2.pdf.

16 See https://www.amnesty.org/en/countries/americas/venezuela/report-venezuela/. Links to other reports at this website fill out the picture of repression.

17 La Patilla, "En 2014 se registraron 9.286 protestas, cifra inéd-
    ita en Venezuela," http://www.lapatilla.com/site/2015/01/19/
    en-2014-se-registraron-9-286-protestas-cifra-inedita-en-venezuela/.

18 From a private email sent to me.

19 Víctor Salmerón, "La pobreza medidas por ingresos se disparó
    hasta 76% en Venezuela, según Encovi (UCV-USB-UCAB),"
    http://prodavinci.com/blogs/la-pobreza-se-disparo-hasta-76-en-
    venezuela-segun-encovi-ucv-usb-ucab-por-victor-salmeron/.

20 The entire process under Chávez and then Maduro has been
    consistent with Dornbusch and Edwards's four phases of populist
    economics. See Rudiger Dornbusch and Sebastian Edwards,
    The Macroeconomics of Populism in Latin America (Chicago:
    University of Chicago Press, 1991), 10–11. The current state of
    Venezuela (early 2016) coincides with their description of the
    final stage of populist cycles when "the collapse of the economy
    makes workers worse off than they were at the beginning of the
    populist period," 50.

21 The Editorial Board, "Free Venezuela's Leopoldo López," http://
    www.nytimes.com/2015/09/14/opinion/free-venezuelas-leopoldo
    -lopez.html?_r=0.

22 Amnesty International, "Venezuela: Sentence against opposition
    leader shows utter lack of judicial independence," https://www.
    amnesty.org/en/latest/news/2015/09/venezuela-sentence-against-
    opposition-leader-shows-utter-lack-of-judicial-independence/.

23 Pedro García Otero, "Leopoldo López's Sentence Is Everything
    Wrong with Venezuela," https://panampost.com/pedro-gar-
    cia/2015/09/17/leopoldo-
    lopezs-sentence-is-everything-thats-wrong-with-venezuela/.

24 Ezequiel Montero, "Soy Chavista y no voté," http://www.aporrea.
    org/ideologia/a219092.html.

25 See the very inspiring article by Francisco Toro, "How a
    Grassroots Movement Defeated Chavista Dirty Tricks" at http://
    caracaschronicles.com/2015/12/11/49649/.

26 See Dornbusch and Edwards, *The Macroeconomics of Populism in
    Latin America*.

27 The best source for information on the history of corporatism in
    Latin American politics is Howard J. Wiarda, *Corporatism and
    National Development in Latin America* (Boulder, CO: Westview
    Press, Inc. 1981). See also my book, *The Map or the Territory*,
    90–91; 125–127.

28 Hal Draper, *Socialism from Below* (Alameda, CA: Center for

Socialist History, 2001), 41.

29 Military caudillos have been president for 140 of the 186 years of Venezuelan history. http://www.el-nacional.com/politica/militares-ocupado-cargos-gobierno_0_325167554. html. See also this piece in English: http://www.foreignaffairs.com/articles/142133/peter-wilson/a-revolution-in-green, and also my article on the military, paramilitary and gang rule in Bolivarian Venezuela at http://dissidentvoice.org/2016/03/news-from-bolivarian-gangland-2/.

30 Álex Vásquez S., "112 diputados de la MUD darán prioridad a la agenda de reivindicación social," http://www.el-nacional.com/politica/diputados-MUD-prioridad-agenda-reivindicacion_0_754724706.html.

31 Diego Ore, "Venezuela's outgoing Congress names 13 Supreme Court justices," http://www.reuters.com/article/us-venezuela-politics-idUSKBN0U626820151223.

32 Mery Mogollon and Chris Kraul, "In power struggle, Venezuela's high court declares parliament in contempt," http://www.latimes.com/world/mexico-americas/la-fg-venezuela-parliament-court-20160111-story.html.

33 Ayatola Núñez, "El TSJ ha dado siete golpes constitucionales a la AN," http://www.el-nacional.com/politica/TSJ-dado-golpes-constitucionales-AN_0_813518956.html.

34 Alfredo Meza, "El chavismo nunca pierde en el Supremo venezolano," http://internacional.elpais.com/internacional/2014/12/12/actualidad/1418373177_159073.html.

35 Javier Mayorca, "Lo que hay detrás de los ejercicios militares Independencia 2016," http://runrun.es/nacional/venezuela-2/262787/lo-que-hay-detras-de-los-ejercicios-militares-independencia-2016.html.

36 Víctor Amaya, "'Yo a Maduro no le doy más de cinco meses,'" http://www.talcualdigital.com/Nota/123222/yo-a-maduro-no-le-doy-mas-de-cinco-meses.

37 Alejandro Palma, "Precio de la Canasta Alimentaria Venezuela Mayo 2016," http://www.notilogia.com/2016/05/precio-de-la-canasta-alimentaria-venezuela-marzo-2016.html.

38 Clifton Ross, "When will the Lights go out in Venezuela?," http://dissidentvoice.org/2016/04/when-will-the-lights-go-out-in-venezuela/.

39 The plans for the Nicaraguan canal have been "temporarily" put on hold: http://www.npr.org/2015/12/18/460312284/

nicaragua-canal-project-put-on-hold-as-chinese-investor-suffers-financially.

40 See Kevin P. Gallagher and Roberto Porzecanski, *The Dragon in the Room: China and the Future of Latin American Industrialization* (Stanford: Stanford University Press, 2010).

41 Rory Carroll, *Comandante: Hugo Chávez's Venezuela*, 99–100.

42 Rick Kearns, "Indigenous Rama Among 15,000 Protesting Nicaragua Canal," http://indiancountrytodaymedianetwork. com/2015/09/03/indigenous-rama-among-15000-protesting-nicaragua-canal-161622.

43 https://www.chevron.com/worldwide/venezuela.

44 I'm referring, of course, to the 2015 election in Argentina that removed Cristina Fernandez de Kirchner from power, the February 2016 referendum in Bolivia that Evo Morales lost, Rafael Correa's slipping control of Ecuador after the 2014 Mayoral elections and the impeachment of Dilma Rousseff in Brazil. While much of this is due to the increased social pain resulting from the commodities bust (after the decade-long boom) and other implications of destructive "developmentalist" policies, there is also widespread concern over the growing authoritarianism, corruption, and nepotism of the progressive governments. See Jorge Castañeda's March 22, 2016 *New York Times* article at http://www.nytimes. com/2016/03/23/opinion/the-death-of-the-latin-american-left. html?_r=0.

45 Translation mine, from an interview in Spanish posted at http:// www.perfil.com/internacional/Noam-Chomsky-La-corrupcion-fue-tan-grande-en-Sudamerica-que-se-desacreditaron-a-si-mismos-y-desperdiciaron-grandes-oportunidades-20151025-0008.html.

Epilogue

1 Nicolas Berdyaev, *The Destiny of Man* (New York: Harper and Row, 1960), 211.

2 Karl Popper, "Utopia and Violence," in *Conjectures and Refutations* (New York: Routledge Classics, 2002).

3 *Revelation* 3:15-16.

4 There was, for example, the Nandaime incident of July 1988, witnessed and experienced by Steven Kinzer when the Sandinista *turbas* (mobs) and Sandinista police were set loose to brutally beat people attending an opposition demonstration. See his book, *The*

Blood of Brothers: Life and War in Nicaragua (NY: Anchor Books, 1992), 381–384. And in early 2014 the Bolivarian government demonstrated it was willing to resort to fairly severe repression against the student demonstrations.

5 Joan Weibel-Orlando, "Indians, Ethnicity and Alcohol," in *The American Experience with Alcohol: Contrasting Cultural Perspectives*, eds. G.M. Ames and L.A. Bennett (NY: Springer Science+Business Media, 1985), 233.

6 http://aimovement.org/ggc/index.html.

7 *A Basic Call to Consciousness: The Hau de no sau nee Address to the Western World* (Geneva, Switzerland: Akwesasne Notes 1977).

8 Ibid., v.

9 From the extraordinary interview with Wade Davis archived at http://www.ttbook.org/listen/89416.

10 Bruce Chatwin, *The Songlines* (New York: Penguin Books, 1987), 123–124.

11 Nicolas Berdyaev, *The End of Our Time* (San Rafael, CA: Semantron Press, 2009), 182–187.

12 Leszek Kolakowski, *Main Currents of Marxism, vol. 2, The Golden Age* (Oxford: Oxford University Press, 1981), 383–384. This was clearly the line Stalin followed, but also Trotsky: See *vol. 3, The Breakdown*, of the same work, especially pgs. 193–200.

13 Leszek Kolakowski, *Main Currents of Marxism, vol. 3, The Breakdown*, 195–196.

14 Ibid., 196–197.

15 See my article, "The Two Lefts and Venezuela," ref. Chapter Nineteen, note 5.

16 This is Kurt Weyland's argument. He writes that "Democracy inherently hinders change by dispersing power and protecting dissent and opposition." Nevertheless, because it also "embodies a healthy dos of skepticism, monitors ongoing reform efforts, and prompts the design of better alternatives… democracy arguably has normative priority over substantive efforts at change." Kurt Weyland, "The Performance of Leftist Governments in Latin America," *Leftist Governments in Latin America: Successes and Shortcomings*, Eds. Kurt Weyland, Raúl L. Madrid and Wendy Hunter (NY: Cambridge University Press, 2010), 16.

17 Ibid., 204.

18 Berdyaev, *The End of Our Time*, 187.

19 Javier Corrales and Michael Penfold, *Dragon in the Tropics*, 1.

20 https://en.wikipedia.org/wiki/Democracy_Index.

21 David C. Unger, *The Emergency State: America's Pursuit of Absolute Security at All Costs* (New York: The Penguin Press, 2012).

22 With the implementation of the new "anti-crime" program, "Operation of the Liberation of the People" extra-judicial killings by police have increased 109% from 2014 numbers, from 220 to 460 (see http://www.larazon.net/2016/05/30/las-violaciones-de-derechos-humanos-detras-de-las-olp/). Particularly hard hit have been low-income and immigrant communities in the country (see https://www.hrw.org/report/2016/04/04/unchecked-power/police-and-military-raids-low-income-and-immigrant-communities).

INDEX